NATIONAL ACADEMIES *Sciences Engineering Medicine*

NATIONAL ACADEMIES PRESS
Washington, DC

K–12 STEM Education and Workforce Development in Rural Areas

Tiffany Neill, Katharine Frase, and
Elizabeth T. Cady, *Editors*

Committee on K–12 STEM
Education and Workforce
Development in Rural Areas

Board on Science Education

Division of Behavioral and
Social Sciences and Education

Consensus Study Report

NATIONAL ACADEMIES PRESS 500 Fifth Street, NW Washington, DC 20001

This activity was supported by a contract between the National Academy of Sciences and the National Science Foundation (49100423C0015). Any opinions, findings, conclusions, or recommendations expressed in this publication do not necessarily reflect the views of any organization or agency that provided support for the project.

International Standard Book Number-13: 978-0-309-73004-4
International Standard Book Number-10: 0-309-73004-X
Digital Object Identifier: https://doi.org/10.17226/28269
Library of Congress Control Number: 2025934036

This publication is available from the National Academies Press,
500 Fifth Street, NW, Keck 360, Washington, DC 20001; (800) 624-6242;
http://www.nap.edu.

Printed in the United States of America.

Suggested citation: National Academies of Sciences, Engineering, and Medicine. 2025. *K–12 STEM Education and Workforce Development in Rural Areas*. Washington, DC: National Academies Press. https://doi.org/10.17226/28269.

The **National Academy of Sciences** was established in 1863 by an Act of Congress, signed by President Lincoln, as a private, nongovernmental institution to advise the nation on issues related to science and technology. Members are elected by their peers for outstanding contributions to research. Dr. Marcia McNutt is president.

The **National Academy of Engineering** was established in 1964 under the charter of the National Academy of Sciences to bring the practices of engineering to advising the nation. Members are elected by their peers for extraordinary contributions to engineering. Dr. John L. Anderson is president.

The **National Academy of Medicine** (formerly the Institute of Medicine) was established in 1970 under the charter of the National Academy of Sciences to advise the nation on medical and health issues. Members are elected by their peers for distinguished contributions to medicine and health. Dr. Victor J. Dzau is president.

The three Academies work together as the **National Academies of Sciences, Engineering, and Medicine** to provide independent, objective analysis and advice to the nation and conduct other activities to solve complex problems and inform public policy decisions. The National Academies also encourage education and research, recognize outstanding contributions to knowledge, and increase public understanding in matters of science, engineering, and medicine.

Learn more about the National Academies of Sciences, Engineering, and Medicine at **www.nationalacademies.org**.

Consensus Study Reports published by the National Academies of Sciences, Engineering, and Medicine document the evidence-based consensus on the study's statement of task by an authoring committee of experts. Reports typically include findings, conclusions, and recommendations based on information gathered by the committee and the committee's deliberations. Each report has been subjected to a rigorous and independent peer-review process and it represents the position of the National Academies on the statement of task.

Proceedings published by the National Academies of Sciences, Engineering, and Medicine chronicle the presentations and discussions at a workshop, symposium, or other event convened by the National Academies. The statements and opinions contained in proceedings are those of the participants and are not endorsed by other participants, the planning committee, or the National Academies.

Rapid Expert Consultations published by the National Academies of Sciences, Engineering, and Medicine are authored by subject-matter experts on narrowly focused topics that can be supported by a body of evidence. The discussions contained in rapid expert consultations are considered those of the authors and do not contain policy recommendations. Rapid expert consultations are reviewed by the institution before release.

For information about other products and activities of the National Academies, please visit www.nationalacademies.org/about/whatwedo.

COMMITTEE ON K–12 STEM EDUCATION AND WORKFORCE DEVELOPMENT IN RURAL AREAS

KATHARINE FRASE (*Cochair*), Vice President of Business Development, IBM (*retired*)
TIFFANY NEILL (*Cochair*), Research Scientist, University of Washington
JUAN-CARLOS AGUILAR, Director for Innovative Programs and Research, Georgia Department of Education
BRADLEY S. BARKER, Professor and Youth Development Specialist, Nebraska 4-H Extension, University of Nebraska–Lincoln
GLORIA BURNETT, Associate Professor, College of Health, Department of Human Services, University of Alaska–Anchorage
LINDA FURUTO, Professor of Mathematics Education, University of Hawai'i at Mānoa
REBEKAH HAMMACK, Assistant Professor of Science Education, Purdue University
ERIC J. JOLLY, President and CEO, St. Paul and Minnesota Foundation
JOHN P. McNAMARA, Professor of Animal Sciences (*emeritus*), Washington State University
AUDREY MEADOR, Assistant Professor of Mathematics, West Texas A&M University
DARRIS R. MEANS, Professor of Educational Leadership, Clemson University
STEPHEN L. PRUITT, President, Southern Regional Education Board
JESSICA SAMPLEY, Academies and Career and Technical Education Director, Gulf Shores City Schools, Gulf Shores, Alabama
GUAN SAW, Associate Professor, School of Educational Studies, Claremont Graduate University
MARA CASEY TIEKEN, Associate Professor of Education, Bates College

Study Staff

ELIZABETH T. CADY, Study Director
AUDREY WEBB, Program Officer
LETICIA GARCILAZO GREEN, Associate Program Officer
LACHELLE THOMPSON, Senior Program Assistant
HEIDI SCHWEINGRUBER, Board Director

BOARD ON SCIENCE EDUCATION

BOARD ON AGRICULTURE AND NATURAL RESOURCES

COMPUTER SCIENCE AND TELECOMMUNICATIONS BOARD

Reviewers

This Consensus Study Report was reviewed in draft form by individuals chosen for their diverse perspectives and technical expertise. The purpose of this independent review is to provide candid and critical comments that will assist the National Academies of Sciences, Engineering, and Medicine in making each published report as sound as possible and to ensure that it meets the institutional standards for quality, objectivity, evidence, and responsiveness to the study charge. The review comments and draft manuscript remain confidential to protect the integrity of the deliberative process.

We thank the following individuals for their review of this report:

SUE ALLEN, Allen & Associates, Maine
LEANNE M. AVERY, Department of Elementary Education and Reading, State University of New York at Oneonta
AMY PRICE AZANO, Center for Rural Education, Virginia Tech
DEVON BRENNER, Social Science Research Center, Mississippi State University
PAM J. BUFFINGTON, Rural STEM Initiatives, Education Development Center, Inc.
XIMENA DOMINGUEZ, Learning Sciences and Early Learning Research, Digital Promise Global
LATONIA M. HARRIS, Biologics Launch & Grow, J&J Innovative Medicine
TOM KELLER, STEM Education Strategies, LLC, Maine
JESSE MOON LONGHURST, School of Education, Southern Oregon University

PETER McLAREN, Next Gen Education, LLC
HELEN R. QUINN, SLAC National Accelerator Laboratory
JEFFREY WELD, STEM Education Executive Consultant, Iowa
BJORN WOLTER, Alaska Department of Education & Early Development, Juneau

Although the reviewers listed above provided many constructive comments and suggestions, they were not asked to endorse the conclusions or recommendations of this report nor did they see the final draft before its release. The review of this report was overseen by **ADAM GAMORAN,** W.T. Grant Foundation, and **CYNTHIA M. BEALL,** Case Western Reserve University. They were responsible for making certain that an independent examination of this report was carried out in accordance with the standards of the National Academies and that all review comments were carefully considered. Responsibility for the final content rests entirely with the authoring committee and the National Academies.

Acknowledgments

The Committee on K–12 STEM Education and Workforce Development in Rural Areas faced a charge mandated by Section 10514 of the CHIPS and Science Act of 2022 to evaluate the quality and quantity of federal programming and research for preK–12 STEM (science, technology, engineering, and mathematics) education and workforce development in rural areas, assess the impacts on STEM and technical literacy of the scarcity and affordability of broadband in rural communities, and assess the research and data needed to understand the challenges facing and assets able to be leveraged in rural communities to promote STEM learning.

Through a contract with the U.S. National Science Foundation (NSF) mandated in the same section of the CHIPS and Science Act, the committee embarked on the project with the goal of making recommendations to federal, state, and local educational agencies, programs, and other relevant stakeholders to advance STEM education and workforce development for rural America. Additionally, Section 10512 of the same legislation authorizes NSF to support research for innovative approaches to STEM education in rural areas to improve the participation of rural students in STEM-related professions and Section 10513 authorizes NSF to support research for online STEM education and mentoring in rural areas. The committee was tasked with providing recommendations to the NSF regarding both activities.

The committee would like to thank our NSF contracting officer, Michelle Parrott, and her representative, Sarah-Kathryn McDonald. We are also grateful to our technical point of contact, Toni Dancstep, for her responsiveness and help in navigating the NSF awards database. We also extend thanks to the congressional staffers of the House Committee on Science, Space, and Technology, who recognized the importance of equitable access to high-quality STEM education in rural areas and included both this study and the new authorizing legislation for NSF in the scope of the CHIPS and Science Act.

The committee benefited from the research and experience of many researchers, policymakers, and practitioners across the United States throughout the information-gathering phase of the study. The goal of the first committee meeting in November 2023 was to clarify the statement of task as well as the kinds of recommendations that would be most useful to the entities called out in the charge. We thank the following invited speakers: Pam Buffington (Education Development Center, Inc.), Toni Dancstep (NSF), Albert Hinman (House Science, Space, and Technology Committee), Cate Johnson (House Science, Space, and Technology Committee, Research and Technology Subcommittee), Victoria Rubin (House Science, Space, and Technology Committee), and Josh Seidemann (Rural Broadband Association).

The goal of the second committee meeting, in January 2024, was to get a broad view of the landscape related to (a) state education policy particular to rural communities, (b) broadband connectivity and student outcomes, and (c) demographic trends in and across U.S. rural areas. The committee thanks Shafiq Chaudhary (New Mexico Public Education Department) and Ellen Ebert (Office of Superintendent of Public Instruction, Washington State) for providing information about their particular state contexts pertinent to the charge, as well as Doug Paulson (American Institutes for Research [AIR]) for speaking about pertinent policy and initiatives across state contexts, David Couch (Kentucky Department of Education) and Keith Hampton (Michigan State University) for providing information about student outcomes related to broadband connectivity, Eduard Bartholme and Jessica Campbell (Federal Communications Commission) for speaking to the state of broadband connectivity and affordability in rural areas as well as current federal efforts to advance access in rural areas, and Ken Johnson (University of New Hampshire) and Jesse Longhurst (Southern Oregon University) for providing both high-level quantitative and nuanced qualitative research on demographic trends and how they interact with current state and federal policy structured to funnel funds to rural schools.

The goal of the entirely virtual third committee meeting in March 2024 was to highlight the needs of (a) both in-service and preservice STEM teachers in rural areas and (b) ongoing rural initiatives to support STEM education and workforce development, including those related to online learning and digital literacy. The committee thanks Patrick Miller (North Carolina East Alliance), Rachel Rosen (MDRC), and Tina Wei Smith (Rural Up! Code Academy) for presenting information about changing STEM workforce needs; Amy Price Azano (Virginia Tech), Abraham Lo (BCSC Science Learning), and Janet Stramel (Fort Hays State University) for discussing research on rural STEM education; and Laurel Ballard (Wyoming Department of Education), Ann Lee Flynn (Center for Digital Government), and Erik Kormos (Ashland University) for discussing online education in rural communities.

To undertake such a large statement of work, the committee commissioned several papers. Dan Aladjem (Policy Studies Associates) took on the monumental task of assessing the quantity of federal programming related to preK–12 STEM education and workforce development in rural areas, as well as examining the quality of several key programs. The committee is grateful for his deep attention to detail, careful methodology, and clarity of results. Doug Paulson (AIR) presented such a robust analysis of state policy and initiatives related to the charge that the committee commissioned him to contribute his analysis in the form of a commissioned paper. The committee is grateful for the examples he was able to highlight. The committee extends thanks to Rachel Rush-Marlow (ResearchEd) for her deep intellectual work that formed the heart of many of the early chapters in this report. She looked at student access and opportunity data for various aspects of K–12 STEM education and workforce development in rural areas to ascertain whether rural students are an underrepresented group in STEM.

Finally, special thanks are due to the staff of this project who together supported the committee in coming to consensus and ushered the report through all its iterations to its current form. Beth Cady, senior program officer for the Board on Science Education (BOSE), directed the study, and was ably assisted by BOSE staff Audrey Webb, program officer, and Leticia Garcilazo Green, associate program officer. Senior program assistants Brittani Shorter (at the beginning of the study) and LaChelle Thompson (after the first committee meeting) managed logistical and administrative needs. BOSE director Heidi Schweingruber provided critical guidance throughout the study.

Staff of the Division of Behavioral and Social Sciences and Education also provided help: Our contracted editor, Cameron Fletcher, substantially improved the readability of the report; Kirsten Sampson Snyder expertly guided the report thought the report review process; and Bea Porter masterfully guided the report through production. The committee also thanks Christopher Lao-Scott in the National Academies Research Center for assistance with literature searches.

Contents

Boxes, Figures, and Tables

BOXES

FIGURES

TABLES

Acronyms and Abbreviations

21CCLC	Nita M. Lowey 21st Century Community Learning Centers Program (U.S. Department of Education)
AL	Federal Assistance Listings
AP	Advanced Placement
BCS	Division of Behavioral and Cognitive Sciences (NSF)
CBSA	core based statistical area
CEOSE	Committee on Equal Opportunities in Science and Engineering (NSF)
CoSTEM	Committee on STEM Education (White House Office of Science and Technology Policy)
CRED	culturally relevant engineering design
CSBG	Community Services Block Grant
CTE	Career and Technical Education
DGE	Division of Graduate Education (NSF)
DRK-12	Discovery Research PreK–12 Program (NSF)
DRL	Division of Research on Learning in Formal and Informal Settings (NSF)
DUE	Division of Undergraduate Education (NSF)

EDU	STEM Education Directorate (NSF)
EES	Division of Equity for Excellence in STEM (NSF)
ELL	English-language learner
ESEA	Elementary and Secondary Education Act
ESSA	Every Student Succeeds Act
FCC	Federal Communications Commission
FoK	funds of knowledge
FPI	Federal Program Inventory
FSCS	Full-Service Community Schools Program
FY	fiscal year
GATE/GT	gifted and talented programs
GYO	Grow Your Own
HRSA	Health Resources and Services Administration
HSLS	High School Longitudinal Study
HSTS	High School Transcript Study
HUD	U.S. Department of Housing and Urban Development
IB	International Baccalaureate
IPEDS	Integrated Postsecondary Education Data System
IRR	Index of Relative Rurality
LEA	local education agency
LRK	local rural knowledge
MSU	Montana State University
NAEP	National Assessment of Educational Progress
NASA	National Aeronautics and Space Administration
NCES	National Center for Education Statistics
NREA	National Rural Education Association
NRHA	National Rural Health Association
NSF	U.S. National Science Foundation
OESE	Office of Elementary and Secondary Education (U.S. Department of Education)
OMB	Office of Management and Budget (White House)
OSTEM	Office of STEM Engagement (NASA)
PLC	professional learning community
PN	Promise Neighborhoods

REAP	Rural Education Achievement Program
RET	Research Experiences for Teachers
RLIS	Rural and Low-Income School program
RPN	Rural Partners Network
RUCC	Rural-Urban Continuum Code
S&E	science and engineering
SBE	Social, Behavioral and Economic Sciences Directorate (NSF)
SCCT	social cognitive career theory
SEA	state education agency
SES	Division of Social and Economic Sciences (NSF); socioeconomic status
SEVT	situated expectancy-value theory
SMA	Division of Multidisciplinary Activities (NSF)
SQSS	school quality and student success
SRSA	Small, Rural School Achievement program (U.S. Department of Education)
STEM	science, technology, engineering, and mathematics
STS	Division of Science and Technology Studies (NSF)
TFA	Teach for America
TQP	Teacher Quality Partnership (U.S. Department of Education)
UA	urbanized area
UC	urban cluster
USDA ERS	U.S. Department of Agriculture Economic Research Service
WBL	work-based learning

Summary

An effective education in science, technology, engineering, and mathematics (STEM) both develops STEM literacy skills and can prepare students for high-quality, well-paying careers. There have been consistent calls to ensure that all students have access to high-quality STEM education, but efforts to expand access to high-quality STEM education and workforce development often overlook rural communities and the students in them.

Improved access to STEM education[1] can enhance rural communities and provide additional options for rural students who choose to stay in place to apply their STEM knowledge in ways that can benefit their communities. But a number of barriers limit rural students' access to STEM education and STEM-related careers. At the same time, unrecognized assets in rural communities can support STEM education for their students. Promoting these assets and removing barriers are both critical for ensuring the inclusion of rural students in STEM education and workforce development and enhancing the ability of rural people to engage in and contribute to their communities or scientific exploration and discovery.

Recognizing both the assets inherent in rural communities and schools and the challenges to providing extensive, rigorous STEM education and workforce development opportunities in those areas, Congress directed the U.S. National Science Foundation (NSF) to establish a program to support work on rural STEM education activities as part of the 2022 CHIPS and

[1]The committee defines STEM education as both the individual disciplines and the interdisciplinary learning experiences that emphasize their connections.

Science Act. In conjunction, the National Academies of Sciences, Engineering, and Medicine (National Academies), sponsored by NSF, was directed to undertake a consensus study to

- take stock of existing federal programs that support rural STEM education and workforce development;
- examine the role of broadband in rural STEM education and workforce development;
- develop recommendations for federal, state, and local action to improve rural STEM education and workforce development; and
- provide guidance to the National Science Foundation on implementing programs focused on rural K–12 STEM education and workforce development and online education.

In response, under the auspices of the Board on Science Education in the Division of Behavioral and Social Sciences and Education, in collaboration with the Computer Science and Telecommunications Board, Board on Higher Education and the Workforce, and Board on Agriculture and Natural Resources, the National Academies established a 15-member committee to develop a consensus report.

COMMITTEE APPROACH

The committee gathered evidence and input relevant to its charge through discussion with outside experts (including staff of the Federal Communications Commission, researchers, and practitioners), examination of existing research and promising programs, and a commissioned scan of federal programs. The committee sought to develop an understanding of the diversity of rural contexts across the United States, including its territories[2] and Freely Associated States.[3] Specifically, we explored the assets for and challenges to K–12 STEM[4] education and workforce development that are unique to rural areas. In reviewing research on effective programs and approaches, the committee determined that few studies focus on rural communities and explore variation across rural areas. For this reason, the committee drew on the broad research literature related to effective STEM

[2]The 14 U.S. territories include the permanently inhabited territories of American Samoa, Guam, the Northern Mariana Islands, Puerto Rico, and the U.S. Virgin Islands; the others are smaller islands, atolls, and reefs.

[3]The Freely Associated States are the Federated States of Micronesia, the Republic of the Marshall Islands, and the Republic of Palau.

[4]While the committee recognizes the importance of examining and supporting STEM education for students at the preK level, the research base for rural preK STEM education is insufficiently robust to support evidence-based conclusions and recommendations.

education and workforce development to make inferences about potential approaches in rural areas.

The following sections summarize the committee's conclusions and present the committee's recommendations and suggested research agenda.

DEFINING AND CHARACTERIZING RURAL COMMUNITIES

The committee began by exploring characteristics of rural communities and examining implications for STEM education and workforce development (see Chapter 2). The members found that multiple definitions of *rural* are used by researchers and across and within federal agencies. This makes it difficult to both accurately identify the number of districts and schools served by federal programs and ensure that resources are equitably distributed. It also makes it difficult to aggregate findings across studies in order to build a rigorous knowledge base about what works to improve rural STEM education and workforce development.

Most federal agencies base their definitions of *rural* communities on one of two sources, one developed by the U.S. Census Bureau and the other by the White House Office of Management and Budget. Both definitions define *rural* mainly as *nonurban*, which fails to adequately capture important characteristics that vary across rural areas, such as population density and remoteness. Rural schools, however, are classified using the U.S. Department of Education's National Center for Education Statistics terms, which are used in much education research.

Rural communities differ tremendously across a variety of dimensions that shape the K–12 STEM education and workforce development landscape: remoteness; geography (i.e., mountainous, desert, island); racial, ethnic, and socioeconomic make-up of the population; and the types of STEM-related resources and industries that are present. This variation leads to differences in the types of challenges a given community may face in implementing K–12 STEM education and workforce development initiatives, the kinds of assets that are available to leverage, and the strategies for improving STEM education and workforce development that are likely to be successful.

Notwithstanding the variability, some challenges to and assets for K–12 STEM education and workforce development are common across many rural communities. Challenges include out-migration, difficulties with recruitment and retention of STEM teachers, absence or low density of STEM-related institutions/organizations (e.g., museums, colleges and universities, industries), and closure and consolidation of schools. Assets include proximity to the natural world, close social ties, community resources, and local rural knowledge.

Recommendation 1: There is a need for a common measure of rurality that goes beyond a rural/nonrural dichotomy to capture dimensions such as population size, population density, extent of urban (built-up) area, and remoteness. This measure should be used both to monitor geographical disparities in STEM education and workforce development and to inform development and administration of programs for rural STEM education and workforce development.

- The federal government, through a statistical agency such as the National Center for Education Statistics or the Bureau of Labor Statistics, should develop this common measure.
- Federal agencies (including the U.S. National Science Foundation), state agencies, nonprofit organizations, nongovernmental organizations, philanthropies, and other groups with rural education portfolios should adopt and use this measure.

Recommendation 2: To monitor geographical disparities in STEM education and workforce development, federal statistical agencies (such as the National Center for Education Statistics, Bureau of Labor Statistics, and National Center for Science and Engineering Statistics) and state education agencies should regularly report indicators of STEM education and employment disaggregated by rurality (using a nondichotomous measure of rurality) in addition to other common demographics (e.g., race/ethnicity, gender, disability status, socioeconomic status).

Recommendation 3: When developing and administering programs for rural STEM education and workforce development, funders should use a nondichotomous measure of rurality to ensure that projects represent different dimensions of rurality and to enable them to target rural communities with specific characteristics when necessary.

It is also important to recognize that many rural areas are undergoing substantial demographic shifts and will continue to do so. While approximately 20 percent of those living in rural communities are people of color, almost a third of children under 18 living in rural communities are people of color. K–12 STEM education and workforce development will need to be responsive to these changes.

Recommendation 4: Education decision makers and leaders at all levels should monitor demographic and other changes in the rural communities they serve and take the changes into account when developing

programming and allocating funding. This might include adoption of culturally responsive and sustaining approaches to teaching, providing supports for multilingual learners, and diversifying the teacher workforce.

FEDERAL AND STATE PROGRAMS AND POLICIES

K–12 STEM education and workforce development programs in schools, districts, and communities are shaped by multiple layers of policy and funding based on federal, state, and district policies. Policies and funding streams at these different levels and across different policy domains (assessment, curriculum, graduation requirements, etc.) interact to facilitate or constrain program implementation at the local level. While all states have a significant population of rural students, federal and state policies do not always attend to the unique needs and strengths of rural communities. As a result, policy decisions and processes often do not take into account potential negative unintended consequences for rural districts and schools.

Recommendation 5: When developing state-level policy for STEM education and workforce development, education policy- and decision makers should ensure that representatives of rural districts are involved in the policymaking process or are given the opportunity to provide feedback on the policies and how they might impact rural districts and schools.

Through a commissioned scan of federal programs focused on rural STEM education and workforce development (see Chapter 3) the committee determined that, although there are many federal programs in K–12 STEM education and workforce development that rural districts, schools, and out-of-school programs can apply to, few target rural districts and schools specifically. In addition, rules for eligibility (including the definition of rurality), program requirements, and the demands of the application process can prevent rural schools, districts, and communities from applying for and receiving funding. Furthermore, some rural communities, districts, and schools lack the capacity (e.g., staffing, time, and expertise) to identify potential funding opportunities to advance STEM education and workforce development opportunities, complete the application process, and meet the reporting requirements if funding is awarded.

Recommendation 6: Because some rural communities (including youth-serving organizations), districts, and schools lack the capacity to identify potential funding opportunities, complete the application process,

and meet the reporting requirements if funding is awarded, federal and state agencies, nonprofit organizations, nongovernmental organizations, philanthropies, and other groups with rural education portfolios should

- consider how timelines or burdens for preparing and submitting applications for funding might create barriers for applicants in rural areas,
- consider how requirements for receiving funding could create barriers for applicants in rural areas, and
- provide opportunities for rural communities, districts, schools, and teachers to build capacity to successfully respond to funding opportunities.

Recommendation 7: There is a need for coordinated attention to K–12 STEM education and workforce development in rural areas across existing federal agencies and initiatives. For example,

- the federal Rural Partners Network, led by the U.S. Department of Agriculture and the White House Domestic Policy Council, should prioritize issues related to K–12 STEM education and workforce development in their work; and
- the White House Office of Science and Technology Policy's National Science and Technology Council's Committee on STEM Education should prioritize K–12 STEM education and workforce development in rural areas in their work.

TRENDS IN AND ACCESS TO STEM EDUCATION AND WORKFORCE DEVELOPMENT OPPORTUNITIES

To develop a baseline understanding of the status of rural K–12 STEM education and workforce development, the committee examined trends in student achievement, aspirations, course taking, and persistence in STEM career pathways. We also examined access to learning opportunities in STEM, including coursework, out-of-school programs, and work-related experiences (see Chapter 4).

Many rural students lack access to STEM coursework (e.g., computer science classes, Advanced Placement and International Baccalaureate courses in math) and programs (e.g., Talented and Gifted and Career and Technical Education [CTE] programs, dual enrollment, and third- and fourth-year CTE courses) that can better prepare them to pursue diverse STEM-related education and careers. These disparities in STEM learning opportunities translate into STEM achievement and aspiration gaps between rural and nonrural students, and these gaps grow as students move through K–12 schooling.

In addition, many students in rural communities lack access to structured out-of-school learning opportunities, which are an important complement to in-school STEM learning. They do, however, often have access to such opportunities at home or in nature, and rural STEM educators can significantly improve students' learning by leveraging these experiences.

Rural districts and schools in remote areas with low population density and limited access to affordable broadband face unique challenges for supporting K–12 STEM education and workforce development initiatives and these challenges are often not adequately addressed by federal and state programs. There is also limited research on these remote communities.

> **Recommendation 8: Federal and state agencies should recognize that many students in rural areas lack opportunities in STEM education and therefore are not able to and/or do not pursue STEM careers at the same rate as their suburban and urban peers. These agencies should direct funding, resources, and policymaking designed specifically for rural districts and schools to address these disparities in STEM education and workforce development.**

KEY COMPONENTS OF K–12 STEM EDUCATION AND WORKFORCE DEVELOPMENT

In developing recommendations for improving K–12 STEM education and workforce development in rural areas the committee considered the major components of education and workforce development where policymakers and education leaders can make impactful policy, programmatic, and funding decisions. These include STEM learning experiences, pathways to STEM careers, the STEM educator workforce, and infrastructure and materials (including school buildings, equipment, internet access, and technology). Where possible, the committee examined evidence related to each of these components that was specific to rural areas. When such evidence was not available, the members drew on the broader body of evidence and considered implications for rural settings. The committee's major conclusions for each component are summarized below.

Learning Experiences and Supportive Pathways

Students' competencies in STEM begin in the early grades (preK–2) and build over time (see Chapter 5 for a detailed discussion of STEM learning experiences and pathways). This means that learning experiences in the core STEM subjects throughout the elementary grades are essential for building the knowledge, skills, and dispositions that develop STEM literacy and lead to later success, including in STEM and related careers.

STEM learning experiences that connect to and leverage students' local rural knowledge and experiences are important components of effective K–12 STEM education in rural settings. Place-based learning experiences, often through local partnerships and the adaptation of instructional materials for local relevance, can be especially productive for building rural students' competency and motivation (e.g., interest, identity) in STEM. Given the diversity and changing demographics of many rural areas, instructional approaches that connect to and leverage learners' cultural knowledge and experiences are especially important. To support teachers in providing effective STEM learning experiences, high-quality instructional materials with connected professional development that can be adapted for local relevance are essential.

Pathways to and through STEM education are enriched by STEM learning opportunities in schools, afterschool programs, summer camps and programs, public libraries, museums, local businesses, and virtual platforms. But in rural communities these learning opportunities are sometimes constrained by funding and availability. Promising models for designing STEM enrichment education and workforce development programs in rural areas (a) involve partnerships among K–12 and local higher education institutions, Tribal Nations and other tribal leaders, and local government and business; (b) provide students with job-relevant experiences (e.g., internships, apprenticeships); and (c) target flexible and transferable knowledge and skills relevant to STEM education and job opportunities available locally. State education agencies maintain accountability systems that can be used to provide incentives to rural school districts to develop these kinds of partnerships.

Educators

Educators are the heart of STEM education and workforce development (see Chapter 6). But rural schools, especially in remote locations and reservations, struggle to fill STEM teacher positions. If a position goes unfilled, a course (or courses) either may not be taught or may be taught by a teacher who does not have the qualifications to teach the subject(s).

Teacher preparation programs often use a generalized approach for training and do not adequately prepare future educators for rural spaces. There are limited opportunities for student teaching in rural areas, and some new educators may not be prepared to deal with associated issues such as how to identify and leverage local assets and knowledge related to STEM, isolation, how to enter and build relationships in a tight-knit community, and lack of professional development opportunities. Promising strategies for addressing the lack of STEM-focused professional learning and mentorship opportunities include use of remote and online options (e.g., repositories of resources and online opportunities to collaborate with other teachers), teacher-industry externships, consortia among districts, and regional service centers. In addition to teachers, school counselors are a key resource for supporting rural youth on their path to STEM degrees and careers. Both teachers and school counselors can play a vital role in improving STEM education and workforce development in rural areas.

STEM Education Infrastructure and Materials

Many rural districts and schools lack adequate infrastructure and materials to support high-quality STEM education and workforce development (see Chapter 7). Specifically, they often have old buildings with outdated systems, lack laboratory space and equipment, lack access to fast and affordable broadband, and have insufficient funding. In addition, some rural schools and districts face pressures to consolidate or close to address infrastructure or funding issues, and such changes can have negative impacts on student outcomes.

Community colleges and tribal and regional colleges and universities play critical roles in supporting STEM education and workforce development in rural areas. The closure of small colleges may hamper the ability of rural areas to build programs and sustain pathways for STEM workforce development.

Inequitable access to broadband in rural communities creates challenges for STEM education and workforce development and digital literacy in preparation for work and life. Improvements require reliable and affordable access to broadband. Recent legislation has led to large investments in broadband connectivity across the United States, and many federal and state agencies are working to improve access and adoption. But broadband access alone will not ensure access to STEM education and workforce development opportunities and resources. It is difficult to determine the extent to which connectivity and access efforts will address broadband-related challenges for rural K–12 STEM education because the efforts are not well coordinated, some do not attend to affordability, and broadband access alone cannot address outdated or lacking computers, routers, or other hardware.

STRATEGIES FOR IMPROVING RURAL STEM EDUCATION AND WORKFORCE DEVELOPMENT

Drawing on the review of evidence related to implementing effective K–12 STEM education and workforce development, the committee developed recommendations primarily for state and local actors to guide improvements in rural areas and focused on the major components identified above. In developing these recommendations, the committee took into account the unique assets and challenges of rural contexts and was attentive to the current and increasing diversity of rural communities (discussed in Chapter 2). The committee also recommends continued funding for existing federal programs that support rural K–12 STEM education and workforce development.

Learning Experiences and Supportive Pathways

Recommendation 9: STEM curriculum developers should take into account the assets, resources, and constraints of rural districts and schools when developing instructional materials and accompanying professional learning resources and opportunities. These materials should be designed to allow for the adaptability of instructional methods to leverage local rural funds of knowledge and take place-based approaches.

Recommendation 10: Rural school districts should explore consortium models for STEM education and workforce development that pool resources to maximize opportunities across regions. Such consortia or other collaborative models could seek to provide

- **opportunities for students to participate in advanced STEM coursework,**
- **job-embedded internships and apprenticeships for students,**
- **professional learning for preK–12 STEM educators, and**
- **improved access to out-of-school STEM learning experiences.**

Recommendation 11: State education agencies should provide funding and other incentives, including in accountability systems, to encourage rural districts to partner with each other and with institutions of higher education, community organizations, out-of-school programs, and industry to advance K–12 STEM education and workforce development and better engage and support preK–12 students, parents, and educators in rural areas.

Recommendation 12: Rural districts should seek community and/or industry partners with whom they can develop a variety of STEM learning opportunities. These opportunities should include project- or placed-based learning experiences that build foundational knowledge in STEM disciplines for students across preK–12, exposure to STEM professions, access to rigorous courses in the core STEM disciplines, opportunities to develop job-related skills, and a requirement to complete

a real-world internship, apprenticeship, or other work-based learning experience. Career-specific exploration and preparation could begin as early as middle school, should be based on an expanded definition of STEM that includes any job that requires proficiency in STEM-related knowledge and skills, and should emphasize STEM fields that can contribute to the viability and sustainability of local areas.

Educators

Recommendation 13: Institutions that offer teacher preparation pathways should incorporate rural-focused coursework and opportunities for rural field placements in their licensure programs. These rural-focused components should provide opportunities to learn about the diversity of rural communities and their assets, how to recognize those assets in different contexts, and ways to leverage the assets in STEM and STEM-based Career and Technical Education curriculum and instruction.

Recommendation 14: Institutions that offer school counselor preparation pathways should incorporate rural-focused coursework and rural internship opportunities for prospective counselors to learn about the diversity of rural communities and their assets, how to recognize those assets in different contexts, and ways to leverage the assets when advising students about STEM courses or career pathways.

Recommendation 15: Rural districts should work with regional teacher preparation programs to explore ways to address the shortage of STEM teachers in rural areas. Strategies to consider include

- housing assistance,
- transportation funds,
- "grow your own" programs in rural areas, and/or
- flexible and ongoing professional learning opportunities.

Infrastructure and Materials

Recommendation 16: When making decisions about adoption of new technology, online services, or equipment, states and districts should take into account the "total cost of ownership," including the initial investment, ongoing costs for access and maintenance, and professional development needed for teachers and administrators to use the technology, service, or equipment effectively. The total cost should explicitly account for challenges in rural areas that might affect costs (for example, costs of professional development for teachers who are spread out geographically, or of tech maintenance if schools are separated by long distances).

Implications for Federal Programs

Recommendation 17: The federal government should continue to support and expand programs that enhance preK–12 STEM education and workforce development initiatives in rural areas, with an emphasis on programs that

- provide funding for training, placement, and continuing education (professional development) for STEM educators in rural schools;
- explore strategies for using technology, including improving internet access to online platforms and AI tools, expanding educators' abilities to teach robust, integrated STEM subjects, and expanding student opportunities to learn and gain experience in STEM fields, rather than as a technique to reduce staff, teachers, or costs, or to close schools; and
- complete connection of all schools and students' homes with internet access at minimal cost and using the technology (fiber optics, cable, satellite, mobile hotspots) available locally.

Recommendation 18: Agencies that fund programs in STEM education and workforce development should conduct evaluations at the portfolio level that examine and document what makes a program or approach successful for rural populations and/or in rural settings. This could include assessing

- how a program overcomes challenges that are unique to rural settings;
- how programs leverage assets of rural communities, including local rural knowledge;
- the capacity of rural organizations to apply for and manage grants (e.g., reporting requirements); and
- effective practices to increase the capacity of rural organizations.

RECOMMENDATIONS TO NSF FOR IMPLEMENTING RURAL STEM EDUCATION AND WORKFORCE DEVELOPMENT PROGRAMS

As stipulated in the statement of task the committee makes specific recommendations to NSF to inform the funding and implementation of programs under sections 10512 (National Science Foundation Rural STEM Activities) and 10513 (Opportunities for Online Education) of the CHIPS and Science Act. The committee first recommends embedding a rural focus in existing relevant programs in order to move forward more quickly.

To qualify for this rural focus, an initiative must clearly show how the questions asked, the programs implicated, and the knowledge generated are relevant to rural communities, schools, students, and families. In addition, throughout its strategies and programs, NSF should attend to the different dimensions of rurality—population size and density, extent of urban (built-up) area, remoteness, and demographic diversity. Further, NSF should require proposers and grantees to describe the settings where the project takes place and the populations and communities involved in ways that will enable NSF to document different dimensions of rural diversity.

NSF should develop a strategy to encourage the development and funding of projects that focus on rural Indigenous communities, including work on reservations and with Tribal Nations, Alaska Natives, Native Hawaiians, and Pacific Islanders. NSF should also develop a strategy to encourage projects that focus on rural migrant, Black, and Latine communities and individuals with intersecting marginalized identities in rural communities.

To kick off development of the strategy for focusing on rural STEM education, it may be useful to convene experts in rural STEM education and workforce development to provide input on the needs and areas for research, building on this report. As more grants are funded for rural preK–12 STEM education and workforce development, NSF should hold a meeting of the project principal investigators to encourage information exchange and the deepening of a professional community around rural STEM education and workforce development.

To accomplish the goals outlined in the legislation, projects must include genuine, trusting, mutually beneficial partnerships between institutions of higher education, nonprofits, preK–12 education, local industries, and communities. In making awards, consideration should be given to how funding is shared with districts, schools, and communities to support their work.

As noted, rural communities have many assets relevant to STEM education and workforce development that are often not leveraged sufficiently. In developing priorities for rural STEM education and evaluating proposals, NSF should explicitly call out the need to clearly describe how a program or project will identify and leverage community resources and be designed to connect to local community priorities and needs.

Recommendation 19: When implementing the suite of programs outlined in articles 10512 and 10513 of the CHIPS and Science Act, NSF should employ the following strategies:

- Build on existing NSF programs when possible.
- Capture the diversity of rural settings and populations.
- Elevate expertise related to rural STEM education and workforce development.
- Support mutually beneficial partnerships between institutions of higher education, nonprofits, preK–12 education, local industries, and communities.
- Emphasize an asset framing of rural communities.
- Create quick-turnaround, short-term funding opportunities to allow for pilot work and strategy development.
- Connect to existing rural STEM education and workforce development programs across other federal agencies.

Recommendation 20: As relates to Section 10512(a), Preparing Rural STEM Educators, NSF should expand the Robert Noyce Teacher Scholarship Program Tracks 1 and 2 to intentionally recruit STEM majors and professionals from rural areas; prepare them to leverage local, natural, and community assets in their STEM teaching; place them in rural areas for their teaching commitments; and support them after placement. In addition, NSF should expand the definition of eligible "STEM major" for the Noyce scholarships to include agricultural and health sciences, given their high relevance to rural areas.

Recommendation 21: As relates to Section 10512(a2B), Rural STEM Collaborative, NSF should leverage regional collaborative structures both within NSF (e.g., INCLUDES, TIP programs) and in higher education or nonprofit organizations (e.g., Regional Hubs in the Rural Schools Collaborative). The new regional structures should include preK–12 formal schooling institutions, organizations that provide informal or out-of-school STEM learning experiences, higher education institutions, and local industries.

Recommendation 22: As relates to Section 10512(b) Broadening Participation of Rural Students in STEM, NSF should

- leverage existing programs like EPSCoR, Advanced Technological Education and other community college–focused programs, and the Division of Research on Learning in Formal and Informal Settings;

- be clear, nuanced, and inclusive when defining *rural*, by requiring use of either the Index of Relative Rurality or the definitional base for rural categorization in applications for funding;
- support longitudinal research in rural STEM education;
- fund participatory research that engages rural students in research methods or includes educators or educational leaders (e.g., research-practice partnerships); and
- consider a variety of partnership models, including fully virtual collaboration, to ensure that all rural areas, including remote areas with few colocated partners, can apply for funding.

Recommendation 23: As relates to Section 10513, Opportunities for Online Education, NSF should attend to the existing technological infrastructure in rural communities and fund research that examines

- the impact of differential connectivity on student and teacher STEM learning outcomes and
- how online tools (including artificial intelligence) and communities can support students and educators in formal and informal settings.

DIRECTIONS FOR RESEARCH

There is an urgent need for more comprehensive, evidence-based, and broad-scale national research that focuses specifically on rural students in STEM. When developing research programs or priorities focused on rural STEM education, funders (federal agencies, foundations, and state agencies) should require applicants to describe how the research team will center the needs and priorities of rural communities, districts, and schools. Funders should also consider calling for research models that require equal partnership and collaboration between researchers and practitioners, such as research-practice partnerships.

Federal agencies and philanthropic organizations should fund education researchers to engage in longitudinal research that examines (a) the impacts of rural STEM and STEM-based CTE programs on rural communities and (b) how broadband infrastructure affects preK–12 STEM education and literacy in rural areas. The committee identifies the following three areas where more research is particularly needed:

- *Intersecting research on preK–12 STEM education and workforce development in rural areas:* There is a lack of studies examining preK–12 STEM education, especially in earlier grades, across the diversity of rural schools and communities. In some cases rurality was a variable but not the study focus. Research is needed to explore the challenges faced by rural students, especially those with intersectional identities, how they impact students' outcomes, and what strategies might alleviate these challenges.

- *Better availability and usability of datasets:* Definitions of rurality should be improved to recognize that rural communities are not monolithic and that rurality exists on a continuum, and datasets are needed that are specific to rural students, teachers, and schools and that leverage the diversity of rural settings and STEM learning.
- *Informal and nonformal STEM learning and workforce development in rural areas:* Research is needed to enhance understanding of the impacts of informal and nonformal STEM learning and workforce development for students in rural areas.

1

Introduction

The disciplines and subfields of science, technology, engineering, and mathematics (STEM) are critical to the global and national economy, and a quality STEM education not only prepares students for high-quality, well-paying careers in the STEM workforce but also develops the STEM literacy that improves decision making and contributes to a well-functioning democracy (National Academies of Sciences, Engineering, and Medicine [NASEM], 2021). There is a clear national interest in increasing the number of qualified candidates for the STEM workforce as this is a rapidly growing, typically well-compensated field, with many roles that have important implications for the country's health, safety, and prosperity. Inherent to STEM education are lessons on understanding the world empirically, and research has shown that individuals who have a comprehensive understanding of science make more evidence-based decisions, leading to a healthier population and informed public, and that this understanding begins in K–12 education (Marksbury, 2017). STEM learning in preschool and early elementary school is critical, as it provides learning experiences that enable students to explore the world around them and pursue their own interests and curiosity (NASEM, 2022, 2024).

Throughout this report, we define STEM education as both the individual disciplines (e.g., science, technology, engineering, and mathematics) and the interdisciplinary learning experiences that emphasize their connections. These learning experiences help children understand their lives and engage in their communities. But when STEM education is seen exclusively through the lens of advanced education or workforce skills, rural families and students may resist it, because pursuing advanced education in general and STEM workforce opportunities in particular are seen as contributing factors to rural brain drain (Short et al., 2020) and out-migration that will take students away from their families and their communities. The reality is that STEM is inherent in most if not all rural communities, including those closely tied to agriculture, coastal communities, and remote communities that rely on a subsistence economy. Thus, improving access to STEM knowledge can enhance rural communities and, if done well, provide additional options for rural students who choose to stay to apply their STEM knowledge for the benefit of their communities. For example, students could learn how to monitor water quality to help preserve a local wetlands ecosystem, acquire predictive modeling and simulation skills that help with monitoring weather patterns, learn how to diagnose problems and use technology to repair their family's automobile or equipment, learn how technology can help emergency response teams in their communities, or learn which native plants will thrive in their garden.

Rural communities have many assets that can enrich and promote STEM learning, such as place-based learning and strong community ties. Identifying and describing the opportunities, supports, and general assets that exist in rural places may also assist in minimizing misconceptions and create a greater understanding of the communities and families. Opportunities in rural STEM education are varied, cover a breadth of subjects, and/or are rooted in the place where the school is centered. Just as there is no one-size-fits-all description of rural areas, there is no one-size-fits-all approach to STEM education in rural schools.

There are also numerous challenges to providing high-quality STEM education and workforce development in rural areas. Rural schools generally have less access to high-quality teachers and school counselors, fewer resources, higher levels of student poverty, and less emphasis on college readiness. Many rural schools, especially those in remote areas, operate with a small staff and low budget that limit advanced course offerings and extracurricular programs in STEM (Saw, 2024; Saw & Agger, 2021). Students in rural classrooms may not receive high-quality STEM instruction because of factors such as lack of technology, insufficient teacher training, and geographic distance from resources (De Mars et al., 2022; Grimes et al., 2019; Johnson & Zoellner, 2016; Marksbury, 2017). Finally, in many rural districts a third or more of students do not have internet connectivity at home, although many do have access at school or in the community library (National Center for Education Statistics, 2023). These limitations, combined with a lack of consistent and agreed-upon definitions of rurality, may result in misalignment of resources meant to be allocated to rural and vulnerable communities.

SCOPE AND FOCUS OF THE REPORT

Recognizing both the assets inherent in rural communities and schools and the challenges to providing extensive, rigorous STEM education and workforce development opportunities in those areas, Congress directed the U.S. National Science Foundation (NSF) to establish a program to support work on rural STEM education activities as part of the 2022 CHIPS and Science Act. In conjunction, the National Academies of Sciences, Engineering, and Medicine (National Academies), sponsored by NSF, was directed to undertake a consensus study to take stock of existing federal programs that support rural STEM education and workforce development and to develop recommendations for federal, state, and local action to improve rural STEM education and workforce development. The work was conducted under the auspices of the Board on Science Education in the Division of Behavioral and Social Sciences and Education in collaboration with the Computer Science and Telecommunications Board, Board on Higher Education and the Workforce, and Board on Agriculture and Natural Resources.

Studies carried out by expert committees convened by the National Academies are guided by a statement of task, which defines the scope of the work and guides both the writing and the peer review of the final report. Committees are instructed to respond to the statement of task and not go beyond it. Reviewers are asked to assess whether the committee's report has responded to the statement of task in an evidence-based way and has not gone beyond it. The statement of task for this study is presented in Box 1-1.

COMMITTEE'S INTERPRETATION OF THE STATEMENT OF TASK

To address the statement of task, the committee first needed to understand rurality and rural populations. Depending on the definition of rurality used (see Chapter 2), between 46 and 66 million U.S. residents live in rural counties, which is between 14 percent and 20 percent of the U.S. population (Davis et al., 2023). Although racial diversity is lower in rural areas than in suburban or urban areas, approximately 20 percent of those living in rural counties are Indigenous, Black, Latine, Asian, Pacific Islander, or multiracial (Parker et al., 2018). And that diversity is increasing; 32 percent of people under the age of 18 in rural America are Indigenous, Black, Hispanic/Latine, Asian, Pacific Islander, or multiracial (Kenneth Johnson, University of New Hampshire, presentation to committee, January 2024). Factors such as immigration and in-migration advance population growth and diversity in rural areas and influence social norms and values to create an array of perspectives and experiences. The funds of knowledge that result when diverse people are gathered in a rural setting where place greatly matters should be celebrated and recognized for the expertise and skill provided to the locale or region (Azano et al., 2021).

BOX 1-1
Statement of Task

The National Academies will undertake a consensus study to take stock of existing federal programs that support rural science, technology, engineering, and mathematics (STEM) education and workforce development, and to develop recommendations for federal, state, and local action to improve STEM education and workforce development in rural areas. For the purposes of this study, "workforce development" includes the interface with preK–12 learning opportunities, with a focus on the interface between postsecondary education institutions and high schools. Rural is defined broadly including population size, density, and remoteness, and it may consider relative degree of rurality (rather than "rural" or "not rural"). Specifically, the committee will

(1) evaluate the quality and quantity of current federal programming and research directed at examining STEM education (in both formal and informal settings) for students in prekindergarten through grade 12 and workforce development in rural areas;
(2) in coordination with the Federal Communications Commission, assess the impact that the scarcity of broadband connectivity in rural communities, and the affordability of broadband connectivity, have on STEM and technical literacy for students in prekindergarten through grade 12 in rural areas;
(3) assess the core research and data needed to understand the challenges rural areas are facing in providing quality STEM education (in formal and informal settings) and workforce development as well as the assets embedded in these communities;
(4) make recommendations for action at the federal, state, and local levels for improving STEM education, including online STEM education, for students in prekindergarten through grade 12 and workforce development in rural areas (whenever possible, findings and recommendations for preK–12 STEM education and workforce development in rural areas will be disaggregated to identify and address regional, racial/ethnic, and economic variability); and
(5) make recommendations to inform the implementation of programs in sections 10512 ("National Science Foundation Rural STEM Activities") and 10513 ("Opportunities for Online Education"), which include the National Science Foundation's funding for rural STEM activities and online STEM education and mentoring in rural communities.

Given this statement of task, a committee was assembled with expertise and experience in preK–12 education research in formal and informal settings, particularly in the areas of learning, teaching, assessment, and policy for STEM in rural spaces. The committee members' expertise includes career and technology education, online STEM education, informal and out-of-school STEM education, educational administration, teacher professional learning, and STEM workforce development. Several committee members are current or former practitioners and/or administrators in rural K–12 education settings. For more information on the committee members, see Appendix A.

The committee also approached its task using asset-based framing. Yosso (2005) developed the concept of *community cultural wealth* to describe the assets that students of color bring to the classroom. She identified six forms: aspirational capital, the capacity for hope in spite of challenges; linguistic capital, the skills inherent in fluency in multiple languages or linguistic styles; familial capital, the knowledge embedded in family systems; social capital, the resources found in relationships and networks; navigational capital, the ability to navigate institutions and systems; and resistant capital, the knowledge and skills that come with challenging injustice. Given the diversity in economy, geography, and people in rural places, there are ample opportunities to grow, nurture, and employ the various forms of capital that constitute community cultural wealth. These forms of capital support rural students both in their preK–12 STEM education pathways (discussed in Chapter 5) and as they enter the workforce. Related, Moll et al. (1992) describe *funds of knowledge*—the knowledge of households, often undervalued by traditional educational systems, that reflect family members' lived experiences and accumulated wisdom. These funds can include, for example, hands-on knowledge of occupations, historical understandings of a region or people, or expertise in languages, traditions, or cultural practices.

We also considered the role of schools, families, and community organizations in rural K–12 STEM education and workforce development. Rural K–12 schools are critical to the well-being and prosperity of their communities (Tieken, 2014). They are often a rural community's largest employer, offering stable, well-paying, middle-class jobs to local residents. They shape the social fabric of rural communities, as a site for both youth and adults to gather, whether in classrooms, at Friday night basketball games, or for community suppers, and in these spaces relationships are nurtured and grown. In communities where schools pull together people across race and class, they can have a significant influence on integration. Schools can also help sustain cultural practices, such as maintaining home languages, or traditions, like homecoming events. They are also a source of political power, as schools are governed by locally elected school boards; this power may be especially important for historically marginalized populations. In all these ways rural schools can have important social, cultural, political, and economic benefits to their communities (Schafft, 2016), and thus policies and programs that support the vitality of rural schools also help sustain rural communities. Besides being the site of many social and recreational activities (Miller, 1995; Seal & Harmon, 1995), the rural school is one of the most visible uses of taxpayer dollars and investments in a rural community.

But some educational policies have resulted in disconnecting schools and communities (Schafft & Harmon, 2010). Although challenges with recruiting and retaining teachers exist nationally, rural schools, which devote a great deal of time to recruiting teachers for open positions but receive few, if any, applicants, experience them more severely. Many positions go unfilled or are covered by long-term substitute teachers. In addition, there is often a lack of local STEM partners to support expansion of learning opportunities in these subjects. Urban areas are often home to many nonprofits and other organizations that provide programming and resources to support STEM learning in formal and informal settings. The dearth of local partners to support STEM education in rural communities means that rural educators and leaders have to think more strategically about who might be able to help them advance their teaching and learning goals, and how to collaborate when those partners are far away. Finally, the historical culture in some rural communities may lead families to devalue education that they think could encourage youth to leave their community or lead children to question whether they can succeed in STEM fields (Allen et al., 2019).

On the other hand, rural schools can leverage place-specific resources, such as place-based learning in the natural world and local rural knowledge, for STEM learning (Smith & Sobel, 2014; Starrett et al., 2021). With small class sizes and increased interactions with families, rural teachers can develop close relationships with their students that result in more individualized instruction and improved student behavior (Tran et al., 2020). While rural teachers can be seen as the "faces" of the rural school (Hammack et al., 2023), school-community partnerships are often enhanced in rural areas (Schafft, 2016). Community-based programs can draw on local expertise and environmental features, such as farms, forests, and rivers, to create meaningful learning experiences (Avery, 2013). This local context helps students see the relevance of science and engineering to their own lives and futures, fostering a stronger connection to the subject matter.

Families, communities, and historical cultural factors also play a large role in determining student access and interest in STEM learning (Allen et al., 2019). Compared to urban parents, rural parents are more likely to volunteer at the school and attend school events (Schafft, 2016). Like parents in other communities, they also tend to engage with their children in family-oriented education activities outside the school, sometimes incorporating family history or ethnic heritage.[1] Using place to educate creates an informed citizenry ready to advocate for their rural home and its relationship in a global context (Eppley, 2017) and prepares rural youth for local STEM employment opportunities (Starrett et al., 2022). The U.S. Department of Agriculture (Cromartie et al., 2015) and Federal Reserve of St. Louis (Davis & Dumont, 2021) have also highlighted the importance of curbing out-migration and promoting rural community renewal. A study showed that a place-based educational unit on environmental science watershed

[1]Parent and Family Involvement in Education Survey of the National Household Education Surveys Program of 2023, https://nces.ed.gov/pubs2024/2024113.pdf

changed the intended future behaviors (i.e., in favor of stewardship and conservation) of rural high school students (Zimmerman & Weible, 2017; Pam Buffington, EDC, presentation to the committee, November 2023).

As the committee gathered evidence from published reports as well as meetings with representatives from the Federal Communications Commission, we noted some inherent assumptions related to the second task, in particular the implied causality between lack of affordable broadband connectivity in rural areas and lower STEM and technical literacy for rural students compared to their urban or suburban peers. Related to this task, the committee stresses two points. First, although *broadband* is often thought of as connection to the internet via fiber-optic cable, it actually encompasses access to high-speed internet via any type of technology, including satellite, cable, and wireless (U.S. Department of Education, 2022), thus the report uses "internet connectivity" interchangeably with "broadband." Furthermore, beyond accessing the internet and adoption of broadband, digital equity, inclusion, and literacy are critical and defined in the 2021 Infrastructure Investment and Jobs Act (see Box 1-2). Chapter 7 discusses broadband in more depth, including stated upload (20 megabits per second [Mbps]) and download (100 Mbps) speeds that count as broadband.

Second, although connectivity, in schools and homes as well as libraries and other community spaces, enables some STEM learning for preK–12 students and their teachers, STEM literacy develops in both physical and virtual spaces. For example, students might learn how to interact with large datasets or other STEM tools as part of an online-enabled lesson. Students and their families could use the internet to search for informal STEM experiences or higher education pathways. Teachers often participate in online professional learning activities. In-person STEM education and workforce development activities can be supplemented by online activities. Students who are unable to access the internet at home are at a disadvantage compared to their peers with home connectivity, and this disadvantage shows up as fewer completed homework assignments and in some cases lower SAT scores, although these effects may be mitigated somewhat by other activities (e.g., sports and other extracurricular activities; Hampton et al., 2021). However, the relationship between broadband access and STEM learning outcomes is complex and multifaceted, and the committee was unable to find evidence of how lack of affordable and reliable broadband connectivity in rural areas affects the STEM and technical literacy of students in those communities.

Another assumption addressed by the committee concerns the definitions of *STEM and technical literacy* as well as *STEM education and workforce*. *STEM literacy* includes "some combination of (a) awareness of the roles of science, technology, engineering, and mathematics in modern

BOX 1-2
Broadband-Related Definitions Used in the Report

Adoption of Broadband: the process by which an individual obtains daily access to the internet—

(A) at a speed, quality, and capacity—
  (i) that is necessary for the individual to accomplish common tasks; and
  (ii) such that the access qualifies as an advanced telecommunications capability;
(B) with the digital skills that are necessary for the individual to participate online; and
(C) on a—
  (i) personal device and
  (ii) secure and convenient network.

Digital Equity: the condition in which individuals and communities have the information technology capacity that is needed for full participation in the society and economy of the United States.

Digital Inclusion: refers to

(A) the activities that are necessary to ensure that all individuals in the United States have access to, and the use of, affordable information and communication technologies, such as—
  (i) reliable fixed and wireless broadband internet service;
  (ii) internet-enabled devices that meet the needs of the user; and
  (iii) applications and online content designed to enable and encourage self-sufficiency, participation, and collaboration; and
(B) includes—
  (i) access to digital literacy training,
  (ii) the provision of quality technical support, and
  (iii) basic awareness of measures to ensure online privacy and cybersecurity.

Digital Literacy: the skills associated with using technology to enable users to find, evaluate, organize, create, and communicate information.

SOURCE: Adapted from Infrastructure Investment and Jobs Act (2021, pp. 1209–1211).

society, (b) familiarity with at least some of the fundamental concepts from each area, and (c) a basic level of application fluency (e.g., the ability to critically evaluate the science or engineering content in a news report, conduct basic troubleshooting of common technologies, and perform basic mathematical operations relevant to daily life)" (National Academy of Engineering [NAE] & National Research Council [NRC], 2014, p. 34).

NAE and NRC (2002) defined *technological literacy* as "an understanding of the nature and history of technology, a basic hands-on capability related to technology, and an ability to think critically about technological development" (pp. 11–12), where *technology* is defined broadly as "not only the tangible artifacts of the human-designed world and the systems of which these artifacts are a part, but also the people, infrastructure, and processes required to design, manufacture, operate, and repair the artifacts" (p. vii).

Many desirable jobs in rural communities do not require advanced education but do require STEM knowledge. Positions in agriculture and manufacturing, for example, call for much of the same advanced STEM knowledge and critical thinking as urban-located STEM professions. K–12 STEM education is therefore as important for students who choose to stay in their community and/or forgo postsecondary education as it is for those interested in pursuing postsecondary education in STEM or leaving their community. But a number of barriers prevent rural students from easily accessing STEM pathways, and useful assets that can support STEM education in rural communities remain unrecognized. Promoting these assets and removing barriers are critical to ensure that rural students are included in STEM education and the workforce.[2]

Rural areas provide a rich context for learning science and engineering. With access to the outdoors, or work in agricultural industries such as farming or fishing, many rural students naturally develop engineering and science skills in their daily lives (Avery, 2013). Thus, opportunities for place-based education in rural areas abound and such learning increases students' access, engagement, and achievement in science content (Avery, 2013).

Because of the nature of STEM learning in rural areas, and as noted in previous National Academies reports, the committee considered STEM education as occurring in a variety of environments, from schoolrooms to museums, zoos, online, the home, and the natural world. Given the charge to examine preK–12 STEM education and workforce development as they relate to preK–12 education, the committee adopted an expansive definition of STEM education based on the fields classified in the Integrated Postsecondary Education Data System (IPEDS), which is used by NSF to analyze the U.S. population with STEM degrees.[3] IPEDS data include the broad category of health sciences and breakout fields such as public or community health, veterinary-related sciences, and premedical sciences, all fields with strong relevance to rural communities. IPEDS also includes fields under the general heading of agricultural sciences, including agriculture economics, natural resources management, forestry, and management of land use or marine resources.

---

[2]The preceding text is based on a commissioned paper by Rachel Rush-Marlowe at ResearchEd. Full citation in references.

[3]https://ncsesdata.nsf.gov/sere/2018/html/sere18-dt-taba001.html

In conceptualizing the STEM workforce, the committee looked to the 2021 National Science Board *Science and Engineering Indicators* report (2021). For years, this report focused on individuals who have at least a bachelor's degree and work in one of five science and engineering (S&E) areas: mathematical and computer sciences, life sciences (e.g., agricultural, environmental, biological), physical sciences (e.g., chemistry, physics), social sciences, and engineering. It also includes workers with bachelor's degrees in S&E-related occupations such as health care, technology fields, or management. But the 2021 report notes that recent discoveries and technological advances have led to questions about the traditional definitions of a STEM workforce, in particular whether STEM work requires a bachelor's degree rather than an associate's degree or certificate. While the previous narrow definition of the S&E workforce estimated 7 million workers, use of "another definition for scientists and engineers, which includes those who have an S&E or S&E-related degree or work in an S&E or S&E-related occupation" (National Science Board, 2021, p. 12), yields 29 million STEM workers in the United States. Because many of the jobs now classified as STEM are performed in rural areas, the committee adopted the newest definition of *STEM worker*, which "not only includes occupations that are historically known to require S&E skills and expertise (e.g., life sciences, physical sciences, engineering, mathematics and computer sciences, social sciences, and health care) but also occupations that require STEM skills but are not historically considered STEM occupations (e.g., installation, maintenance, and repair; construction trades; and production occupations)" (National Science Board, 2021, p. 16).

In conceptualizing U.S. rural areas and how the recommendations in this report could impact them, the committee includes the 50 states, District of Columbia, Commonwealth of Puerto Rico, four Insular Areas (the territories of American Samoa, Guam, the U.S. Virgin Islands, and the Commonwealth of the Northern Mariana Islands), and the Freely Associated States of the Republic of the Marshall Islands, the Republic of Palau, and the Federated States of Micronesia.[4] However, much of the research and statistical information cited in the report focuses solely on the 50 states.

Finally, the original statement of task called on the committee to consider the preK–12 system in its entirety, but we found the literature base on preK STEM education challenging to analyze and integrate into the report. While the committee recognizes the importance of examining and supporting STEM education for students at the preK level, the research base for rural preK STEM education is insufficiently robust to support evidence-based conclusions and recommendations. This limitation prevented us from exploring the preK space as thoroughly as we were instructed in

[4]https://www.doi.gov/library/internet/insular

our statement of task. Thus, much of the evidence discussed and our conclusions focus on K–12 STEM education; when evidence exists from the preK level it is included.

STUDY APPROACH

The committee met five times between November 2023 and July 2024. The meetings included three public information-gathering sessions with expert presentations on issues in rural STEM education, rural broadband and connectivity, definitions of rurality, examples of state systems, broadband connectivity and student outcomes, changing STEM workforce needs in rural communities, research on rural STEM education challenges, and online education in rural communities. In addition, the committee engaged with the sponsoring agency (NSF) and learned more about the development of the 2022 CHIPS and Science Act from congressional staffers.

The goal of the first committee meeting in November 2023 was to clarify the statement of task as well as the kinds of recommendations that would be most useful to the entities identified in the charge. The committee also heard from experts on rural education and rural broadband access. The goal of the second committee meeting in January 2024 was to get a broad view of the landscape related to (a) state education policy particular to rural communities, (b) broadband connectivity and student outcomes, and (c) demographic trends within and across U.S. rural areas. The committee also met with representatives of the Federal Communications Commission to discuss broadband connectivity and affordability.

The virtual third committee meeting in March 2024 included panels on the needs of both in-service and preservice STEM teachers in rural areas and on existing rural initiatives to support STEM education and workforce development, including those related to online learning and digital literacy. In the entirely closed fourth committee meeting in May 2024 the committee heard from the authors of the three commissioned papers and continued writing the report. The goal for the final, entirely closed, committee meeting in July 2024 was to come to consensus and refine the report text.

Beyond the three information-gathering sessions, the committee reviewed literature pertaining to its charge, including peer-reviewed materials, book chapters, reports, working papers, government documents, white papers and evaluations, editorials, and previous reports of the National Academies. The committee also commissioned three papers to help address questions in the statement of task. One commissioned landscape scan evaluated the quantity and quality of federal programming and research in preK–12 STEM education (in both formal and informal settings) and workforce development in rural areas (*Strategic Priorities or Distributed Choice? Federal Education and Workforce Development Investments in*

Rural Areas by Dan Aladjem). A second commissioned paper examined the landscape of state policies and programs that can advance or hinder K–12 STEM education and workforce development in rural areas (*State-Driven Rural STEM Education Policies and Programs* by Doug Paulson). The third commissioned paper examined underrepresentation of the rural population in STEM education and the workforce (*Rural Students as an Underserved Population in STEM Education and Workforce* by Rachel Rush-Marlowe). The findings from the committee's review of these evidence sources informed the members' deliberations, conclusions, and recommendations (presented in Chapter 8).

STANDARDS OF EVIDENCE

The committee believes that "a wide variety of legitimate scientific designs are available for education research" (NRC, 2002, p. 6). From that standpoint, to be considered scientific (NASEM, 2015, p. 21),

> the design must allow direct, empirical investigation of an important question, [use methods that permit direct investigation of the question], account for the context in which the study is carried out, align with a conceptual framework, reflect careful and thorough reasoning, and disclose results to encourage debate in the scientific community.

As in previous National Academies studies, the committee examined research articles that had been peer reviewed to help ensure the quality of design, methods, and conclusions. The articles spanned multiple disciplines and included quantitative, qualitative, and mixed-methods studies related to rural STEM education and workforce development as well as rural education and communities more broadly. The committee took an expansive view of evidence in developing this report and drew on diverse methods and evidence types. While the committee's conclusions rely primarily on peer-reviewed journals and books, the members also, as noted above, commissioned three papers and reviewed many other types of relevant resources. As appropriate, throughout the report, the committee articulates the type of research being reviewed and its strength. The committee is also careful to qualify the conclusions and resulting recommendations based on the type and strength of evidence.

ORGANIZATION OF THE REPORT

In developing recommendations for improving K–12 STEM education and workforce development in rural areas the committee considered the major components of education and workforce development where policymakers and education leaders can make impactful policy, programmatic, and funding decisions. These include STEM learning experiences, pathways to STEM careers, the STEM educator workforce, and infrastructure and materials (including school buildings, equipment, internet access, and technology). The chapters in this report are organized to first provide background information about rurality, education policy, and current trends in rural STEM education before describing these major components and how the evidence related to them builds support for the committee's conclusions and recommendations.

Chapter 2 explains why *rural* is difficult to define and easy to misunderstand. It also addresses the implications of the multiple definitions and assumptions about rural areas, including the demographic and geographic characteristics of rural communities as well as the many definitions used to define rural areas. This chapter provides foundational knowledge needed to address the statement of task.

Chapter 3 describes the education system in rural settings, highlighting similarities and differences between rural and nonrural settings, and describing unique policy and funding structures that support or hinder STEM learning in rural areas. It includes formal, informal, and nonformal education systems and how they are structured (federal constructs, local control, collaboration outside the classroom). The chapter includes portions of the commissioned landscape scan of federal programming (task 1) and provides evidence for tasks 3, 4, and 5.

Chapter 4 gives an overview of national trends in rural STEM education, including statistics on STEM achievement, aspirations, enrollment, and persistence. This addresses task 3 and sets up the recommendations called for in tasks 4 and 5.

The next three chapters present the evidence and committee deliberations to address tasks 3, 4, and 5. Chapter 5 discusses the research base on effective learning for K–12 STEM education in rural settings, considering instructional and experiential learning constructs and their benefits and challenges, including online learning. It also provides an overview of how STEM pathways in rural settings serve as mechanisms to integrate K–12 education and workforce development skills to help students transition to higher education or the workplace.

Chapter 6 explores the needs for educator recruitment, retention, and professional learning in rural settings and describes some promising new methods to increase these for rural STEM teachers.

Chapter 7 examines the physical and fiscal requirements for effective STEM education and the challenges of providing them (including internet connectivity) in rural settings.

Chapter 8 presents the committee's conclusions and recommendations as well as a research agenda.

REFERENCES

Aladjem, D. (2024). [Strategic priorities or distributed choice? Federal education and workforce development investments in rural areas]. Paper commissioned for the Committee on K-12 STEM Education and Workforce Development in Rural Areas.

Allen, P. J., Chang, R., Gorrall, B. K., Waggenspack, L., Fukuda, E., Little, T. D., & Noam, G. G. (2019). From quality to outcomes: A national study of afterschool STEM programming. *International Journal of STEM Education*, *6*(1), 1–21. https://doi.org/10.1186/s40594-019-0191-2

Avery, L. M. (2013). Rural science education: Valuing local knowledge. *Theory into Practice*, *52*(1), 28–35.

Azano, A. P., Callahan, C. M., & Kuehl, R. (2021). Challenges and innovative responses in rural gifted education. In *Bloomsbury handbook of rural education in the United States* (pp. 294–303). Bloomsbury Academic.

Cromartie, J., von Reichert, C., & Arthun, R. (2015). *Factors affecting former residents' returning to rural communities* (ERR-185). Economic Research Service, U.S. Department of Agriculture. https://www.ers.usda.gov/webdocs/publications/45361/52906_err185.pdf?v=498

Davis, D. P., & Dumont, A. (2021). The "TRIC" to fostering shared economic prosperity in rural America. In A. Dumont, & D. P. Davis (Eds.), *Investing in rural prosperity* (pp. 135–152). Federal Reserve Bank of St. Louis. https://www.stlouisfed.org/-/media/project/frbstl/stlouisfed/files/pdfs/community-development/investing-rural/9_tric_fostering_shared_economic_prosperity_rural_america.pdf

Davis, J. C., Cromartie, J., Farrigan, T., Genetin, B., Sanders, A., & Winikoff, J. B. (2023). *Rural America at a glance: 2023 edition*. Economic Research Service, U.S. Department of Agriculture. https://www.ers.usda.gov/webdocs/publications/107838/eib-261.pdf?v=3379.2

De Mars, A., Taken Alive, J., Burns Ortiz, M., Ma, Z., & Wang, M. (2022). Educators' perspectives on factors impacting STEM achievement in rural indigenous student-serving schools. *The Rural Educator*, *43*(1), 24–36.

Eppley, K. (2017). Rural science education as social justice. *Cultural Studies of Science Education*, *12*, 45–52. https://link.springer.com/content/pdf/10.1007/s11422-016-9751-7.pdf

Grimes, L. E., Arrastía-Chisholm, M. A., & Bright, S. B. (2019). How can they know what they don't know? The beliefs and experiences of rural school counselors about STEM career advising. *Theory & Practice in Rural Education*, *9*(1), 74–90. https://doi.org/10.3776/tpre.2019.v9n1p74-90

Hammack, R., Stanton, C. R., & Boyle, J. (2023). "Step outside": A portrait of an exemplary rural K-8 science educator. *Journal of Research in Science Teaching*, *60*(3), 544–567. https://onlinelibrary.wiley.com/doi/epdf/10.1002/tea.21809

Hampton, K. N., Robertson, C. T., Fernandez, L., Shin, I., & Bauer, J. M. (2021). How variation in internet access, digital skills, and media use are related to rural student outcomes: GPA, SAT, and educational aspirations. *Telematics and Informatics*, *63*, 101666.

Infrastructure Investment and Jobs Act, Pub. L. No. 117-58, 135 Stat. 429 (2021). https://www.congress.gov/117/plaws/publ58/PLAW-117publ58.pdf

Johnson, J. D., & Zoellner, B. P. (2016). School funding and rural districts. In S. M. Williams & A. A. Grooms (Eds.), *Educational opportunity in rural contexts: The politics of place* (pp. 3–20). Information Age Publishing.

Marksbury, N. (2017). Monitoring the pipeline: STEM education in rural US. *Forum on Public Policy Online*, *2017*(2). Oxford Round Table.

Miller, B. (1995). *The role of rural schools in community development: Policy issues and implications. Program report.* Northwest Regional Lab. https://files.eric.ed.gov/fulltext/ED393617.pdf

Moll, L., Amanti, C., Neff, D., & Gonzalez, N. (1992). Funds of knowledge for teaching: Using a qualitative approach to connect homes and classrooms. *Theory into Practice*, *XXXI*(2). https://education.ucsc.edu/ellisa/pdfs/Moll_Amanti_1992_Funds_of_Knowledge.pdf

National Academies of Sciences, Engineering, and Medicine (NASEM). (2015). *Science teachers' learning: Enhancing opportunities, creating supportive contexts.* National Academies Press.

———. (2021). *Call to action for science education: Building opportunity for the future.* National Academies Press.

———. (2022). *Science and engineering in preschool through elementary grades: The brilliance of children and the strengths of educators.* National Academies Press. https://doi.org/10.17226/26215

———. (2024). *A new vision for high-quality preschool curriculum.* National Academies Press. https://doi.org/10.17226/27429

National Academy of Engineering & National Research Council (NAE & NRC). (2002). *Technically speaking: Why all Americans need to know more about technology.* National Academies Press.

———. (2014). *STEM integration in K–12 education: Status, prospects, and an agenda for research.* National Academies Press.

National Center for Education Statistics. (2023). *Rural students' access to the internet: Condition of education.* U.S. Department of Education, Institute of Education Sciences. https://nces.ed.gov/programs/coe/indicator/lfc

National Research Council. (2002). *Scientific research in education.* National Academies Press.

National Science Board. (2021, August 31). *The STEM labor force of today: Scientists, engineers, and skilled technical workers* (NSB-2021-2). https://ncses.nsf.gov/pubs/nsb20212

Parker, K., Horowitz, J., Brown, A., Fry, R., Cohn, D. V., & Igielnik, R. (2018). *What unites and divides urban, suburban and rural communities.* Policy Commons. https://coilink.org/20.500.12592/6q6tkh

Paulson, D. (2024). [State-Driven Rural STEM Education Policies and Programs]. Paper commissioned for the Committee on K-12 STEM Education and Workforce Development in Rural Areas.

Rush-Marlowe, R. (2024). [Rural students as an underserved population in STEM education and workforce]. Paper commissioned for the Committee on K-12 STEM Education and Workforce Development in Rural Areas.

Saw, G. K. (2024). STEM education and pathways of rural and small-town students: Disparities by geographical remoteness [Presentation]. 2024 National Forum to Advance Rural Education, Savannah, GA.

Saw, G. K., & Agger, C. A. (2021). STEM pathways of rural and small-town students: Opportunities to learn, aspirations, preparation, and college enrollment. *Educational Researcher*, *50*(9), 595–606.

Schafft, K. A. (2016). Rural education as rural development: Understanding the rural school–community well-being linkage in a 21st-century policy context. *Peabody Journal of Education*, *91*(2), 137–154. https://doi.org/10.1080/0161956X.2016.1151734

Schafft, K. A., & Harmon, H. L. (2010). Schools and community development. In J. W. Robinson & G. P. Green (Eds.), *Introduction to community development: Theory, practice, and service-learning.* Sage.

Seal, K. R., & Harmon, H. L. (1995). Realities of rural school reform. *Phi Delta Kappan*, *77*(2), 119–124. https://eric.ed.gov/?id=EJ513379

Short, R. A., Struminger, R., Zarestky, J., Pippin, J., Wong, M., Vilen, L., & Lawing, A. M. (2020). Spatial inequalities leave micropolitan areas and Indigenous populations underserved by informal STEM learning institutions. *Science Advances*, 6(41), eabb3819.

Smith, G. A., & Sobel, D. (2014). *Place- and community-based education in schools.* Routledge. https://doi.org/10.4324/9780203858530

Starrett, A., Irvin, M. J., Lotter, C., & Yow, J. A. (2022). Understanding the relationship of science and mathematics place-based workforce development on adolescents' motivation and rural aspirations. *American Educational Research Journal*, *59*(6), 1090–1121. https://doi.org/10.3102/00028312221099009

Starrett, A., Yow, J., Lotter, C., Irvin, M. J., & Adams, P. (2021). Teachers connecting with rural students and places: A mixed methods analysis. *Teaching and Teacher Education*, *97*, 103231. https://doi.org/10.1016/j.tate.2020.103231

Tieken, M. C. (2014). *Why rural schools matter*. University of North Carolina Press.

Tran, H., Hardie, S., Gause, S., Moyi, P., & Ylimaki, R. (2020). Leveraging the perspectives of rural educators to develop realistic job previews for rural teacher recruitment and retention. *The Rural Educator*, *41*(2), 31–46. https://files.eric.ed.gov/fulltext/EJ1277657.pdf

U.S. Department of Education. (2022). *Advancing digital equity for all*. https://tech.ed.gov/advancing-digital-equity-for-all/

Yosso, T. J. (2005). Whose culture has capital? A critical race theory discussion of community cultural wealth. *Race Ethnicity and Education*, *8*(1), 69–91. https://doi.org/10.1080/1361332052000341006

Zimmerman, H. T., & Weible, J. L. (2017). Learning in and about rural places: Connections and tensions between students' everyday experiences and environmental quality issues in their community. *Cultural Studies of Science Education*, *12*, 7–31.

2

Defining and Characterizing Rural America

Discussion of science, technology, engineering, and mathematics (STEM) education in rural America requires an understanding of how rural America is defined in federal, state, local, and societal terms. This chapter first reviews some definitions of rurality, including the committee's approach to defining it, and then considers consequences of those definitions on funding and other outcomes for rural schools and communities in the context of rural STEM education. The chapter also discusses diversity in rural areas and the changing rural landscape. Subsequent chapters will discuss in more detail the effects of these definitions and characteristics on effective STEM education and workforce development in rural settings.

Throughout this chapter and report, the terms *United States* and *America* are inclusive of U.S. territories (American Samoa, Guam, the Commonwealth of the Northern Mariana Islands, and the U.S. Virgin Islands), the Commonwealth of Puerto Rico, and the Federated States of Micronesia, Republic of the Marshall Islands, and Republic of Palau.

THE CHALLENGE OF DEFINING RURALITY

What is rural? The word encompasses a multitude of definitions, making it difficult to determine what types of communities are classified as rural. In many ways, the definition is dependent on the audience. Most definitions focus on "where is rural" and assume that "who is rural" is contained in those definitions.

Rurality varies by geography unique to each region of the United States. It includes, for example, the following types of communities, which exist all over the country:

- a remote village located off the road system, accessible only by air, and dependent on traditional subsistence activities for livelihood;
- a remote town inhabited by families with very low or high income levels, with growing school and job opportunities nearby;
- an island teeming with vibrant life and diverse culture but isolated geographically, resulting in a high cost of living;
- a picturesque mountain community with seasonal influx of population yet lacking affordable housing for year-round residents; and
- a two-building school district serving a farming community 80 miles from the nearest services.

Rurality is distinctly linked to local culture, which frequently involves a profound connection to the land. Connections are further defined by economic drivers that attract or retain certain types of people who thrive in these environments. Perhaps most importantly, the combination of these factors creates a deep-rooted sense of community with strong relational ties that are sometimes difficult to find outside of rural settings.

It is also important to recognize that rural people have their own self-definitions based on their lived experiences. People tend to create their understanding of the term *rural* based on where they have lived in comparison to places they have visited or heard about. Ardoin and Koon (2024) describe three main categories of rural individuals' self-definitions: (a) *Prevalence of nature/land* may be related to the vast openness or unique geographic features of the land as well as the wildlife and people's synergistic relationship with the local fauna. Most rural residents also self-report a high level of appreciation for and reliance on the land. (b) *Proximity to stores* is a factor of rural life, as residents refer to the distance and modality of travel involved in getting to the nearest grocery store, gas station, or shopping mall, or they may use proximity to a large city or metropolitan area to place their hometown. (c) *Close-knit community* is often mentioned by rural residents, who note the level of interconnectedness in their community—statements like "everyone knows everyone" or "the people make the place" are common. There is also an emphasis on familial relationships and the value of being a good neighbor.

The next section surveys various definitions of rurality across both policy and research, and the following section discusses various implications of several approaches to defining rurality.

Formal Definitions of Rural Populations and Areas

The federal government relies on two main geographic/demographic definitions of what is considered rural. The U.S. Census Bureau defines *rural* as any population, housing, or territory not in an urban area, which is defined as an area with either 5,000 or more people or 2,000 units of housing.[1] The Office of Management and Budget (OMB) defines *rural* in the context of county classifications as *metropolitan* (if it includes an urban area with a population of 50,000 or more), *micropolitan* (if it includes an urban area with a population between 10,000 and 50,000), or neither.[2] These definitions present measurement challenges, with the Census definition often reporting larger numbers and OMB consistently reporting lower numbers of rural areas, and both running the risk of missing communities that may self-identify as rural (Castle & Tak, 2021).

The U.S. Department of Education's National Center for Education Statistics (NCES) created urban-centric locale codes that divide public schools into four categories: city, suburb, town, or rural (Geverdt, 2019). Each group is then further delineated by population size or proximity to urban areas or clusters. The NCES locale criteria rely on three primary geographic concepts to define and classify territory—urban areas, core based statistical areas (CBSAs), and places. "To qualify as an urban area, the territory must encompass at least 2,500 people, at least 1,500 of which reside outside institutional group quarters. Urban areas that contain 50,000 or more people are designated as Urbanized Areas (UAs); urban areas that contain at least 2,500 and less than 50,000 people are designated as Urban Clusters (UCs)" (Geverdt, 2019, pp. 2–3). The following NCES definitions influence many of the datasets used in education research:

City: territory located within principal cities (incorporated places with a large population of residents) of CBSA;
Suburban: territory in a UA that is located outside the boundary of a principal city of a CBSA;
Town: all UCs; and
Rural: territory outside of urban areas.

---

[1]https://www.census.gov/programs-surveys/geography/guidance/geo-areas/urban-rural.html. It should be noted that this definition of urban increased from a threshold of 2,500 people, which increased the numbers of places classified as rural that were previously classified as town. In addition, most studies and reports published prior to 2023, including NCES data, were based on the 2,500 cutoff, which may have implications for interpreting the evidence base.

[2]https://www.ers.usda.gov/topics/rural-economy-population/rural-classifications/what-is-rural/

Each of these areas can be further subdivided to create 12 different categories, or consolidated into a rural-town vs. suburban-city comparison. For most purposes in this chapter, the consolidated (rural-town vs. suburban-city) view of rural areas is used when discussing NCES data.

The U.S. Department of Agriculture's Economic Research Service (USDA ERS) maintains the Rural-Urban Continuum Code (RUCC),[3] which delineates the OMB definition into nine categories (codes 1–3 representing metropolitan counties and codes 4–9 representing nonmetropolitan counties) based on a county's population and whether it is adjacent to a metropolitan area. Because the RUCC uses threshold values for the population criteria, it may be deceptive because "similar counties may be classified as different, whereas counties that are very dissimilar may be grouped together in the same category" (Waldorf, 2006, p. 6).

The Rural-Urban Density Typology (Isserman, 2005), an alternative to the RUCC, defines thresholds for the following variables: percentage of urban residents, total number of urban residents, population density, and population size of the county's largest urban area, yielding four types of counties: rural, mixed rural, mixed urban, and urban. The committee notes that (a) although the typology improves the definitions for rural and urban counties, it does not adequately define the two "mixed" categories and is applicable only to counties; and (b) although definitions based on thresholds are simple and result in a finite number of categories, thresholds can be controversial because they rely on arbitrary figures that do not adequately adjust for small changes (Waldorf, 2006).

One approach to defining rural using multiple measures without the dichotomous classification of rural versus nonrural was proposed in 2022 by the Alliance for Research on Regional Colleges to define regional institutions of higher education as "rural-serving institutions" (Koricich, 2022). This definition incorporates five variables from three data sources and creates an index that can be used to compare institutions. Two variables use Census data for the percentages classified as rural in both the county where the institution is located and the counties adjacent to it. The index also incorporates USDA ERS classifications for the home county, with six threshold-based definitions for metro, urban, or rural populations as well as a dichotomous variable of whether the county where the institution is located is adjacent to a metro area. Finally, the index uses Integrated Postsecondary Education Data System data for the percentage of parks and recreation, natural resources, and agriculture degrees conferred at the institution (Koricich, 2022). This work thus uses multiple data points to conceptualize a framework of rurality on a spectrum and affords a more nuanced view of postsecondary institutions that serve rural areas.

---

[3]https://www.ers.usda.gov/data-products/rural-urban-continuum-codes.aspx

Perhaps the most comprehensive definition of rurality is the Index of Relative Rurality (IRR) proposed by Waldorf (2006). This all-encompassing measure produces a spectrum of rurality on a 0–1 scale, with 0 being most urban and 1 most rural. The scale includes four dimensions: population size, population density, extent of urban (built-up) area, and remoteness. These dimensions are components of existing definitions of rurality, and the IRR uses the unweighted average of the dimensions rescaled to the 0–1 scale to create a comparative index. This approach allows the measure to be applicable to a wider array of groupings, from individual counties to groups of counties, regions, townships, and census tracts. It also allows rurality to become a relative measure, useful for research on trajectories of rurality over periods of time. This IRR also reflects the multidimensional nature of rurality that varies across locations. The committee discusses the affordances and limitations of this approach to defining rurality later in this chapter.

Visualizing Discrepancies

The discrepancies among these definitions are clearly illustrated in Figure 2-1, a visual representation of three definitions used in the state of Indiana and the resulting differences in which counties are considered "rural." For example, Newton, Benton, and Warren counties in northwest Indiana are labeled metro in the OMB map designating metropolitan areas (left), yet in the RUCC map (center), Newton and Benton counties are classified with one of the three metro designations, while Warren is one of the most nonmetropolitan counties in the state and. Further, in the IRR (right) map all three are designated nonmetropolitan and some of the counties with the highest degree of rurality in the state.[4]

In addition to divergent meanings, definitions are used in different ways by federal agencies, national organizations, individual states, localities, private organizations, and philanthropic foundations. The resulting datasets are therefore not always comparable. Table 2-1 outlines further variability in definitions of *rural* for selected federal agencies and national organizations most relevant to the charge of this consensus study, and Figure 2-2 shows these discrepancies graphically.

---

[4]The preceding paragraph and Figure 2-1 were changed after release of the report to accurately reflect the classification of "rural" on the maps.

Office of Management and Budget

Area Designation	*Number*
Metropolitan	*44*
Nonmetro Micropolitan	*24*
Nonmetro Noncore	*24*

Rural-Urban Continuum Codes

Metropolitan		*Nonmetropolitan*	
1	*23*	*4*	*6*
2	*7*	*5*	*3*
3	*14*	*6*	*30*
		7	*4*
		8	*5*
		9	*0*

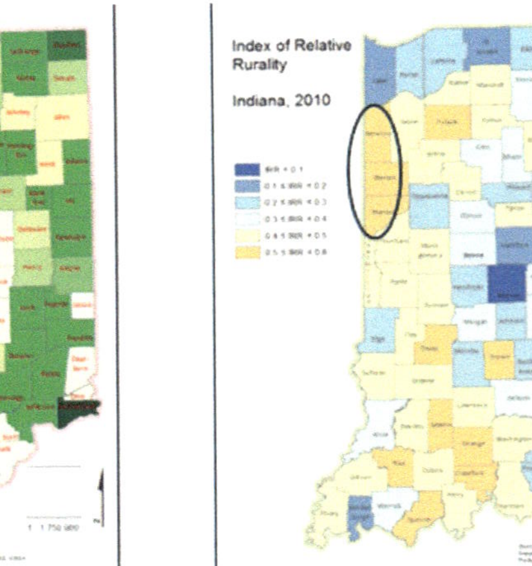

Index of Relative Rurality

IRR	*Number*
IRR < *0.1*	*1*
0.1 ≤ *IRR* < *0.2*	*5*
0.2 ≤ *IRR* < *0.3*	*14*
0.3 ≤ *IRR* < *0.4*	*18*
0.4 ≤ *IRR* < *0.5*	*39*
0.5 ≤ *IRR* < *0.6*	*15*

FIGURE 2-1 Definitions of rurality used in Indiana.
SOURCE: Adapted from Purdue University Center for Regional Development.

TABLE 2-1 Federal Agencies' and National Organizations' Definitions of *Rural*

Federal Agency/National Organization	Definition of Rural
Census Bureau	Rural areas are all population, housing, and territory that is not urban: Open country, Settlements with fewer than 5,000 residents, and Settlements with fewer than 2,000 housing units
Office of Management and Budget	Rural areas are counties that are not part of a Metropolitan Statistical Area. This includes counties that do not meet minimum population requirements, do not have a central city (with a population of at least 10,000), do not relate closely to larger urban places
National Center for Education Statistics (NCES; Department of Education)	Urban-centric locale codes (city, suburb, town, rural) further delineated by population size or proximity to urban areas
Sustainable Regional Systems (National Science Foundation)	Rural systems are any settlements with population, housing, economic activity, or areas not in an urban geographical area.
Department of Agriculture Economic Research Service (USDA ERS)	Population of 20,000 or less for Rural Development programs; population limit can vary for other programs. For Rural Housing Service Population limit may be higher, such as 35,000
Health Resources and Services Administration (HRSA; Department of Health and Human Services)	Determined by factors including population density, distance from urban areas, and healthcare shortages
Federal Communications Commission (FCC)	Factors include population density, broadband availability, and proximity to urban areas
Department of Housing and Urban Development (HUD)	Criteria may include population size, location, and specific program requirements
Department of Transportation (DOT)	Criteria may include population size, distance from urban centers, and road access
National Rural Health Association (NRHA)	Areas with populations of 2,500 or less are considered rural
National Rural Education Association (NREA)	Criteria similar to those of the U.S. Department of Education, including factors related to population size and geographic isolation
National Rural Electric Cooperative Association (NRECA)	Areas served by rural electric cooperatives are considered rural
National Rural Water Association (NRWA)	Based on size and population of communities served by water and wastewater systems

(*continued*)

TABLE 2-1 Continued

Federal Agency/National Organization	Definition of Rural
National Association of Development Organizations (NADO)	Factors such as population density and geographic isolation are considered when defining rural regions
National Rural Transit Assistance Program (RTAP; DOT)	Defines rural areas based on population density and distance from urbanized areas
National Rural Economic Developers Association (NREDA)	Definitions based on economic indicators, population, and access to resources

SOURCE: Committee generated.

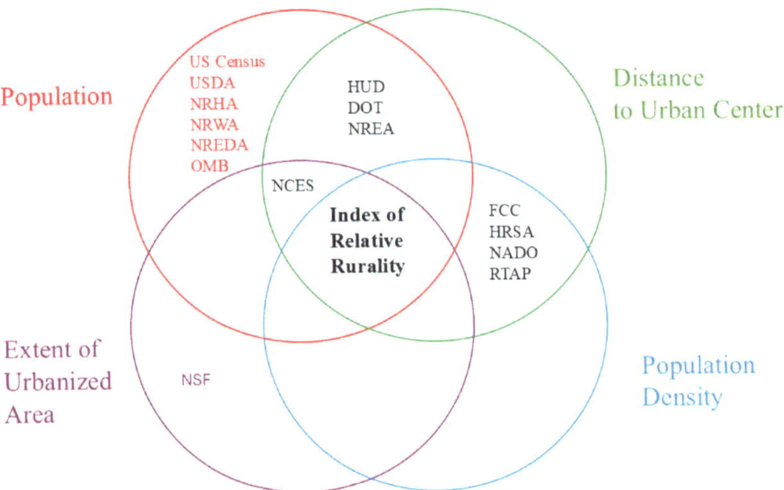

FIGURE 2-2 Criteria used in federal agencies' and national organizations' definitions of rurality.
NOTE: See Table 2-1 for definitions of abbreviations. Organizational definitions not based on any of the four dimensions included in the Index of Relative Rurality are listed in Table 2-1 but not present in Figure 2-2 (NRECA).
SOURCE: Committee generated.

IMPLICATIONS OF THE VARIOUS DEFINITIONS OF *RURAL*

Given the broad variability of definitions, both formal and informal, the committee acknowledges both the difficulties of delineating what is and is not rural and the implications of the lack of a standard definition of rurality.

Consistency and Challenges in Research

The various definitions of what is rural create inconsistency and fragmentation across research on rural STEM education, making it difficult to draw clear conclusions. The literature referenced in this report includes a variety of definitions of the word *rural*, so although related findings are helpful, they do not provide comprehensive reliable results. Consensus definitions in rural-related education research are needed to better inform the development of effective programming and funding opportunities.

Rural populations also present challenges to research on STEM education methods and outcomes. Small population sizes in some communities make it difficult to determine statistical significance, and differing characteristics among rural communities hamper efforts to compare or combine datasets or research results. Research based on governmental data carries with it the specific definition of rurality under which the data were collected; the resulting research papers may appear to be contradictory simply because their underlying definitions and datasets were inconsistent. Many governmental datasets do not identify *rural* as a keyword or a concept in the data, further limiting the practicality of conducting research in this space. These factors comport with the observation by the U.S. National Science Foundation (NSF) Committee on Equal Opportunities in Science and Engineering (NSF, 2024, p. 6) that "demographic statistics for rural students in NSF-supported activities over time were not readily available regarding students reached and served," and reports often rely on examples. The lack of agreed-upon definitions used across federal agencies and researchers, as well as limited data collection on rural students, results in an incomplete and inconsistent picture of rural K–12 STEM education.

Implications for Schools and Districts

The NCES designations, when translated into definitions of school districts, can have a profound effect on the ability of a rural school district to obtain federal funding. For example, the Rural Education Achievement Program (REAP), funded through Title V-B of the Every Student Succeeds Act, requires that every school in a district be classified as NCES 41, 42, or 43 for the district to qualify for REAP funds meant to support schools with small student population sizes. The Eagle Point High School on the Rogue River in southern Oregon is coded 22 (suburb midsize) because of the proximity of a micropolitan area. But the district extends far north along the river, with elementary and middle schools that are small and isolated: The Lake Creek Learning Center (K–5) is about 35 miles from the high school, has 40 percent of its students in poverty, and is coded appropriately as 43 (remote). Yet the Lake Creek school cannot receive REAP support because of the NCES coding of the high school at the other end of the district (Jesse Longhurst, Southern Oregon University, presentation to the committee, January 2024).

These definitions also have implications for community colleges. For example, Iowa is the 15th least populous state in the country, with a population density of 57 people per square mile and more than 85 percent of the land used for farming. Iowa has the third highest number of farms in the country and over 50 percent of its micropolitan statistical areas are considered rural by Census definitions. By these metrics it seems the state is overwhelmingly rural. But application of a different metric suggests otherwise. Iowa is also home to 15 community colleges. Even considering these community colleges in the context of urban-centric definitions and population density, we would anticipate many of them to be classified as rural, as 10 of the 15 are in communities with fewer than 25,000 residents, and six of those 10 communities have fewer than 10,000 residents. Yet, according to the NCES definition of rurality, only 3 of Iowa's 15 community colleges are classified as rural (Rush-Marlowe, 2024): those 3 would be eligible for rural-specific funding programs, but others with very similar characteristics and infrastructure would not. In addition, the community colleges that are not classified as rural by NCES could end up competing for grants with institutions that have much higher levels of staffing and administrative capacity.

Funding Inequity

Inconsistent definitions of what is considered rural, as well as threshold numbers that differently classify similar communities, schools, or districts, can result in inequitable and inconsistent funding for rural communities as well as less access to opportunities targeted to rural populations. In addition to the two examples above, consider two communities applying for the same grant that is specific to rural communities as based on the Census definition (rural is a community of fewer than 5,000). One has a population of 1,000 and is 45 miles from the nearest UA and 30 miles from a UC; it is classified as *remote* by NCES. The other has 4,900 inhabitants and is only 5 miles from a UA and 2.5 miles from a UC; it is classified as *fringe* by NCES. Both communities would qualify for a grant aimed at rural communities, but the second, by virtue of its size and proximity to more populous areas as well as educational institutions and resources, would more likely be able to access the administrative capacity and expertise needed to write a successful proposal for that funding. Thus although the communities are viewed as equivalent by the funding agency, it is likely that the proposals written by those with more resources and capacity will have an advantage over requests from those with very limited resources, staffing, or expertise in federal grant applications and management. This inequity results in a lack of awards to the most rural and remote schools and communities simply because they do not have the human capital and expertise to put together a competitive application.

THE INDEX OF RURALITY: A COMMON DEFINITION FOR RURALITY

Given the differing definitions used by federal agencies, state agencies, policymakers, and researchers, and the implications of that inconsistency on rural communities and schools, the committee argues that future research and policy relevant to rural K–12 STEM education and workforce development should reframe the conversation around a more nuanced and flexible definition of rurality. We find that the spectrum definition of rurality provided by the IRR acknowledges that the variability, challenges, and strengths of each community are unique. As Waldorf (2006, p. 2) explains, "It does not answer the question 'Is a county rural or urban?' but instead addresses the question 'What is a county's degree of rurality?'" In short, the tool recognizes that a series of factors delineate the scale to which a community is rural. For these reasons we are confident that the IRR is well aligned with the context of this report. Although all of the definitions discussed can be relevant for improving K–12 STEM education and workforce development, the IRR better enables users to determine the level of rurality for each community.

Another benefit of the IRR is that it avoids what Waldorf calls the "*threshold trap*," the likes of which can lead to funding inequities faced by rural schools in urban counties like Lake Creek Learning Center, by pigeonholing "counties, thereby potentially separating similar counties and joining dissimilar counties" (Waldorf, 2006, p. 2). One example considers three communities with populations of 20, 497, and 502, with a definition threshold of under 500 people to be considered in one category: thus the first two will be grouped together although they are quite different, and the second pair will be grouped separately although they are quite similar (Waldorf & Kim, 2015).

The IRR also allows for small changes in variables to impact classification. Other definitions that are more aligned with threshold tend to require large changes to shift categorization. The reality is that, in rural settings, small changes to variables have significant implications for small communities. The IRR can be applied to a variety of spatial scales and offer a regional perspective across communities that may not otherwise be working together. These regional snapshots could identify opportunities for partnerships and coordinated regional development efforts that maximize human capital for smaller communities. The map in Figure 2-3 shows the IRR as applied to counties throughout the United States, clearly highlighting both the difference between urban centers and other counties in a state and the presence of rural counties in every state.

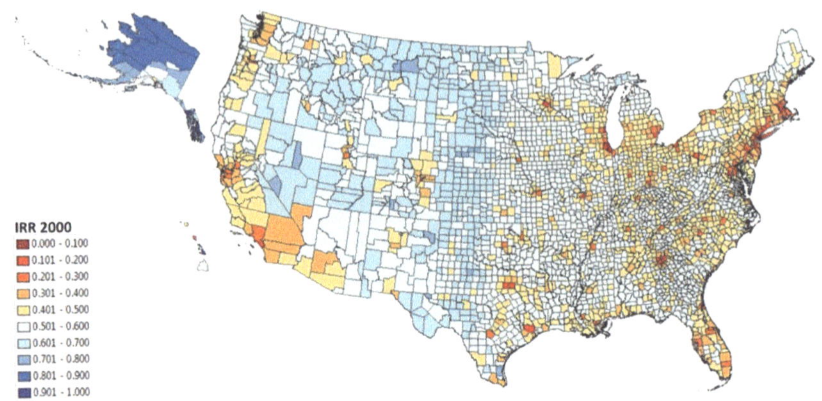

FIGURE 2-3 Map of rural U.S. counties according to the Index of Relative Rurality (IRR).
SOURCE: Waldorf and Kim (2015).

CHARACTERISTICS OF RURAL AMERICA

The common narrative of the rural-urban divide is not only inaccurate, it is also harmful to both rural and urban communities. Just as no two cities are alike, there is no singular version of rurality and, contrary to common narratives, rural communities are not all defined by whiteness, agriculture, or political conservatism. The reality is that rural America is diverse in every way—geographically, economically, and racially (Showalter et al., 2023). Its diverse ideas, people, and economies are also inherently linked to urban communities, which provide support functions and access to hospitals and other public services that are often unavailable in rural communities, while the latter are critical contributors of food, energy, and economic growth. Rural and nonrural areas are thus deeply interconnected (Cattaneo et al., 2022).

Furthermore, the composition of U.S. rural communities continues to evolve. Common misconceptions of rural America as either a nostalgic remnant of a simpler and more wholesome time or a provincial undereducated backwater influence attitudes and undermine support for rural communities. The outdated idea that rural areas have been "left behind" began with a 1967 Presidential Advisory Report that described the economic depression in rural America at the time (Carnevale et al., 2024). The resulting overemphasis on rural challenges (e.g., lower educational attainment, higher poverty rates, and declining population sizes) without recognizing the assets of rural communities has created a problematic dichotomy, where the "struggling rural" is unfavorably compared to the "thriving urban" (Carnevale et al., 2024). Rural areas are often viewed from deficit perspectives, characterized as underdeveloped and needing to be saved (Brenner, 2022, 2023; Crain & Newlin, 2021; Fulkerson & Lowe, 2016; Tieken, 2014). They are also often presented as a monolith (Brenner, 2022; Burrola et al., 2023).

This outlook contributes to stereotypical views and misconceptions about the people who live in rural areas, their cultures, and their values. For example, there is an assumption that rural America is largely White, agriculturally based, and uneducated. In reality, rural communities are increasingly diverse (Center for Public Education, 2023) and have industries in the social sectors (e.g., education, health care) as their largest employers (Kusmin, 2016), and chronic problems such as poverty and workforce development are experienced by both urban and rural areas alike (Liu & Peng, 2023).

The diversity of people, economics, and geography across rural areas makes it understandably difficult to pin down a precise definition of what it means to be rural. However, as discussed, existing definitions are both deficient and deficit based, and confusing or misaligned definitions of rurality can be a barrier for rural communities attempting to access state, federal, or philanthropic funding. Improved definitions are critical to better understand rural communities and help ensure that they have access to the resources they need. In essence, there is no one-size-fits-all definition of *rural* and it should be acknowledged that this fact makes understanding the rural context complicated.

Demographics of Rurality

According to a USDA report, 46 million U.S. residents—approximately 14 percent of the population—live in nonmetropolitan or rural counties (Davis et al., 2023). The Census Bureau classified 66.3 million U.S. residents (20%) as nonurban in 2020. The percentage of the population classified by the OMB as nonmetropolitan has declined from 33 percent in 1974 to 14 percent in 2023, largely from an increase in the effective size of urban centers (Kenneth Johnson presentation to the committee, January 2024). While some rural areas have seen an increase in population since 2022, rural areas overall have experienced a decrease (Carnevale et al., 2024; Davis et al., 2022, 2023), attributed in part to a declining birth rate and an increasing death rate driven by an aging population.

Some nonmetropolitan counties that saw a slight population increase in 2020–2022 after a decade of population loss (Davis et al., 2023) benefited from the state and local economy, proximity to larger metropolitan areas, association as a destination for retirement or recreational activities, or the ability to work remotely from a rural setting, including the availability of broadband (Kenneth Johnson presentation; Davis et al., 2023;

Dobis et al., 2021). Slight population growth in some nonmetropolitan counties is due to the increase in remote work and out-migration from metropolitan areas during the COVID-19 pandemic, but out-migration rates in 42 percent of such counties decreased their population, especially in the Great Plains (Davis et al., 2023).

Rural America has also seen demographic changes related to racial and ethnic diversity, age, and poverty. While White residents constitute the largest share of rural populations, communities of color and immigrant populations are growing (Davis et al., 2022; Parker et al., 2018). For example, while not true for all rural counties, in aggregate roughly 20 percent of people living in rural counties are Indigenous, Black, Latine, Asian, Pacific Islander, or multiracial (Parker et al., 2018). The rural Latine population grew by almost 20 percent and the rural multiracial population increased by 148 percent between 2010 and 2020 (HAC, 2021). The increase in diversity is particularly large among children: 32 percent of people under the age of 18 in rural America are from historically minoritized groups (Kenneth Johnson presentation). At the same time, the average age of adults is higher than in nonrural places (Carnevale et al., 2024; Davis et al., 2022; Parker et al., 2018): in 2021 rural counties had a larger share of adults 65 and older (more than 20%) than nonrural counties (Davis et al., 2022).

The 2020 Census marked the first time that rural America lost population (Johnson & Lichter, 2022): it showed declines in about two thirds of nonmetropolitan counties from 2010 to 2020 and chronic population loss in nearly a third. These losses were most extreme in the most remote places (Kenneth Johnson presentation). With this population loss, these places face additional challenges maintaining critical services and programs, including education.

Rural America has also experienced persistent inequities due to poverty (Davis et al., 2023), affecting housing, health care, and education. A 2006 study noted that high school students in rural areas in the Appalachian region were more likely than their urban counterparts to have grown up in poverty (Ali & McWhirter, 2006). These students were more likely than urban youth in the region at the time to say that "postsecondary education is unaffordable and not necessary" (Carnevale et al., 2024). Today, approximately 14 percent of children ages 5 to 17 in rural areas live in poverty. This is higher than in suburban areas (12%) but lower than town and city locales (21%; NCES, 2023). In addition, Black/African American, Hispanic/Latine, and Indigenous/Native communities in rural areas experience higher rates of poverty than White communities (Carnevale et al., 2024). Many studies have shown that poverty is associated with lower academic achievement. For example, rural students begin school with lower reading achievement than their suburban peers, and this gap continues through elementary and middle school in both mathematics and reading. But it is important to note that when controlling for poverty the reading achievement scores are no longer significantly different (Clarke, 2014).

Spatial Inequities

Notwithstanding the strengths, assets, and resources of rural communities, they face inequities and challenges related to infrastructure. Opportunity is unevenly distributed across rural U.S. counties (Brown & Schafft, 2011; Galster & Killen, 1995; Lobao & Saenz, 2002; powell, 2008; Soja, 2010; Tieken & Auldridge-Reveles, 2019), as some enjoy more resources, like grocery stores or good medical care or quality housing, than others. Factors that create this "spatial injustice" (Soja, 2010), or "the fair and equitable distribution in space of socially valued resources and opportunities to use them" (Soja, 2009, p. 2), include discriminatory policies and practices, the political and social organization of space, and uneven economic development.

Both rural and urban communities are subject to spatial injustice, though the isolation and distance of the latter tend to exacerbate disparities. For example, many rural communities are food deserts, lacking access to healthy and affordable food (Beaulac et al., 2009), and more than 85 percent of U.S. counties facing persistent poverty—that is, where more than 20 percent of the population has lived in poverty for the past 40 years—are nonmetropolitan counties (Davis et al., 2023). These challenges often intersect in ways that create unique and overlapping challenges for rural communities and schools.

Spatial injustice tends to intersect with racial and economic inequities (powell, 2008; Tieken, 2014, 2017). For Black, Indigenous, and Latine communities, spatial injustice is both a manifestation and continuation of historic practices of exploitation. Enslavement, Jim Crow laws, gerrymandering, and racial violence, for example, have prevented many Black residents in rural communities from accumulating wealth, land, or power, resulting in generational poverty, entrenched isolation, and neglect from policymakers. Indigenous communities also face spatial injustices tied to colonization, including dispossession of land, erasure of cultural practices, and a continuing fight for sovereignty and recognition. Rural Latine communities, too, have histories of territorial disputes, linguistic oppression, and cultural erasure as well as nativist immigration policies and exploitative labor practices. The legacy of these histories, coupled with the impact of current policies and practices, is that rural communities of color experience the most severe spatial injustices, such as higher rates of persistent poverty and child poverty, greater levels of segregation, and more limited employment options (Duncan, 1999; Lichter & Parisi, 2008; Lichter et al., 2012; Schaefer et al., 2016; Tieken, 2022).

One of the most critical spatial injustices facing rural communities, especially related to STEM education and workforce development, is the digital divide, the inequitable and uneven distribution of broadband connectivity that prevents many rural communities from accessing the internet (Center for Public Education, 2023; Federal Communications Commission, 2024; Morehart et al., 2009). At the Federal Communications Commission's new benchmark speed of 100/20 Mbps, 72 percent of rural areas and 76 percent of tribal areas have access to fixed broadband (which includes technologies such as T1, cable, DSL, and FiOS and excludes cellular data), compared to 98 percent of urban areas (Federal Communications Commission, 2024, pp. 32–33). In addition, whereas about 63 percent of urban households have at least two provider options at this speed, the same is true of less than 24 percent of rural households and 31 percent of households on tribal land (Federal Communications Commission, 2024, pp. 37–38). Rural Black and Latine households are particularly likely to lack access to affordable fixed broadband (Center for Public Education, 2023). The committee discusses the issue of broadband connectivity in more detail in Chapter 7.

Many policies and practices may also intensify spatial inequalities. Policymakers and practitioners often take a "place-neutral" approach when crafting policies and developing practices, failing to consider the unique funding opportunities and challenges or the strengths and needs of local communities that shape implementation, or they assume an urban context, with large schools and big population sizes (Brenner, 2022; Eppley, 2009; Johnson & Howley, 2015). Such approaches ignore the particular challenges presented by distance and sparsity, such as teacher shortages, multiage classrooms, long bus rides, or small staffs (and they also overlook the unique strengths of rural schools, such as nimbleness and close relationships). Related, much of the "evidence" cited in "evidence-based practice" comes from urban settings, especially given the difficulty in producing adequate *n*-sizes in many small, rural contexts. Thus, many policies may not work as intended in rural settings, and recommended practices—even so-called best practices—may be ill suited for rural communities and schools.

Rural Workforce

Although rural communities are often portrayed as primarily relying on agriculture, the workforce in rural America has become much more diverse (Davis et al., 2022; Laughlin, 2016). The six largest employment industries in rural U.S. areas are health, social assistance; accommodation, food services; government; retail; agriculture; and manufacturing. In addition, real estate, education, administrative and professional services, health, and finance are the highest growth industries in rural America (Davis et al.,

2022), and the number of clean energy jobs has also increased as a result of federal legislation (Davis et al., 2023).

On the other hand, agriculture, mining, logging, and other resource-dependent industries have all shrunk in recent years, because of resource exhaustion, mechanization, outsourcing, and industry consolidation (Green, 2020; Lyson & Falk, 1993). And the number of farms in the United States has dropped from a high of 7 million in 1935 to only 2 million in 2022 (Keller & Kassel, 2024), and jobs in extractive industries have been declining since 1920 (Freudenburg, 1992). Today, only about 10 percent of rural workers are employed in traditional rural industries like agriculture and mining (Laughlin, 2016), and another 12 percent work in manufacturing.

As explained in Chapter 1, the committee defines rural STEM occupations both as those that require focused STEM skills and expertise (e.g., jobs in the life sciences, physical sciences, engineering, mathematics and computer sciences, social sciences, and health care) and as those that require STEM skills but not an advanced STEM degree, such as construction; manufacturing installation, maintenance, and repair of infrastructure; and production.

Restructuring continues to impact rural economies (Smith & Tickamyer, 2011; Ulrich-Schad & Duncan, 2018), with automation, globalization, and resource depletion reducing rural jobs and wages (Freudenburg, 1992; Johnson & Lichter, 2019; Pender et al., 2019; Smith & Tickamyer, 2011). Employment in each industry varies greatly across regions. For example, in rural counties in the West a larger percentage of the workforce is employed in agriculture, forestry, fishing, hunting, and mining compared to the manufacturing industry (Laughlin, 2016).

Two factors have recently affected industries in rural America: technological advances and the COVID-19 pandemic (Davis et al., 2022). Technological advances in agriculture led to higher labor productivity, and the manufacturing and mining industries also saw an increase in labor productivity. And although the COVID-19 pandemic had a devastating effect on job and career opportunities in rural (and other parts of) America, as of 2023 they had almost fully rebounded (Davis et al., 2023). However, a lack of economic diversity in many rural places means that, as industries shrink and leave, rural workers have substantially fewer options than their urban or suburban counterparts: they must find employment in a new sector—underscoring the critical need for good workforce development in rural places—or leave to find work elsewhere, often in cities, where jobs are more available and better paid (Marré, 2017).

The demographics of the workforce in rural America have also changed. The working-age population in nonmetropolitan areas declined between 2010 and 2020 (Carnevale et al., 2024; Davis et al., 2022). Carnevale et al. (2024) note that some of the most common occupations in rural America require physical labor and are more likely than urban jobs to result in workplace injuries. Given both the average age of the rural population and workplace injuries from physical labor demands, 15 percent of rural individuals have disabilities compared with 10 percent in urban areas.

While the largest share of workers in rural America are White, a recent study reports that "the rural Black, Asian, and Hispanic workforces each increased, with rural growth in the Hispanic workforce outpacing metro area growth. In addition, employment growth rates were higher for all other races and/or Hispanic workers than for White workers in every rural industry except agriculture" (Davis et al., 2022, p. 3). However, Carnevale et al. (2024) find gender, racial/ethnic, educational, and regional disparities in access to good rural job[5] opportunities. Women in rural areas are less likely to have a good job than both rural men and urban women, and Asian, Black, and Latine individuals are less likely than both their urban counterparts and White workers (both urban and rural) to have a good job. Although fewer rural than urban individuals hold bachelor's degrees, rural individuals with high school or associate's degrees are more likely to have a good job than urban individuals with similar educational backgrounds. But rural workers with bachelor's or advanced degrees are less likely than their urban counterparts to have good jobs, and across educational levels gender differences persist, a notable statistic in light of the average compensation for licensed rural public school teachers with a bachelor's degree meeting the minimum pay required to be considered a "good job" ($53,750).[6] Although over half of rural workers in the Northeast and Midwest areas of the United States have good jobs, across all regions the likelihood of having a good job is higher in urban areas compared to rural (Carnevale et al., 2024).

Rural Education

In *Making the Invisible Visible: STEM Talent of Rural America* (NSF, 2024), the NSF Committee on Equal Opportunities in Science and Engineering (CEOSE) describes five characteristics associated with rural education: It (a) takes place at a distance from large urban areas and (b) in small schools; (c) has access to fewer resources, such as high-quality professional development and curricula; (d) cooperates with and tries to meet the needs of the community and local economy; and (e) is placed or rooted in the lives of the

[5]A good job is defined as "one that pays a minimum of approximately $43,000 for workers ages 25–44 and a minimum of approximately $55,000 for workers ages 45–64 (in 2022 dollars)" (Carnevale et al., 2024, p. 8).

[6]https://nces.ed.gov/programs/digest/d22/tables/dt22_211.10.asp

community. The committee notes that while these characteristics can reflect the experience of many rural schools, no one rural school must exhibit all or even most of these characteristics to be classified as rural, and many rural schools exhibit many more assets than are described here. For example, there are many large rural schools in Florida, Oklahoma, California, and elsewhere (Showalter et al., 2023).

Rural Districts and Schools

State definitions of district boundaries determine whether districts are classified as rural or not. In addition, NCES defines three subcategories of rural districts: *fringe* refers to a community less than 5 miles from a UC, *distant* districts are between 5 and 10 miles from a UC, and *remote* rural districts are more than 25 miles from a UC (Geverdt, 2019). However, the definitions do not discriminate between 10 miles of highway, dirt road, mountain switchbacks, or access by float plane. In western states, rural districts cover greater areas of land than in other states and are less likely to be designated rural because they include one or more urban areas and so are classified as urban, whereas districts in eastern and midwestern states are smaller and unlikely to include urban areas. Rural districts are more likely to be classified as remote in the northern and western U.S. regions (Gutierrez & Terrones, 2023).

In addition to the term *rural*, states use the words *small*, *sparse*, and *isolated* to describe certain school districts that may need additional support. The term *small* is generally based on an enrollment threshold (generally around 200 students), *sparse* is based on a student density threshold metric, and *isolated* is based on a school's distance to other state districts with schools that teach the same grade level. However, each state sets its own metrics; in the 25 states that use the term *small*, enrollment thresholds vary from 244 in Wyoming to 24,000 in Florida, while in the 15 states that use *sparse*, student density thresholds vary from 1.2 students per square mile in Arkansas to 35 in Massachusetts. Some states' definition of *small* categorizes most of their districts as small; for example, more than 70 percent of the school districts in Alaska, Idaho, Kansas, Louisiana, Nebraska, New Mexico, and Utah are considered small by their state definition. In contrast, just 20 percent or less of the school districts in Arkansas, North Dakota, and West Virginia are considered small by their state definition (Gutierrez & Terrones, 2023).

Roughly 7.3 million public school students are enrolled in rural school districts—more than one in every seven students across the United States. Nearly one in seven of those rural students experiences poverty, one in 15 lacks health insurance, and one in ten has changed residence in the previous 12 months. Significantly, the number of children attending rural schools is greater than the number of students in rural school districts because many children attend rural schools in districts that are not designated "rural" by the National Center for Education Statistics (Showalter et al., 2023). Over half of U.S. school districts are rural, and in 28 states they may account for at least one third of public schools. In fact, "more students in the United States attend rural schools than attend the 100 largest U.S. school districts combined," making rural students a critical population to pay attention to in policy, practice, and research (Showalter et al., 2023, p. 2). One in five U.S. students attends a rural school, half of which are considered small, enrolling fewer than 493 students (Showalter et al., 2023). However, because every state has its own methodology for defining school districts and determining whether they are rural, the percentages of rural students in some states may be underestimated; and this inconsistent methodology can compromise the availability of government support for rural school districts. Table 2-2 shows the number and percentage of rural students in each state.

Rural School Staff

Over a million staff—instructional, support services, and school- and district-level administrators—were employed in rural school districts in fall 2019 (Irwin et. al., 2022). The majority (69%) are school staff: teachers and instructional aides, counselors, assistant principals, principals, support staff, and librarians. All kinds of U.S. public schools and districts have had difficulties filling teacher vacancies and addressing teacher turnover (Ingersoll & Tran, 2023). Turnover rates in rural areas broadly (15.4%) mirror those in urban (17.7%) and suburban areas (15.1%), but on closer inspection, high-poverty rural public schools experience significantly more teacher turnover each year (28%) than high-poverty urban schools (19.1%) (Ingersoll & Tran, 2023). Addressing this turnover is critical, as there is a strong correlation between high teacher turnover and low student achievement, especially for students from low-income backgrounds and students of color (Djonko-Moore, 2016; Ronfeldt et al., 2013).

Rural students are often viewed as a monolith, but they are diverse in race and ethnicity, language, social class, and learning needs (Greenough & Nelson, 2015). There is a significant difference in the percentage distribution by race/ethnicity of public elementary and secondary students between rural communities and urban or suburban ones (NCES, 2023). Though the largest percentage of students enrolled in public schools is White (68%), approximately one in three students is Indigenous/Native, Asian, Pacific Islander, Black/African American, Latine/Hispanic, and/or multiracial (NCES, 2023); and 3.5 percent of rural students are multilingual learners

TABLE 2-2 Number and Percentage of Rural Students per State, 2019

State	Number of Rural Students	Percentage of Rural Students	State	Number of Rural Students	Percentage of Rural Students
Vermont	44,805	56	Wisconsin	199,755	24
Maine	90,456	54	Ohio	395,390	24
Mississippi	209,883	48	New Mexico	81,610	26
South Dakota	63,810	45	Virginia	319,605	26
West Virginia	107,652	43	Minnesota	198,382	23
North Dakota	48,819	43	Delaware	29,980	21
Alabama	294,484	39	Michigan	298,249	21
Montana	56,462	38	Texas	1,102,648	20
Kentucky	243,345	37	Pennsylvania	299,924	18
North Carolina	562,428	37	Oregon	88,809	17
Arkansas	174,666	36	Colorado	139,833	16
Iowa	178,155	35	Utah	100,164	15
New Hampshire	58,703	35	Maryland	121,769	14
South Carolina	262,340	34	Florida	387,113	14
Wyoming	29,707	32	Washington	137,307	13
Idaho	97,704	31	Arizona	129,785	11
Tennessee	305,510	31	Connecticut	56,671	11
Oklahoma	212,694	31	New York	285,804	11
Alaska	39,401	30	Illinois	208,098	11
Kansas	144,986	30	Hawaii	18,273	11
Nebraska	94,652	29	Rhode Island	13,883	10
Indiana	296,784	29	Massachusetts	81,229	9
Georgia	498,995	29	Nevada	39,032	8
Missouri	250,564	28	New Jersey	104,853	8
Louisiana	189,438	28	California	406,504	7

SOURCE: NCES Table 203.72 Public elementary and secondary school enrollment by local and state: Fall 2021.

(Showalter et al., 2017). Across rural school districts, 13.6 percent of children aged 5–17 are experiencing poverty, and 15 percent of students have a documented disability and an Individualized Education Plan (Showalter et al., 2023). Among the parents/guardians of children in rural schools in 2019, 71 percent had education beyond high school: an associate's degree (13%), bachelor's degree (26%), graduate/professional degree (16%), or a vocational/technical certificate or some college (16%; NCES, 2023).

RURAL STEM EDUCATION AND WORKFORCE DEVELOPMENT LANDSCAPE

While it is not in the scope of this report to present an exhaustive discussion of future workforce trends in rural America, it is important to note that across all employment sectors, technical and digital skills are increasing in importance. There has been a growing demand for individuals to enter STEM fields (Harris & Hodges, 2018), across all employment areas and geographic zones. Digital literacy, facility with computerized equipment and software, and awareness of the benefits and pitfalls of data analysis and statistics pervade every discipline. These skills are grounded in STEM education subjects throughout the K–12 experience, and play a vital role in the transition from school to workforce. These trends are as true for rural schools, rural students, and rural employment as they are for urban or suburban settings.

However, there is a conflict in attitudes about STEM education in rural communities, between encouraging youth to explore STEM careers, which may result in out-migration, and pressuring them to remain close to home. Many jobs in STEM fields, especially those that require a bachelor's degree and pay well, are located in major cities (Rothwell, 2013). Although STEM and related careers are available in rural communities, there is a notion that STEM careers exist only in urban and suburban areas. Rural families may be conflicted about their children pursuing STEM education if it may lead to a college education and then an adult life far from home—a cost that suburban and urban families, living in places rich with both colleges and STEM jobs, do not have to pay. Indeed, much research has documented the feelings of conflict that rural youth and parents alike experience around college going and its implications for their community (Corbett, 2007; Grimes et al., 2019; Hektner, 1995; Petrin et al., 2014; Tieken, 2016); for this reason, some parents may discourage college attendance (Grimes et al., 2019; Tieken, 2016). In addition, new STEM economies may be perceived as at odds with traditional industries, such as fishing or millwork or agriculture, such that pursuing a career in a new STEM-related industry feels like a rejection of local lifeways (Rush-Marlowe, 2024). For all these reasons, STEM education and workforce development may be seen as perpetuating rural out-migration and furthering the decline of traditional rural industries—and, understandably, viewed with skepticism or misgivings.

The recent CEOSE report (NSF, 2024) highlights this tension as an important opportunity for NSF programming to improve awareness of local STEM employment opportunities. The out-migration concern of rural communities may also have funding implications. If a community believes that STEM careers are not available or accessible, they will not prioritize applying for those funding opportunities. Effective recruitment activities to combat out-migration should be considered in this context. STEM professionals who are trained in urban settings may not consider the opportunities that exist in rural areas when there is a lack of intentional exposure activities such as internships, place-based learning, and community-based experiential learning.

As of 2019 (NSB, 2021) STEM workers represented 23 percent of the total U.S. workforce, and this portion has been growing more rapidly than other workforce segments—three times faster than non-STEM over the past 20 years—and healthcare-related employment is expected to grow the most rapidly. In 2021 the National Science Board expanded its definition of STEM workers to include those that do not have bachelor's degrees but do highly technical work. These *skilled technical workers* are in all employment categories but particularly in health care, construction (including electricians, carpenters, and plumbers), equipment installation and repair, production (including mining), and agriculture (including forestry, fishing, and hunting). With this expanded definition, the number of STEM workers in the United States more than doubled.

Another recent change in rural workforce trends is the shifting community demographics that result in older residents choosing to age in place (Davis et al., 2022). A larger aging population correlates to an increased need for healthcare workers in areas already experiencing workforce shortages. Hospitals are often one of the largest employers in rural communities. Because of staffing shortages, and given adaptations in the post-COVID-19 world, rural healthcare facilities, like those in other areas, are leaning into telehealth practices, which provide opportunities to expand both medical services and educational supervision of professionals. These new methods of healthcare practice will redefine the rural STEM workforce, requiring both digital and healthcare literacy.

Health care is not the only STEM-related rural workforce experiencing this transformation. A variety of other industries now rely on remote workers, who can live and work from wherever they choose so long as it has reliable internet access, a criterion that may compel residence in a nonrural area (Hylton et al., 2022). In some regions, for example in the Pacific Northwest and Mountain West states, the number of STEM job postings involving remote work in certain rural and small-town areas has risen significantly and even outpaced urban areas since the COVID-19 pandemic (Western Governors University Labs, 2023).

Schools are often a major employer in rural areas, and capable STEM educators are essential to create learning opportunities that can inspire youth to pursue a STEM-related career, whether by leaving their home community or staying in a local STEM occupation, thus fighting out-migration trends and improving retention and community vitality. Effective STEM teachers can help ensure that every student, regardless of background and home community, has the confidence and, ideally, the opportunity to explore their potential and choose the path of their interest.

In terms of opportunities, place-based learning and industry engagement in rural communities are not always straightforward by nature because priorities for STEM education are not necessarily aligned with local industry needs. Partnerships between schools and industry can help bridge the gaps so that STEM education provides students with transferable skills that will be beneficial to professional growth and development regardless of their field of study and occupation.

Given increasing reliance on web-based services and technologies across all employment sectors, affordable and reliable internet access is central to the development of relevant skills, in addition to its direct impacts on the delivery of educational content and the support of individual curiosity and creativity. Pandemic-era programs made significant headway in bringing broadband connectivity to underserved schools and communities (predominantly rural and tribal), yet the digital divide persists. Studies in Michigan (Hampton et al., 2023) reported that while home broadband access improved in 2020–2021, much of it was through school-based hotspots, and access declined from 2021 to 2022 as school resources declined. Furthermore, any expansion of broadband access in rural America must be paired with training to enhance technical literacy. Rural residents who suddenly gain access to unfamiliar technology must learn how to use, understand, and manage it. Failure to provide adequate technical training could result in access without use or vulnerability to scams or unsafe digital environments.

SUMMARY AND CONCLUSIONS

This chapter provides a high-level overview of some definitions of rurality, potential consequences of different definitions on rural schools and communities, and the committee's approach to the development of a more nuanced and useful definition of rurality. It discusses misconceptions about rural areas, demographic diversity in them, and the changing rural landscape. Finally, it provides an overview of rural K–12 STEM education and workforce development.

Conclusion 2-1: Multiple definitions of rural *are used across and within federal agencies, making it difficult to both accurately identify the number of districts and schools served by federal programs and ensure that resources are equitably distributed.*

Conclusion 2-2: Multiple definitions of rural *are used by researchers, making it difficult to aggregate findings across studies in order to build a rigorous knowledge base about what works to improve rural STEM education and workforce development.*

Conclusion 2-3: Most federal agencies base their definitions of rural *on one of two sources, one developed by the U.S. Census Bureau and the other by the Office of Management and Budget. Both define* rural *mainly as* nonurban. *This approach fails to adequately capture important characteristics that vary across rural areas, such as population density and remoteness.*

Conclusion 2-4: Many rural areas are undergoing substantial demographic shifts and will continue to do so. While approximately 20 percent of those living in rural communities are people of color, almost a third of children under 18 in rural communities are people of color. K–12 STEM education and workforce development need to be responsive to these changes.

REFERENCES

Ali, S. R., & McWhirter, E. H. (2006). Rural Appalachian youth's vocational/educational postsecondary aspirations: Applying social cognitive career theory. *Journal of Career Development*, *33*(2), 87–111. https://doi.org/10.1177/0894845306293347

Ardoin, S., & Koon, K. (2024). Rural students self-definitions and characterizations of rurality. *ACPAAdmin*, *21*(1). https://developments.myacpa.org/private7J9pRkXzLq/02/rural-students-self-definitions-and-characterizations-of-rurality-ardoin-koon/2290/

Beaulac, J., Kristjansson, E., & Cummins, S. (2009). A systematic review of food deserts, 1966-2007. *Preventing Chronic Disease*, *6*(3). https://pmc.ncbi.nlm.nih.gov/articles/PMC2722409/pdf/PCD63A105.pdf

Brenner, D. (2022). Toward a rural critical policy analysis. In A. P. Alan, K. Eppley, & C. Biddle (Eds.), *The Bloomsbury Handbook of Rural Education in the United States* (pp. 30–42). Bloomsbury.

———. (2023). Rural critical policy analysis: A framework for examining policy through a rural lens. *The Rural Educator*, *44*(1), 71–73. https://doi.org/10.55533/2643-9662.1393

Brown, D. L., & Schafft, K. A. (2011). *Rural people and communities in the 21st century: Resilience and transformation*. Polity Press.

Burrola, A., Rohde-Collins, D., & Anglum, J. (2023). Conceptualizing rurality in education policy: Comparative evidence from Missouri. *The Rural Educator*, *44*(3), 17–33. https://doi.org/10.55533/2643-9662.1389

Carnevale, A. P., Kam, L., & Van Der Werf, M. (2024). *Small towns, big opportunities: Many workers in rural areas have good jobs, but these areas need greater investment in education, training, and career counseling*. Georgetown University Center on Education and the Workforce. https://cew.georgetown.edu/cew-reports/ruralgoodjobs/

Castle, M. E., & Tak, C. R. (2021). Self-reported vs RUCA rural-urban classification among North Carolina pharmacists. *Pharmacy Practice*, *19*(3). https://scielo.isciii.es/scielo.php?pid=S1885-642X2021000300008&script=sci_arttext

Cattaneo, A., Adukia, A., Brown, D. L., Christiaensen, L., Evans, D. K., Haakenstad, A., McMenomy, T., Partridge, M., Vaz, S., & Weiss, D. J. (2022). Economic and social development along the urban–rural continuum: New opportunities to inform policy. *World Development*, *157*, 105941. https://www.sciencedirect.com/science/article/pii/S0305750X22001310

Center for Public Education. (2023). *Educational equity for rural students: Out of the pandemic, but still out of the loop*. https://www.nsba.org/-/media/CPE-Parent-and-Community-Supports-Are-Assets-of-Rural-Schools.pdf

Clarke, B. L. (2014). *Rurality and reading readiness: The mediating role of parent engagement* (Working Paper No. 2014-1). National Center for Research on Rural Education. http://r2ed.unl.edu/resources/downloads/2014-wp/2014_1_Clarke.pdf

Corbett, A. C. (2007). Learning asymmetries and the discovery of entrepreneurial opportunities. *Journal of Business Venturing*, *22*(2), 97–118. https://doi.org/10.1016/j.jbusvent.2005.10.001

Crain, A. M., & Newlin, M. (2021). Rural first-generation students: A practical reflection on urbanormative ideology. *Journal of First-Generation Student Success*, *1*(1), 57–69. https://doi.org/10.1080/26906015.2021.1891822

Davis, J. C., Cromartie, J., Farrigan, T., Genetin, B., Sanders, A., & Winikoff, J. B. (2023). *Rural America at a glance: 2023 edition*. Economic Research Service, U.S. Department of Agriculture. https://www.ers.usda.gov/webdocs/publications/107838/eib-261.pdf?v=3379.2

Davis, J. C., Rupasingha, A., Cromartie, J., & Sanders, A. (2022). *Rural America at a glance: 2022 edition*. Economic Research Service, U.S. Department of Agriculture. https://www.ers.usda.gov/webdocs/publications/105155/eib-246.pdf?v=5931.9

Djonko-Moore, C. M. (2016). An exploration of teacher attrition and mobility in high poverty racially segregated schools. *Race and Ethnicity and Education*, *19*(5), 1063–1087. https://www.tandfonline.com/doi/epdf/10.1080/13613324.2015.1013458?needAccess=true

Dobis, E. A., Krumel, T., Cromartie, J., Conley, K. L., Sanders, A., & Ortiz, R. (2021). *Rural America at a glance: 2021 edition*. Economic Research Service, U.S. Department of Agriculture. https://ageconsearch.umn.edu/record/327363/?v=pdf

Duncan, L. E. (1999). Motivation for collective action: Group consciousness as mediator of personality, life experiences, and women's rights activism. *Political Psychology*, *20*(3), 611–635. https://doi.org/10.1111/0162-895X.00159

Eppley, K. (2009). Rural schools and the highly qualified teacher provision of No Child Left Behind: A critical policy analysis. *Journal of Research in Rural Education*, *24*(4), 1.

Federal Communications Commission (FCC). (2024). *Inquiry concerning the deployment of advanced telecommunications capability to all Americans in a reasonable and timely fashion*. https://docs.fcc.gov/public/attachments/FCC-24-27A1.pdf

Freudenburg, W. R. (1992). Addictive economies: Extractive industries and vulnerable localities in a changing world economy. *Rural Sociology*, *57*(3), 305–332. https://doi.org/10.1111/j.1549-0831.1992.tb00467.x

Fulkerson, G. M., & Lowe, B. (2016). Representations of rural in popular North American television. In G. M. Fulkerson & A. R. Thomas (Eds.), *Reimagining rural: Urbanormative portrayals of rural life* (pp. 9–34). Rowman & Littlefield.

Galster, G. C., & Killen, S. P. (1995). The geography of metropolitan opportunity: A reconnaissance and conceptual framework. *Housing Policy Debate*, *6*(1), 7–43. https://www.tandfonline.com/doi/epdf/10.1080/10511482.1995.9521180?needAccess=true

Geverdt, D. E. (2019). *Education Demographic and Geographic Estimates (EDGE) Program: Locale Boundaries File Documentation, 2017* (NCES No. 2018-115). National Center for Education Statistics, U.S. Department of Education.

Green, G. P. (2020). Deindustrialization of rural America: Economic restructuring and the rural ghetto. *Local Development & Society*, *1*(1), 15–25.

Greenough, R., & Nelson, S. R. (2015). Recognizing the variety of rural schools. *Peabody Journal of Education*, *90*(2), 322–332. https://doi.org/10.1080/0161956X.2015.1022393

Grimes, L. E., Arrastía-Chisholm, M. A., & Bright, S. B. (2019). How can they know what they don't know? The beliefs and experiences of rural school counselors about STEM career advising. *Theory & Practice in Rural Education*, *9*(1), 74–90. https://doi.org/10.3776/tpre.2019.v9n1p74-90

Gutierrez, E., & Terrones, F. (2023). *Small and sparse: Defining rural school districts for K–12 funding*. Urban Institute. https://files.eric.ed.gov/fulltext/ED629039.pdf

Hampton, K. N., Hales, G. E., & Bauer, J. M. (2023). *Broadband and student performance gaps after the COVID-19 pandemic*. Michigan State University Quello Center.

Harris, R. S., & Hodges, C. B. (2018). STEM education in rural schools: Implications of untapped potential. *National Youth-At-Risk Journal*, *3*(1). https://doi.org/10.20429/nyarj.2018.030102

Hektner, J. M. (1995). When moving up implies moving out: Rural adolescent conflict in the transition to adulthood. *Journal of Research in Rural Education*, *11*(1), 3–14. https://jrre.psu.edu/sites/default/files/2019-08/11-1_3.pdf

Housing Assistance Council (HAC). (2021). *Annual report*. https://ruralhome.org/wp-content/uploads/2022/05/HAC-2021-Annual-Report.pdf

Hylton, S., Ice, L., & Krutsch, E. (2022). What the long-term impacts of the COVID-19 pandemic could mean for the future of IT jobs. *Beyond the Numbers: Employment & Unemployment*, *11*(3). U.S. Bureau of Labor Statistics. https://www.bls.gov/opub/btn/volume-11/what-the-long-term-impacts-of-the-covid-19-pandemic-could-mean-for-the-future-of-it-jobs.htm

Ingersoll, R. M., & Tran, H. (2023). Teacher shortages and turnover in rural schools in the US: An organizational analysis. *Educational Administration Quarterly*, *59*(2), 396–431. https://doi.org/10.1177/0013161X231159922

Irwin, V., De La Rosa, J., Wang, K., Hein, S., Zhang, J., Burr, R., Roberts, A., Barmer, A., Mann, F. B., Dilig, R., & Parker, S. (2022). *Report on the Condition of Education 2022* (NCES No. 2022-144). National Center for Education Statistics.

Isserman, A. M. (2005). In the national interest: Defining rural and urban correctly in research and public policy. *International Regional Science Review*, *28*(4), 465–499. https://doi.org/10.1177/0160017605279000

Johnson, J., & Howley, C. B. (2015). Contemporary federal education policy and rural schools: A critical policy analysis. *Peabody Journal of Education*, *90*(2), 224–241. https://doi.org/10.1080/0161956X.2015.1022112

Johnson, K. M., & Lichter, D. T. (2019). Rural depopulation: Growth and decline processes over the past century. *Rural Sociology*, *84*(1), 3–27. https://doi.org/10.1111/ruso.12266

———. (2022). *Growing racial diversity in rural America: Results from the 2020 census* (Issue Brief No. 163). Carsey Research National. https://scholars.unh.edu/cgi/viewcontent.cgi?article=1450&context=carsey

Keller, A., & Kassel, K. (2024). *The number of US farms continues slow decline*. Economic Research Service, U.S. Department of Agriculture. https://www.ers.usda.gov/data-products/chart-gallery/gallery/chart-detail/?chartId=58268

Koricich, A. (2022). Crafting better rural-focused postsecondary policy by identifying rural-serving institutions. *The Rural Educator, 43*(4), 67–70. https://scholarsjunction.msstate.edu/cgi/viewcontent.cgi?article=1374&context=ruraleducator

Kusmin, L. (2016). *Rural America at a glance: 2016 edition.* Economic Research Service, U.S. Department of Agriculture. https://www.ers.usda.gov/webdocs/publications/80894/eib-162.pdf?v=4783.9

Laughlin, L. (2016). *Beyond the farm: Rural industry workers in America.* U.S. Census Bureau. https://www.census.gov/newsroom/blogs/random-samplings/2016/12/beyond_the_farm_rur.html

Lichter, D. T., & Parisi, D. (2008). Concentrated rural poverty and the geography of exclusion (Policy brief). *Carsey Institute Rural Realities.* https://scholars.unh.edu/cgi/viewcontent.cgi?article=1054&context=carsey

Lichter, D. T., Parisi, D., & Taquino, M. C. (2012). The geography of exclusion: Race, segregation, and concentrated poverty. *Social Problems, 59*(3), 364–388. https://doi.org/10.1525/sp.2012.59.3.364

Liu, T., & Peng, R. (2023). Globalization, urbanization and rural transformation. *Rural and Regional Development, 1,* 10010. https://doi.org/10.35534/rrd.2023.10010

Lobao, L., & Saenz, R. (2002). Spatial inequality and diversity as an emerging research area. *Rural Sociology, 67*(4), 497–511. j.1549-0831.2002.tb00116.x20161207-15702-19183le-libre.pdf

Lyson, T. A., & Falk, W. W. (Eds.). (1993). *Forgotten places: Uneven development in rural America.* University Press of Kansas.

Marré, A. (2017). *Rural education at a glance: 2017 edition.* Economic Research Service, U.S. Department of Agriculture. https://www.ers.usda.gov/publications/pub-details/?pubid=83077

Morehart, M. J., Cromartie, J., & Stenberg, P. L. (2009, September 1). *Broadband internet service helping create a rural digital economy. The economics of food, farming, natural resources, and rural America, amber waves.* U.S. Department of Agriculture, Economic Research Service. https://www.ers.usda.gov/amber-waves/2009/september/broadband-internet-service-helping-create-a-rural-digital-economy

National Center for Education Statistics (NCES). (2023). *Children in rural areas and their family characteristics.* Institute of Education Sciences, U.S. Department of Education. https://nces.ed.gov/programs/coe/indicator/lfa

National Science Board (NSB). (2021). *The STEM labor force of today: Scientists, engineers, and skilled technical workers* (NSB-2021-2). https://ncses.nsf.gov/pubs/nsb20212/assets/nsb20212.pdf

National Science Foundation (NSF). (2024). *Making visible the invisible: STEM talent of rural America.* https://nsf-gov-resources.nsf.gov/files/CEOSE_STEM-Talent_of_Rural_America_Report.pdf?VersionId=Jr.NV_HxMT0eVnFm12wZA5EPZ0DgxAXJ

Parker, K., Horowitz, J., Brown, A., Fry, R., Cohn, D., & Igielnik, R. (2018). *What unites and divides urban, suburban and rural communities.* Pew Research Center. https://coilink.org/20.500.12592/6q6tkh

Pender, J., Hertz, T., Cromartie, J., & Farrigan, T. (2019). *Rural America at a glance: 2018 edition.* Economic Research Service, U.S. Department of Agriculture. https://www.ers.usda.gov/publications/pub-details/?pubid=95340

Petrin, R. A., Schafft, K. A., & Meece, J. L. (2014). Educational sorting and residential aspirations among rural high school students: What are the contributions of schools and educators to rural brain drain? *American Educational Research Journal, 51*(2), 294–326. https://doi.org/10.3102/0002831214527493

powell, j. (2008). Race, place, and opportunity. *The American Prospect, 19.*

Ronfeldt, M., Loeb, S., & Wyckoff, J. (2013). How teacher turnover harms student achievement. *American Educational Research Journal*, *50*(1), 4–36. https://doi.org/10.3102/0002831212463813

Rothwell, J. (2013). The hidden STEM economy: The surprising diversity of jobs requiring science, technology, engineering, and math knowledge. *Brookings Scholar Lecture Series*. https://digitalscholarship.unlv.edu/cgi/viewcontent.cgi?article=1059&context=brookings_lectures_events

Rush-Marlowe, R. (2024). [Rural students as an underserved population in STEM education and workforce]. Paper commissioned for the Committee on K-12 STEM Education and Workforce Development in Rural Areas.

Schaefer, A. P., Mattingly, M. J., & Johnson, K. M. (2016). *Child poverty higher and more persistent in rural America* (Issue Brief No. 97). Carsey Research National. https://scholars.unh.edu/cgi/viewcontent.cgi?article=1265&context=carsey

Showalter, D., Hartman, S. L., Eppley, K., Johnson, J. D., & Klein, R. M. (2023). *Why rural matters 2023: Centering equity and opportunity*. National Rural Education Association. https://wsos-cdn.s3.us-west-2.amazonaws.com/uploads/sites/18/WRMReport2023_DIGITAL.pdf

Showalter, D., Klein, R., Johnson, J., & Hartman, S. L. (2017). *Why rural matters 2015-2016: Understanding the changing landscape*. Rural School and Community Trust.

Smith, K. E., & Tickamyer, A. R. (2011). *Economic restructuring and family well-being in rural America*. Penn State University Press.

Soja, E. (2009). The city and spatial justice. *Justice Spatiale/Spatial Justice*, *1*(1), 1–5.

———. (2010). Spatializing the urban, Part I. *City*, *14*(6), 629–635. https://www.tandfonline.com/doi/epdf/10.1080/13604813.2010.539371?needAccess=true

Tieken, M. C. (2014). *Why rural schools matter*. University of North Carolina Press.

———. (2016). College talk and the rural economy: Shaping the educational aspirations of rural, first-generation students. *Peabody Journal of Education*, *91*(2), 203–223. https://doi.org/10.1080/0161956X.2016.1151741

———. (2017). The spatialization of racial inequity and educational opportunity: Rethinking the rural/urban divide. *Peabody Journal of Education*, *92*(3), 385–404. https://www.tandfonline.com/doi/epdf/10.1080/0161956X.2017.1324662?needAccess=true

———. (2022). Rural poverty and rural schools. In A. P. Azano, K. Eppley, & C. Biddle (Eds.), *Bloomsbury handbook of rural education in the United States* (pp. 62–71).

Tieken, M. C., & Auldridge-Reveles, T. (2019). Rethinking the school closure research: School closure as spatial injustice. *Review of Educational Research*, *89*(6), 917–953. https://doi.org/10.3102/0034654319877151

Ulrich-Schad, J. D., & Duncan, C. M. (2018). People and places left behind: Work, culture and politics in the rural United States. *The Journal of Peasant Studies*, *45*(1), 59–79. https://www.tandfonline.com/doi/epdf/10.1080/03066150.2017.1410702?needAccess=true

Waldorf, B. S. (2006). *A continuous multi-dimensional measure of rurality: Moving beyond threshold measures*. Paper presented at American Agricultural Economics Association Annual Meeting, Long Island, CA, US. https://ageconsearch.umn.edu/record/21383/?v=pdf

Waldorf, B., & Kim, A. (2015). [Defining and measuring rurality in the US: From typologies to continuous indices]. Commissioned paper presented at the Workshop on Rationalizing Rural Area Classifications, Washington, DC, US. https://sites.nationalacademies.org/cs/groups/dbassesite/documents/webpage/dbasse_167036.pdf

Western Governors University Labs. (2023). *Shifting winds: Examining employment trends in rural northwest regions*. Western Governors University. https://www.wgu.edu/content/dam/wgu-65-assets/western-governors/documents/other-reports/NW-Rural-WF.pdf

3

Education Policy, Funding, and Programs in Rural Areas

The U.S. public education system has multiple interacting components that are influenced by policy and funding decisions at the federal, state, and local levels (National Academies of Sciences, Engineering, and Medicine [NASEM], 2022). Schools are typically divided into three levels—elementary (grades K–5 or sometimes preK–5), middle (grades 6–8), and high school (grades 9–12)—and three types: traditional public school, public charter school, or private school. A vast majority of students in rural areas are enrolled in traditional public schools. In 2019 approximately 9.8 million students were enrolled in rural public elementary and secondary schools—nearly one in five (19%) of all U.S. public school students (National Center for Education Statistics [NCES], 2023).

States have different variations or combinations of these school categories, and educational priorities are set by policies enacted by state education agencies and legislatures. These policies guide the development and implementation of academic standards, accountability measurements, and funding allocations. Most states also support "local control," in which final decisions about instruction, scheduling, and academic programs are made by local education agencies.

Federal funding allocations for education also play a major role in how well educational priorities can be implemented in various communities. The policies and decisions made by multiple entities can influence whether students become interested in science, technology, engineering, and mathematics (STEM) and pursue future STEM career opportunities.

In this chapter, we give an overview of the potential STEM learning opportunities for students both in and out of school and discuss policies and funding that can support or hinder students' opportunities to learn in rural areas.

STEM LEARNING OPPORTUNITIES FOR RURAL STUDENTS

Similarities between rural, suburban, and urban schools include the general structure of school days for students and educators and the type of content that must be taught for compliance with state standards. There are also similar challenges in providing quality STEM learning opportunities to students in different types of school locations. In the elementary grades, instructional time for reading and mathematics are emphasized over time for science instruction, and instruction for science and engineering are underresourced and not highly prioritized (NASEM, 2022).

Beyond the similarities, rural students can encounter unique challenges for obtaining quality STEM education in terms of access to courses, quality instructors, and appropriate logistical needs (e.g., broadband access, transportation), any or all of which can impact their education and their decision or ability to pursue STEM-related interests, whether in their schooling or as a future career. The Center for Public Education (2023) identified five areas that may affect rural students' access to quality learning opportunities:

- insufficient funding due to declining rural populations and economies in some areas,
- a digital divide that impedes students from accessing learning resources and developing digital literacy,
- local schools that lack the capacity to meet students' needs,
- a worsening teacher shortage made even more apparent in rural schools by the COVID-19 pandemic, and
- a lack of research on policy and praxis issues relevant to rural education.

As more and more families leave rural areas, potential available funding for schools further declines, affecting school districts' capacity to offer either the STEM programming and coursework offered in suburban and urban schools or qualified educators to provide instruction. The lack of qualified STEM teachers is particularly acute. Inadequate funding also contributes to the lack of technological access for students, whether by restricting the availability of quality broadband in classrooms and homes or preventing participation in digital learning opportunities (De Mars et al., 2022; Grimes et al., 2019; Kormos & Wisdom, 2021; Marksbury, 2017).

ACCESS TO STEM COURSES IN RURAL SCHOOLS

STEM pathways are in large part a function of students' academic preparation and training throughout their K–12 schooling, particularly their access to and completion of high-quality and rigorous STEM coursework (Saw & Agger, 2021; Tyson et al., 2007). Students may choose or be guided to different STEM curricular paths through their performance and motivation in STEM subjects, and their choice or decision depends on the curriculum structures and resources of the schools they attend (Irizarry, 2021; Wang, 2013). Similarly, their college and workforce readiness in STEM can be significantly influenced by the course offerings and programming of their school or district. For example, STEM-focused schools, gifted and talented programs, and Career and Technical Education (CTE) programs at both the elementary and secondary education levels offer more intensive or advanced learning experiences and credentialing opportunities for STEM postsecondary education and careers (Gottfried et al., 2016; Saw, 2019; Steenbergen-Hu & Olszewski-Kubilius, 2017). Chapters 4 and 5 provide more information about STEM learning and pathways in rural areas.

Research has shown that inequities in access to advanced math and science courses begin well before high school, sometimes as early as kindergarten (Graham & Provost, 2012; Wolfe et al., 2023). Rural students have fewer opportunities to take STEM courses: 62 percent of rural schools offered at least one STEM course, compared to 88 percent of urban schools and 93 percent of suburban schools. Rural students also have less access to Advanced Placement (AP) STEM courses (Banilower et al., 2018; Crain & Webber, 2021; Mann et al., 2017; Saw & Agger, 2021; Showalter et al., 2017); data from 2015 showed that rural schools were much less likely to offer any AP STEM courses compared to schools in urban and suburban districts (Mann et al., 2017).

Dual enrollment programs allow students to earn postsecondary credit while still in high school and are available in about 90 percent of all rural high schools (NCES, 2020). In most cases, the relevant courses are offered online or at the postsecondary institution campus (Thomas et al., 2013). But rural districts face greater challenges than their counterparts in other locales, in providing transportation for students enrolled in such programs and finding qualified dual enrollment instructors (Zinth, 2014), who, in most states, need to meet requirements such as a master's degree or the same qualifications as faculty in the partner postsecondary institution.

CTE programs are designed to help students develop technical, academic, and workforce skills that can be applied to employment and postsecondary education (Mobley et al., 2017; Stone, 2014; Stringfield & Stone, 2017). Rural students may attend CTE courses through area technical centers, which serve students from multiple institutions at the same time

(Advance CTE, 2017). These centers can provide diverse course offerings and make up for limited availability in a student's home school district. While technical centers are not available in all states, they can build strong partnerships with business and industry partners, which could ultimately lead to more STEM-related courses and work in rural communities. Involvement in quality CTE pathways increases overall achievement, the probability of high school completion, college readiness, and employability skills (Lindsay et al., 2024).

Students who have access to and can complete advanced STEM courses are more likely to pursue STEM college degree programs and careers (Hu & Chan, 2024). But geographical disparities in STEM coursework offerings and completion favor nonrural over rural students, contributing to the underrepresentation of rural students in postsecondary STEM programs (Saw & Agger, 2021). One possible factor is that rural schools have, in general, smaller student populations than suburban and urban schools, and the smaller student population means a smaller teaching staff, which limits the number of courses the school can offer. And when rural schools do offer STEM courses, these are much more likely to be "alternative" or "applied" courses, which decrease access to advanced coursework (Wolfe et al., 2023).

STEM Teachers

As has been noted in this report, schools across the country are facing teacher shortages; these are most extreme in low-income areas, and some of the highest vacancy rates are in science and math (García & Weiss, 2019a, 2019b; Schmitt & deCourcy, 2022), which can negatively impact students' STEM access and success (Rogers & Sun, 2019; Saw & Agger, 2021; Showalter et al., 2017). The shortage also appears to be worse in rural districts, especially for low-income rural areas (Ingersoll & Tran, 2023).

Using three decades of data from the Schools and Staffing Survey and its successor, the National Teacher and Principal Survey, Ingersoll and Tran (2023) show that vacancies are most prevalent in science and math: at the start of the 2015–2016 school year nearly 40 percent of rural public high schools had science vacancies and more than 35 percent had math vacancies. Many principals at rural schools with those vacancies reported serious difficulties filling them (Ingersoll & Tran, 2023). These STEM teacher shortages are exacerbated by inadequate rural school district funding that makes it more difficult to recruit and retain STEM teachers (De Mars et al., 2022). With fewer qualified STEM teachers, rural teachers may find themselves assuming responsibility for teaching multiple, diverse courses in the same semester or school year, (e.g., needing to prepare for and teach biology, chemistry, and physics at the high school level), increasing the need for preparation time (Goodpaster et al., 2012). Additionally, a study found that rural science teachers had lower self-efficacy (i.e., confidence in their ability to teach science) compared to suburban science teachers (Saw & Agger, 2021).

In summary, the rural STEM teacher shortage impacts rural students' ability to access STEM pathways through postsecondary education or workforce development opportunities. Chapter 5 discusses effective STEM pathways in rural areas and Chapter 6 presents a more in-depth look at educator recruitment, retention, and professional learning.

Transitioning to Postsecondary Education or the Workforce

Like their K–12 counterparts, rural postsecondary institutions play a significant financial and community role by providing pathways to careers that can help sustain rural communities. However, research has shown a disparity between rural postsecondary opportunities compared to urban. According to Wells et al. (2023), the rural-nonrural enrollment gap is affected by academic preparation, economic factors, and proximity, among others.

Rural students may feel underprepared for higher education, face challenges once in college, and experience hurdles that prevent them from completing their degree. Because many rural schools are small and have high proportions of low-income students they are less often able to provide a college-preparatory curriculum (Koricich et al., 2018).

The relationship between low socioeconomic status and rurality is important (Cain & Smith, 2020; Koricich et al., 2018), as poverty remains one of the strongest threats to rural students' completing a postsecondary degree (Byun et al., 2012; Wells et al., 2019). For example, they may want to complete a degree without going into debt but not be aware of financial aid options (McNamee & Ganss, 2023). Based on High School Longitudinal Study data, the Postsecondary National Policy Institute (2024) observed that rural students took higher loan amounts ($7,005 vs. $6,354 nationally) and received lower grant amounts ($7,864 vs. $8,460 nationally).

Proximity to a postsecondary institution is a primary concern for rural students. Most students attend classes within 50 miles of their permanent home address (Hillman et al., 2021). But numerous rural areas face a significant shortage of educational opportunities because they are not near a postsecondary institution. In 2019 there were 516 rural colleges, compared to 2,439 nonrural. With the lack of educational options, rural students may leave the community to attend college and possibly seek employment away from the community, or they may skip postsecondary education and simply join the local workforce (Wells et al., 2023). This may explain why rural students have lower college enrollment and degree completion rates than urban or suburban students even though they have similar educational aspirations (Koricich et al., 2020). Proximity also plays a role in the type of institution rural students attend. For instance, students attending a high school near a community colleges are less inclined to enroll in a four-year university (Hirschl & Smith, 2020). Two-year colleges predominantly enroll students living in areas with limited access to higher education facilities.

As with students in urban and suburban areas, community colleges can offer important STEM pathways for rural students. A 2023 Aspen Institute report (Barrett et al., 2023) reported 1.5 million rural students attending 444 rural community colleges. Postsecondary coursework at a community college can reduce financial and geographic obstacles to higher education for rural students. Graduates from rural community colleges play a crucial role in local economies. Research indicates that compared to their counterparts with a bachelor's degree or higher, rural students who earn an associate's degree often maintain stronger family connections and are more inclined to remain in their communities to seek employment opportunities (Muraskin & Lee, 2004). But rural students who seek to transfer to a four-year institution may encounter difficulties with credit transfer, inadequate academic support, limited financial aid, and differences in campus environment that may make them feel unwelcome (Byun et al., 2017). These difficulties often hinder their ability to successfully transfer or complete a four-year degree. Compared to their urban and suburban counterparts, rural students have the highest completion rates for certificates and associate's degrees, but the lowest rates for bachelor's degrees (NCES, 2023).

Broadband access is another barrier for rural postsecondary education (Rosenboom & Blagg, 2018). Without access to affordable high-speed internet, rural students are limited in their access to quality online postsecondary education options (Chen & Koricich, 2014).

Locational differences in financial resources also play a role. Postsecondary institutions in urban and suburban areas generate more revenue per student and have higher expenditures than rural institutions, limiting their ability to address the unique needs of rural students (Koricich et al., 2020).

Boynton and Hossain (2010) added a cultural component to the barriers facing rural STEM education by recognizing an idea in rural communities that students must move away to have a successful career. Research has shown that students who pursue studies in STEM fields often end up leaving their rural communities (Peterson et al., 2015). Byker (2014) suggests that to successfully implement quality STEM curriculum and learning experiences in rural communities, the first step should be to convince families and other community groups of the importance of STEM education. For example, offering tours of farms with chip-implanted cows, robotic milking machines, or high-tech barns can provide examples of work in rural areas involving computational thinking, computer science, and data science. In other rural businesses, such as lumber mills and other forestry operations, orchards, and ski slopes, employees generate, collect, and analyze data using a combination of high-tech equipment and STEM proficiency. Many members of these rural workforces have certifications but not four-year STEM-related degrees, and other rural industries employ civil engineers, biologists, and workers with degrees in environmental science.

Out-of-School STEM Programs

Out-of-school educational environments can be classified as *informal* and *nonformal*, each offering enrichment activities to foster cognitive development. Informal learning experiences are voluntarily pursued outside traditional classroom settings (NRC, 2009) and usually self-determined by the learner, without a formal curriculum or formal evaluative processes. Examples of these experiences in rural areas include observing and understanding changing seasons for crops and hunting, learning agriculture from family members, or noting changing ecosystems on mountain hikes. Nonformal education occurs at a location other than a school (e.g., a zoo, museum, nature center) and is more likely to be aligned with formal curriculum. It may include clear learning goals but is usually not evaluated to determine the impact on learning (Eshach, 2007). Most out-of-school activities are usually classified as informal as a blanket term to include informal and nonformal learning environments.

Rural students and their families have fewer out-of-school and co-curricular STEM learning opportunities (Saw & Agger, 2021; Showalter et al., 2017). For example, Saw and Agger (2021, p. 600) report that rural communities are less likely "to hold math or science fairs, workshops, or competitions; inform students about math or science contests, websites, blogs, or other online programs; and sponsor a math or science after-school program." However, an increasing number of STEM enrichment opportunities in online settings can provide students with valuable exposure to real-world learning experiences of STEM professions (such as virtual lab tours or field trips; Lakin et al., 2021) and potential careers (Culbertson et al., 2023; Nye et al., 2017). For example, the Nebraska Innovation Maker Co-Laboratory project developed a model to establish and support makerspaces in rural communities (Barker et al., 2018). The model supports collaboration between university faculty and staff and rural makerspaces by utilizing virtual reality and telepresence robots. The exploratory research project deployed telepresence robotics to teach, coteach, and provide project support to a rural community (population 7,000) makerspace. Virtual reality was used to teach creativity concepts, digital creation, and digital-to-physical manifestation of projects.

Research has consistently shown that middle and high school students who engage in STEM learning opportunities with in-person and/or online mentorship provided by near-peers or professionals in STEM fields tend to report higher levels of STEM workforce readiness and interest in pursuing a STEM college degree and career (Beauchamp et al., 2022; Finkel, 2017; Stoeger et al., 2013; Tenenbaum et al., 2017). Research is needed to understand how rural students can overcome disparities in out-of-school STEM experiences between rural and nonrural districts.

Informal Learning Opportunities

Rural communities lack large informal built environments for STEM, such as science centers, zoos, and botanical gardens, which are often found in urban ecosystems, but numerous local assets such as schools, libraries, museums, clubs, and supportive organizations like 4-H and Scouting America are available. Rural libraries and museums play a critical role in educating and supporting the learning of rural students.

About half of public libraries in the United States are in rural areas (Swan et al., 2013). They often provide access to public computers and the internet (Real & Rose, 2017), workforce development opportunities (e.g., assistance with applying for jobs), and afterschool STEM and other programs and events (Lopez et al., 2019; Real & Rose, 2017).

Approximately one in four museums are in rural communities, and they play a vital role in supporting learning and education related to history, culture, and science.[1]

Rural and some Indigenous communities are more likely to be near national parks and other large federal or state nature reserves (Byun et al., 2012). Students in these communities have almost immediate access to and can engage in real-life outdoor learning experiences not found in suburban and urban settings (Avery & Kassam, 2011). But the extent to which these resources are used for rural and Indigenous students as informal learning institutions has not been adequately studied, and may be worth examining as these places have the potential to serve as informal learning environments for place-based STEM education.

Research shows that youth and families need direct engagement with these multiple informal assets to explore and build STEM interest and skills (Allen et al., 2020). Families' greater exposure to and engagement in STEM learning increase the likelihood that they will encourage and support their students' interest and curiosity in STEM. Families and students in rural areas can also benefit from "collaborative partnerships between teachers and informal STEM practitioners that capitalize on the unique environmental

[1]https://www.aam-us.org/wp-content/uploads/2024/02/Museum-Facts-2024.pdf

offerings of rural areas in an authentic, hands-on way that makes learning come to life for young children within the context of their own backyards" (Hartman et al., 2017, p. 36).

POLICIES THAT SUPPORT OR LIMIT STEM LEARNING OPPORTUNITIES FOR RURAL STUDENTS

While all communities benefit from federal and state initiatives promoting high-quality STEM education and workforce development, rural communities have enjoyed disproportionately less attention and funding from both. One of the functions of government at all levels is to address such inequities. Historically, the foundational premise of the federal role in education has been to counter inequities in state and local education systems (Griffen, 2020; Hanushek,1989; Kaestle, 2016; Vinovskis, 2022). So efforts to improve STEM education and workforce development in rural communities require an understanding of the current state of federal and state support.

One of the most significant barriers faced by rural schools is inadequate funding. Considering that rural school systems serve populations with high poverty rates, a growing number of English learners, and hard-to-fill staff positions, the lack of funding is critical. The National Rural Education Association's report *Why Rural Matters 2023: Centering Equity and Opportunity* (Showalter et al., 2023) found that the majority of states do not fund rural schools equitably: rural districts receive on average 17 percent of state education funding although they account for almost 30 percent of all districts. Other studies have found evidence that rural schools tend to have lower levels of per-pupil funding than nonrural schools (Irvin et al., 2012). And what it takes to reach equitable funding may be even more difficult than it seems, as inadequate economies of scale limit rural schools' ability to provide cost-effective programming. In addition, the isolation of rural communities makes some resources and opportunities more expensive than in nonrural environments; for example, both the actual cost and opportunity cost of sending teachers away for professional development is higher in rural than in nonrural environments.

A 2014 case study surveyed K–12 teachers in rural Colorado about the challenges of providing STEM education and found that they were much more likely than teachers in nonrural schools to mention funding as a significant barrier (Henley & Roberts, 2016). The study also found that rural schools regularly forgo opportunities to apply for state or federal STEM grant funding because the administrative burdens associated with both applying for and winning these grants was too high. In fact, rural schools are often not even eligible for STEM grant funding as most formulas for state and federal grants use enrollment size as a primary qualifying factor, and private foundations often require applicants to demonstrate scalability or impact as measured by the number of students served.

The next sections look at federal policies that contribute to the disparities described above, and then consider the local costs that challenge rural school districts, sometimes leading to school consolidation.

FEDERAL POLICY

Research shows that STEM-related activities and programs have been integrated in many K–12 curricula and course offerings but that there is a significant gap in the ability of rural schools to access these resources. Barriers to access are not a function of rural communities but of the current social and political landscape, which includes legislation that routinely ignores or discounts rural experiences and needs (Williams & Grooms, 2016). Most legislation concerning education policy and education funding mechanisms never mentions rural schools (Dahill-Brown & Jochim, 2018).

In the U.S. Department of Education's Office of Elementary and Secondary Education (OESE), the Office of Formula Grants manages the Rural Education Achievement Program (REAP), which is one of the few mechanisms that provides exclusive support for rural education funding. However, although REAP provides much-needed funds to rural districts, many rural schools may not benefit from the funds because of the administrative burdens of the program (Apling, 2007; Yettick et al., 2014). In addition, the U.S. Department of Education's Office of Postsecondary Education manages the Rural Postsecondary & Economic Development Program, which awards grants to institutions of higher education so they can develop career pathways aligned with local high-wage industry needs in order to increase the percentage of rural students who enroll, persist, and complete postsecondary education pathways.

Administrative burdens are often due to restrictions on the way funding is awarded, such as requiring some percentage of the award to be set aside for a specific purpose. Characteristics of rural school systems hamper their ability to comply with these requirements and in some cases make compliance cost prohibitive. Competitive grant opportunities, which require detailed applications followed by extensive review by the grant-making agency, could supplement state and local dollars but often include requirements that are impractical for rural schools (Brenner, 2016). For example, conditions of a professional development grant might make it too costly to implement the professional development compared to the amount of money allocated for it (Yettick et al., 2014). In addition, completing grant applications, which usually require a detailed description of the organization, problem to be solved, budget and justification for the budget, and other documentation, involves a substantial amount of work. Rural districts often employ a small administrative staff, and few have the experience or time available to complete a lengthy grant application (Johnson et al., 2014).

In 2023 Congress approved $215 million to be split evenly between the two REAP subprograms: the Small Rural School Achievement (SRSA) program, which provides grants directly to local education agencies (LEAs), and the Rural Low-Income School (RLIS) program, which provides grants to states, which then award subgrants to LEAs. Although not a major source of funding for the operation of rural schools, these supplemental funds for both subprograms can be used to support activities described in the Elementary and Secondary Education Act (ESEA), Title I-A (grants to LEAs for education of children from disadvantaged backgrounds), Title II-A (grants to support effective instruction), Title III (language instruction for English learners and immigrant students), or Title IV-A (student support and academic enrichment). In addition, SRSA funds can be used for Title IV-B (21st Century Community Learning Center) initiatives. Parent involvement activities can be supported only by RLIS. In addition, Title VIII of the Higher Education Act includes a clause in Part Q that was specifically written to create rural development grants. This program was authorized but has not received any funding in appropriations.

Most of the federal support for rural education originates in the U.S. Department of Agriculture, but rural schools are rarely aware of these funding opportunities (Rush-Marlowe, 2021). Research from the Brookings Institution found that federal assistance for rural communities is "outdated, fragmented, and confusing," with over 400 programs housed in 10 different agencies and more than 50 offices or subagencies (Pipa & Geismar, 2022). Navigating how to apply for these programs, where they originate, and who might be eligible is often an insurmountable challenge for many rural communities. This lack of equitable, accessible funding for rural communities is a barrier to improvements in their STEM education.

Another challenge in rural schools' access to federal funding is that most programs allocate funds based on population and community poverty. Since rural schools tend to be small and many of them experience depopulation, the amount of funding they receive is limited although their needs are greater than those in other locales.

Federal Programs

As the committee grappled with the funding inequities seen in many rural areas, it became evident that a thorough exploration of the number of federal programs supporting rural students, preK–12 STEM education, and workforce development was necessary. This section reviews federal programs across analytic groups: preK–12 education, STEM, rural, and workforce development. We start by reviewing the federal government as a whole, then explore programs in the U.S. National Science Foundation (NSF). Appendix B describes the methods used to identify programs and includes tables listing programs across federal agencies in the analytic groups.

Overall, the committee found the following:

- Federal assistance is broad in scope, concentrated in cabinet-level agencies, and weighted toward project grants.
- There is an abundance of STEM-related programs across the federal government, though just three agencies administer over half of all STEM-related programs.
- Relatively few programs prioritize rural communities.
- Even fewer programs prioritize preK–12 STEM education in rural communities.
- A small percentage of NSF grants focus on rural communities, and an even smaller percentage on preK–12 STEM in those communities.
- Given the differences in how *rural* is coded across agencies, it is challenging to draw firm conclusions about the overall picture of federal investments in rural preK–12 STEM education and workforce development.

Federal agencies provide assistance predominantly through competitively awarded project grants rather than formula grants that might require an application but without applicants competing for those funds. The use of project grants implies that agencies likely have greater flexibility to target resources effectively by leveraging agency expertise, but rural districts often do not have the capacity to submit competitive grant applications.

The Federal Program Inventory (FPI) dataset catalogues 1,946 formula and project grant programs across all federal agencies. Of these, 87 percent (1,689) are project grant programs and 13 percent (257) are formula grant programs. Seven (of 44) agencies—the Departments of Agriculture, Education, Health and Human Services, Justice, Interior, and Transportation and the Environmental Protection Agency—account for almost 70 percent of the grant programs across all agencies.[2] Health and Human Services accounts for over 21 percent of all programs, administering 334 project grant programs and 75 formula grant programs. Interior and Agriculture account for about 12 percent each (238 project grants and 10 formula grants, and 215 and 27, respectively). The distribution of grants across agencies by the four analytic categories of interest in this chapter implies both the importance of

[2]Although many other federal agencies, including the Departments of Defense and Energy, support STEM education, those programs are primarily aimed at higher education and not at rural areas, so they are not described in this chapter. See Table B-5 in Appendix B for more information.

STEM across agencies and a narrower constituency for preK–12 education and workforce development. Cabinet-level agencies operate all but a few of the federal programs related to preK–12, STEM, rural communities, and workforce development. This is unsurprising as noncabinet-level agencies tend to be smaller and focused on highly specific policy issues.

In addition to the agencies mentioned above, the National Aeronautics and Space Administration (NASA) and NSF stand out. Both are organized into directorates, and their Federal Assistance Listings numbers are assigned at the directorate level rather than to individual programs in the directorates. This approach can make it appear that NASA and NSF fund very few programs. And in other ways the data do not accurately reflect the breadth and depth of the agencies' work, as a single program may be counted in none, one, several, or all of the analytic categories.

The next two sections detail the number of federal programs in the four analytic groups: preK–12 education, STEM education, workforce development, and rural. Based on the available data, the committee analyzed the intersectionality of both (a) STEM education programs and (b) workforce development programs with preK–12 education and programs targeted to rural communities.

STEM Education Programs That Intersect with PreK–12 Education and Rural Communities

Over half (58%) of all federal preK–12 education programs are administered by just three agencies: Education (90 programs, 29.6%), Health and Human Services (62 programs, 20.4%), and Agriculture (25 programs, 8.2%). The 339 preK–12 education programs constitute 15.6 percent of all federal programs. In contrast, almost 70 percent of all federal programs relate directly or indirectly to science, technology, engineering, or mathematics. Three agencies account for about half (52%) of the 1,355 STEM-related programs: Health and Human Services (351 programs, 25.9%), Interior (198 programs, 14.6%), and Agriculture (154 programs, 11.4%). While STEM abounds across federal programs, 13.6 percent (265 programs) of federal programs explicitly mention rural communities as a focus or beneficiary, and they are highly concentrated in a few agencies: Agriculture alone accounts for 34 percent (90 programs); Agriculture, Health and Human Services, and Interior combined account for 54.3 percent. Adding Transportation and the Environmental Protection Agency brings the total to 68.3 percent of rural programs in five cabinet departments.

Of the 170 programs (8.7% of all programs) that can be characterized as both preK–12 and STEM, almost two thirds (63.5%) are administered by the Departments of Health and Human Services, Education, Commerce, and Agriculture and the Environmental Protection Agency. Sixty-five programs

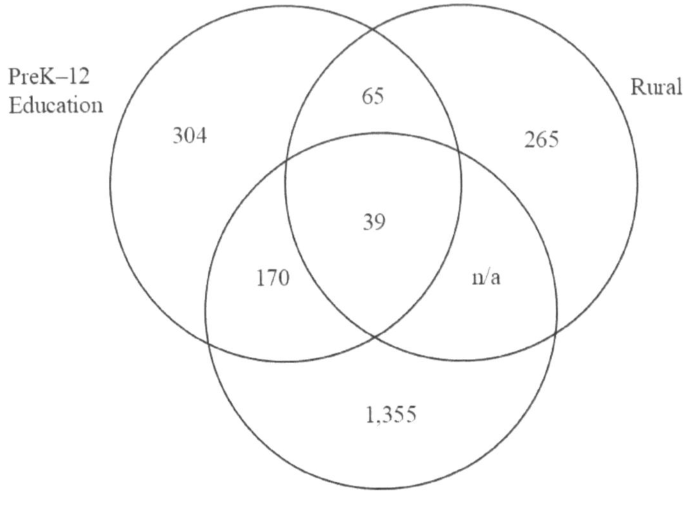

FIGURE 3-1 Number of federal programs for preK–12 education, STEM education, and rural communities.
NOTE: n/a denotes lack of information on the number of STEM education programs targeted for rural communities.
SOURCE: Committee generated.

(3.3% of all programs) can be characterized as relevant to both preK–12 education and rural. These are relatively evenly distributed across 15 agencies. Within these 15, 46 percent are administered by Agriculture, Health and Human Services, State, Commerce, and the Environmental Protection Agency. Eleven agencies offer 39 programs—37 project grant and two formula grant programs—at the intersection of preK–12 education and STEM programs in rural communities. Figure 3-1 shows the distribution of federal investments across the analytic groups of preK–12 education, rural communities, and STEM education, and the intersectionality of the funds across these groups. The committee found programs at the intersection of preK–12 education and STEM education, preK–12 education and rural, and the intersection of all three analytic groups, but no information on the number of STEM education programs targeted for rural communities.

Workforce Development Programs That Intersect with PreK–12 Education and Rural Communities

The funding agencies and funding patterns of federal workforce development programs are similar to those of STEM education programs (Figure 3-2). Four agencies—Health and Human Services (107 programs,

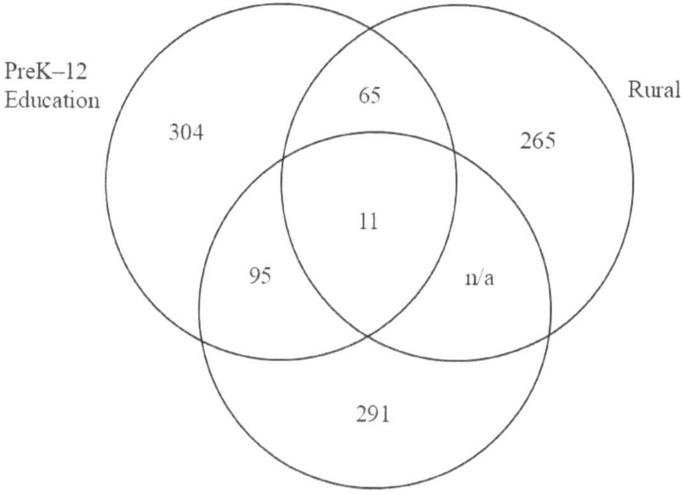

FIGURE 3-2 Number of federal programs for preK–12 education, workforce development, and rural communities.
NOTES: n/a denotes lack of information on the number of workforce development programs targeted for rural communities. The intersections between preK–12 education and workforce development do not also illustrate programs focused on STEM; the middle number shows the intersection of preK–12 education, workforce development, rural areas, and STEM.
SOURCE: Committee generated.

36.8%), Education (39 programs, 13.4%), Labor (26 programs, 8.9%), and Agriculture (19 programs, 6.5%)—administer two thirds (66%) of federal workforce development programs. Twenty agencies administer 95 programs at the intersection of preK–12 education and workforce development; Education and Health and Human Services administer about half (50.5%), and Labor and Defense administer another 14 percent. Fourteen agencies offer 62 programs—51 project grant and 11 formula grant programs—at the intersection of preK–12 education, STEM, and workforce development; here too, Health and Human Services offers half of these programs.

The purpose of this inventory is to identify federal efforts supporting preK–12 STEM education and workforce development in rural areas. The committee found 11 such programs, shown in Figure 3-2, and they illustrate the main conclusion of this report: that while the federal government invests broadly in terms of the sheer number of programs, very many of them are at best tangentially related to preK–12 education, STEM, rural communities, or workforce development. Many of those that are more directly connected to these topics rely on grantees choosing to focus on them rather than the programs or agencies encouraging a specific focus on rural preK–12 STEM education (see, for example, the discussion below of Community Services Block Grants). NASA's Office of STEM Engagement (a collection of programs)[3] offers a different, strategic approach to supporting preK–12 STEM education and workforce development. Even this program, however, could be more strategically targeted to rural communities.

National Science Foundation Programs

As noted above, the NSF directorates rather than individual programs appear in the FPI data. To better capture the full inventory of federal programming focused on rural preK–12 STEM education and workforce development, the committee analyzed datasets provided by NSF, focusing on awards made in fiscal year (FY) 2024 (October 1, 2023, through September 30, 2024) with the word "rural" in either the title or the abstract. Importantly, the committee did not include awards made to an institution located in a rural area unless the title or abstract of the project included the word rural. Similarly, the committee did not consider work with Tribal Nations, Alaska Natives, Native Hawaiians, and Pacific Islanders to be rural unless it was explicitly mentioned to be in a rural area. The committee acknowledges that this method may undercount work conducted in rural areas or focused on rural communities (e.g., work done on a reservation but not described as rural in the title or abstract), but chose to not risk overstating the investment in these communities. This tension highlights the difficulties of accurately counting grants using the existing databases, although NSF's relatively new reference code for awards focused on rural America may help researchers examine this work in future fiscal years. The committee recognizes the possibility that grants on general topics in K–12 STEM or workforce development will have implications for rural settings, but those implications should not be assumed given the diversity both within rural areas and between rural and nonrural areas

Table 3-1 shows the number and amount of total awards and rural-related awards made across the nine directorates. The award amounts are only for FY 2024. In other words, some grants may have had only part of their funding awarded for FY 2024, so the dollar amount listed does not reflect the total amount awarded over multiple fiscal years. Although collaborative awards can be awarded to a single institution that provides subawards to collaborating institutions, the collaboratives listed in the table are for a single research project made in two or more separate awards to the collaborating institutions.

[3]NASA's Office of STEM Engagement is one example of the idiosyncratic and inconsistent way agencies provide data to SAM.gov and in turn to the FPI.

TABLE 3-1 NSF Awards and Amounts Awarded, FY 2024

NSF Directorate	Total Number of Awards FY 2024	Total Amount Awarded FY 2024	Number of Rural Awards FY 2024	Rural Amount Awarded FY 2024
Biological Sciences (BIO)	1021	$584,958,427	24	$18,932,492
Computer and Information Science and Engineering (CISE)	1815	$778,966,305	37 (3 part of a collaborative)	$15,701,005
Engineering (ENG)	1645	$653,427,494	39 (6 awards part of 3 different collaboratives)	$14,615,879
Geosciences (GEO)	1321	$472,592,680	55 (28 part of 11 different collaboratives	$25,215,776
Mathematical and Physical Sciences (MPS)	2486	$880,980,535	26 (2 part of a collaborative)	$8,037,672
Office of the Director (O/D)	331	$275,668,598	43 (28 part of 5 collaboratives)	$37,116,313
Social, Behavioral and Economic Sciences (SBE)	769	$192,072,645	18 (2 part of a collaborative)	$4,617,654
STEM Education (EDU)	1284	$812,092,569	117 (30 part of 8 different collaboratives)	$78,409,468
Technology, Innovation and Partnerships (TIP)	1015	$610,378,201	47 (10 part of 4 different collaboratives)	$117,672,611
Total	**11687**	**$5,261,137,454**	**406 (109 part of 34 different collaboratives)**	**$320,318,870**

NOTE: Numbers for total grants for SBE and EDU provided by NSF. Numbers for total grants for the other directorates determined using the NSF public awards database (searching by directorate for grants awarded between October 1, 2023, and September 30, 2024). Award amounts reflect only the award amount for FY 2024, not the total amount awarded over multiple fiscal years.
SOURCE: Committee generated.

NSF's Office of the Director had the highest percentage of its grants and funding awarded for work described as related to rural areas, but the fewest grants awarded overall in FY 2024. Most relevant to the committee's work, of the 1,284 total grants awarded by the EDU directorate in FY 2024, 117 awards for 95 different projects (accounting for the number of collaborative grants) went to organizations that described their work as occurring in or related to rural areas. This is 9 percent of the total awards and 10 percent of the total amount awarded by EDU in that timeframe. Across directorates, over $300 million was awarded in FY 2024 for work described as related to rural areas, which is approximately 6 percent of the total award amount for that year, although the total number of awards for this work was 3.5 percent of the total number of NSF awards.

Further, although all of the rural-related grants are related to STEM, only a subset of those are related to preK–12 education and/or workforce development. Using the 406 awards with the word rural in the title or abstract, the committee reviewed the titles and abstracts of the awards to identify awards made to projects that included aspects related to learning experiences for youth in the preK–12 age range, including references to formal preK–12 schools or students; informal or out-of-school-time education activities (including citizen science and other youth learning) that were specified to be for preK–12 students; and/or teacher learning (which includes both preservice teacher education and inservice teacher professional learning). In addition, many of the awards were connected to STEM workforce development as it relates to postsecondary education in bachelor degree programs, but given the committee's statement of task, only awards that described workforce development related to preK–12 education, including dual enrollment, certifications, transitions to associate degree programs, and STEM teacher education, were included in this analysis. In order to be coded for preK–12 education the abstract needed to provide a level of specificity about how the work would reach rural preK–12 students or educators in formal or informal settings. For example, abstracts describing "outreach" without more information were not included. Although it is possible that this coding undercounts educational experiences provided to rural preK–12 students either in or out of school time, the committee again chose to not risk overcounting the investment in these students. Coding was conducted by one person and checked by a second person; discrepancies were resolved through discussion. In an effort to count all of the awards that might relate to rural STEM preK–12 education and workforce development, the committee chose to be inclusive of all directorates as well as focusing more closely on all of the divisions within EDU. Table 3-2 shows the number of awards in each directorate coded as "rural" and included one or more of these aspects of preK–12 education among the rural awards.

TABLE 3-2 Learning for PreK–12 Aged Children in NSF Rural Awards

NSF Directorate	Rural Youth Learning	Percent of Directorate Awards	Rural Youth Learning Award Amount	Percent of Directorate Awarded Amount
Biological Sciences (BIO)	10	1.0	$7,409,542.00	1.3
Computer and Information Science and Engineering (CISE)	9	0.5	$4,942,349.00	0.6
Engineering (ENG)	18	1.1	$7,621,740.00	1.2
Geosciences (GEO)	25	1.9	$7,621,740.00	1.6
Mathematical and Physical Sciences (MPS)	12	0.5	$3,775,881.00	0.4
Office of the Director (OD)	18	5.4	$9,836,767.00	3.6
Social, Behavioral and Economic Sciences (SBE)	0	0	0	0
STEM Education (EDU)	81	6.3	$47,617,206.00	5.9
Technology, Innovation and Partnerships (TIP)	4	0.4	$16,353,838.00	2.7
Total	**177**	**1.5**	**$112,328,874.00**	**2.1**

NOTE: Numbers for total grants for SBE and EDU provided by NSF. Numbers for total grants for the other directorates determined using the NSF public awards database (searching by directorate for grants awarded between October 1, 2023, and September 30, 2024). Award amounts reflect only the award amount for FY 2024, not the total amount awarded over multiple fiscal years.
SOURCE: Committee generated.

Note that it is not possible to disaggregate the funds directed to rural youth STEM learning from the funding to support other activities of the grant, and many grants addressed learning experiences for youth in a variety of ways, including developing classroom modules or conducting summer camps. Of the 117 grants coded as rural and related to youth learning, many included activities for informal or out-of-school-time learning (including citizen science activities), either as the only educational experience or in conjunction with formal preK–12 education. In addition, several grants included activities for postsecondary education and workforce development and/or teacher learning. Table 3-3 shows the other foci of awards from all directorates except EDU, which is shown in Table 3-4. A single grant may be coded as more than one category, so the total across categories for each directorate might sum to more than the total number of grants awarded as shown in Table 3-2. In addition, because some awards focused on more than one of these, the award amounts are not shown.

TABLE 3-3 Relevant Foci for Rural Youth Learning Grants

Directorate	Formal	Informal	Workforce	Teacher Learning
Biological Sciences (BIO)	7	4	1	3
Computer and Information Science and Engineering (CISE)	9	0	8	6
Engineering (ENG)	12	7	7	5
Geosciences (GEO)	21	5	11	1
Mathematical and Physical Sciences (MPS)	9	4	6	0
Office of the Director (OD)	13	13	13	8
Technology, Innovation and Partnerships (TIP)	4	0	4	1

SOURCE: Committee generated.

Given its mission, the EDU directorate included a wider variety of activities related to preK–12 STEM education than the other directorates (see Table 3-4). Many of the awards included aspects of educational research: one in DGE (focused on turnover in the STEM teacher workforce in high-needs areas such as rural communities) and 48 in DRL. Note that because some awards focused on more than one of these, the award amounts are not shown. Within DRL, one of the awards for informal learning also included an aspect for formal preK–12 education. Also note that the Division of Equity for Excellence in STEM did not make any FY 2024 awards that included an aspect of rural youth learning. A single grant may be coded as more than one category, so the total across categories for each division might sum to more than the total number of grants.

TABLE 3-4 Relevant Foci for EDU Rural Youth Learning Grants

EDU Division	Formal	Informal	Workforce	Teacher Learning	Total Rural Youth Learning
Graduate Education (DGE)	1	0	0	1	1
Research on Learning in Formal and Informal Settings (DRL)	43	7	10	22	49
Undergraduate Education (DUE)	31	0	8	26	31

SOURCE: Committee generated.

In DRL, the Discovery Research PreK–12 (DRK-12) program funded 12 of the teacher learning awards, while Innovative Technology Experiences for Students and Teachers funded four, National STEM Teacher Corps funded five, and CSforAll funded one. In DUE, 22 teacher learning awards were through the Robert Noyce Scholarship program, 2 in Advanced Technological Education, and 1 each in IUSE and National STEM Teacher Corps. In FY 2024, DRK-12 made 80 awards and Noyce made 98; the percent of teacher learning awards with a rural focus in those programs is 15 percent for DRK-12 and 27 percent for Noyce. The committee did not conduct a quality analysis of the professional learning initiatives.

In addition to the categories previously mentioned, the committee's coding of rural awards from NSF's data revealed a small number of grants related to the portion of its charge concerning broadband and connectivity in rural areas. One doctoral dissertation improvement grant in the SBE Social and Economic Sciences division is examining the environmental and socioeconomic consequences low-earth-orbit satellites that could help provide broadband connectivity to remote areas. A collaborative CISE grant across three universities aims to improve broadband connectivity for schools, hospitals, and libraries that serve rural communities, and another CISE grant aims to improve internet connectivity and digital literacy in rural tribal communities. Finally, three different Small Business Innovation Research projects in the TIP directorate focus on connectivity through mobile broadband and other wireless communications that could serve remote areas.

Quality of Federal Programs

The number of federal programs provides some insight into the level of federal support for preK–12 STEM education and workforce development in rural communities. A more complete picture requires knowledge of the quality of the programs offered. But just as counting federal programs presents more challenges than one might expect, so too does assessing the quality of federal support. Federal programs are not interventions with standardized theories of change, logic models, inputs, activities, and resources. Rather, they are funding streams that support grantee projects that may (or may not) resemble more evaluable social interventions. This defining characteristic of federal programs makes it very difficult to conduct rigorous research consistent with National Research Council (2002) and NSF (2013) standards.

A recent report by the Committee on Equal Opportunities in Science and Engineering (NSF, 2024) describes features of successful strategies for rural STEM programs:

- access to experiential activities,
- financial support to increase access to a STEM degree,

- leveraging of technology to improve STEM pathways,
- bridging of formal and informal STEM education experiences,
- leveraging of investments in place-based research, and
- strengthened mentorship opportunities.

The programs listed below are examples of those at the intersection of preK–12 STEM education and workforce development in rural areas. For each program, the committee describes the primary objective, application priorities (for nonformula programs), range of grants (including overall funding), features of quality rural STEM programming, and kinds of performance data collected.

- Nita M. Lowey 21st Century Community Learning Centers
- Innovative Approaches to Literacy; Promise Neighborhoods; Full-Service Community Schools; and Congressionally Directed Spending for Elementary and Secondary Education Community Projects
- Rural Education Achievement Program
- Community Services Block Grant
- NASA Office of STEM Engagement

The committee presents these with the following observations. First, performance measures are generally simple measures of inputs and outputs that provide little insight into program improvement. In the case of the Community Services Block Grant, where somewhat more detailed data are collected, the collection imposes a substantial burden on grantees. Second, although several of these programs support preK–12 STEM education and workforce development in rural communities, they do so primarily or exclusively because grantees choose to do so, not because of a strategic prioritization of resources to support rural STEM learning. Finally, while the distributed choice model is the default for federal programs, NASA demonstrates that a more strategic prioritization can guide federal support for rural STEM, and NSF illustrates a blending of the two.

Nita M. Lowey 21st Century Community Learning Centers

The U.S. Department of Education's Nita M. Lowey 21st Century Community Learning Centers (21CCLC) support academic enrichment in out-of-school, afterschool, and summer programming. This preK–12 formula grant program requires a focus on STEM insofar as improved mathematics achievement is a key outcome measure. It encourages grantees to offer additional STEM learning opportunities for students as well as workforce development, but these are at grantees' discretion and not integral to the program's operation.

Nothing in 21CCLC runs counter to the research features of quality rural STEM programs. Other than providing access to a STEM degree, the other features are well within the scope of the program's intent.

The Government Performance and Results Act indicators for 21CCLC reduce a complex and varied program to student improvement on state reading/language arts and mathematics assessments, improvement in middle and high school student grades, improved student attendance, reduced in-school student suspension, and improved teacher-reported student engagement in learning. These indicators are preferable to counts of students participating in funded activities, but they shed little light on program performance and so are at best weak proxies for the features of quality rural STEM programming.

Promise Neighborhoods and Full-Service Community Schools

The Promise Neighborhoods (PN) program focuses on outcome improvement for children and youth in "the most distressed communities."[4] The Full-Service Community Schools (FSCS) program funds grantees to support "full-service community schools that improve the coordination, integration, accessibility, and effectiveness of services for children and families."[5] Like 21CCLC, PN and FSCS require a focus on STEM insofar as improved mathematics achievement is a key outcome measure and, although they consider additional STEM learning opportunities and workforce development, the integration of such activities is left to the discretion of grantees.

PN grants have a term of up to 24 months, and FSCS grants up to 60 months. Funding for PN in FY 2023 was $102 million and in FY 2024 $74 million; the president's request for FY 2025 is $91 million. For FSCS, funding for fiscal years 2023 and 2024 was $76 million and $149 million, respectively; the president's FY 2025 request is $200 million (OMB, 2024, p. 308).

PN and FSCS are both place-based, collective impact programs to support student and family success, school improvement, and community and workforce development. PN applications include three absolute priorities: nonrural and nontribal communities, rural communities (as defined by the NCES locale codes), and tribal communities. Competitive priorities include career and technical education programs. FSCS applications include an absolute priority for serving small and rural or rural and low-income schools as defined by the Small Rural School Achievement Program or the Rural and Low-Income School Program.

---

[4]https://www.govinfo.gov/content/pkg/FR-2024-06-27/pdf/2024-14054.pdf

[5]https://www.govinfo.gov/content/pkg/FR-2023-06-07/pdf/2023-12145.pdf

PN performance indicators include measures of student academic performance on state reading and language arts and mathematics assessments, student transitions from middle to high school, student absenteeism, postsecondary educational enrollment, postsecondary educational attainment, student nutrition, student safety, student mobility rates, family reading, family college and career discussions, and home broadband access.

The FSCS performance indicators include numbers of individuals served, student chronic absenteeism, student discipline, school climate, measures of implementation of key dimensions of full-service community schools, school staff qualifications and retention, graduation rates, and school spending.

Rural Education Achievement Program

Described earlier in this chapter, REAP is intended to help rural districts meet their particular needs and to "participate more fully and effectively in many of the ESEA programs and allow them to provide better educational services to their students" (U.S. Department of Education, 2021). LEAs can use SRSA and RLIS funds to support any allowable activities under ESEA Title I Part A, Title II Part A, Title III, and Title IV Parts A and B. These uses are consistent with both STEM education and workforce development, but nothing in REAP requires a focus on either.

Both programs are formula grant programs: SRSA provides assistance via formula to LEAs and RLIS by formula to state education agencies that in turn make subgrants to LEAs. Funding for REAP in both FY 2023 and FY 2024 was $215 million; the president's request for FY 2025 is $218 million (OMB, 2024, p. 307). As with 21CCLC, PN, and FSCS, some REAP grantees use funds consistent with at least some of the Committee on Equal Opportunities in Science and Engineering features, but none of that activity is intentional; it is at best coincidental.

Performance reporting for REAP is by means of the Consolidated State Performance Report of the U.S. Department of Education OESE. This report provides a way for state education agencies to report performance across a number of U.S. Department of Education formula grant programs. As such, there are minimal data focused on REAP. The most salient data are brief narratives on outcomes per the state's plan.

Community Services Block Grant

The Community Services Block Grant (CSBG) program is a cornerstone antipoverty program in the U.S. Department of Health and Human Services (2022), and many grantees of this formula grant program support preK–12 STEM education and workforce development in rural communities. None of these uses is required under CSBG, but all are allowed and implemented by grantees (known as Community Action Agencies). CSBG funds activities in all 50 states, the District of Columbia, the Commonwealth of Puerto Rico, and U.S. territories (American Samoa, Guam, the Northern Mariana Islands, and the U.S. Virgin Islands), and conducted by federally recognized tribes and tribal organizations (U.S. Department of Health and Human Services, 2022). Funding for CSBG was $771 million in FY 2023 and $770 million in FY 2024; the president's request for FY 2025 is $770 million (OMB, 2024, p. 443).

The CSBG portfolio encompasses a greater range of services than 21CCLC, PN, or FSCS, but many projects share commonalities with projects funded by all three of those programs and likely (though perhaps to a lesser extent) with REAP projects. The balance of academic programming in CSBG, both generally and focused on STEM education, is unclear. The antipoverty focus of CSBG suggests that there may be a greater emphasis on workforce development and other postsecondary outcomes than the more school-focused 21CCLC and FSCS.

While the education programs discussed above require relatively few measures and they are generally distal to likely program effects, the CSBG annual report asks grantees and subgrantees for a wealth of data. The Community National Performance Indicators related to education and cognitive development provide somewhat more detailed information than similar indicators in the education programs. This additional detail should be of use to both government program officers and grantee and subgrantee project managers. Unfortunately, the estimated public reporting burden for each grant is 198 hours for grantees (i.e., states) and 697 hours for subgrantees (i.e., project staff).

NASA Office of STEM Engagement

NASA's Office of STEM Engagement (OSTEM), like NSF's directorates, is a collection of programs focused on promoting STEM engagement, learning, pathways, and workforce development. Of the five programs in OSTEM, Next Gen STEM supports a portfolio of work on preK–12 education. The projects include activities similar to those of 21CCLC, PN, and FSCS, but with an explicit focus on STEM engagement and/or workforce development. The OSTEM budget for FY 2023 was $154 million and for FY 2024 $144 million; the president's request for FY 2025 is $144 million. Approximately $14 million was devoted to Next Gen STEM in FY 2023. While these numbers pale in comparison to the funding for 21CCLC, PN, and FSCS, OSTEM activities in rural areas could provide valuable examples for U.S. Department of Education programs and grantee projects. It should be noted that this funding does not explicitly focus on rural education; strategic planning could help move toward that focus.

Federal Interagency Working Groups

There are two relevant interagency working groups, but neither targets the intersection of preK–12 STEM education or workforce development and rural communities.

U.S. Department of Agriculture Rural Partners Network

Primarily led by the U.S. Department of Agriculture and the White House, the Rural Partners Network (RPN) is a program meant to link rural communities to resources that promote infrastructure and economic development. Other participating agencies are the Departments of Commerce, Education, Energy, Health and Human Services, Homeland Security, Housing and Urban Development, Interior, Labor, Transportation, Treasury, and Veterans Affairs; the Environmental Protection Agency; the Appalachian Regional Commission; Consumer Financial Protection Bureau; Delta Regional Authority; Denali Commission; Federal Deposit Insurance Corporation; Northern Border Regional Commission; Small Business Administration; Social Security Administration; Southeast Crescent Regional Commission; and Southwest Border Regional Commission.

RPN provides a search engine that rural communities can use to find open grants across federal agencies based on need type (e.g., housing, job creation, transportation). As of September 2024, a search of grant programs related to STEM education yielded zero hits. And although workforce development programs abound, none are connected to K–12 students. The resource page for programs developed specifically for tribes, Native Americans, and Alaska Natives yielded one resource for K–12 education, the Indian Education Formula Grants from the U.S. Department of Education OESE (Rural.gov).

White House Office of Science Technology Policy Committee on STEM Education

In the Office of Science and Technology Policy, the National Science and Technology Council operates the Committee on STEM Education (CoSTEM), established in 2011 through the America COMPETES Reauthorization Act. CoSTEM has six interagency working groups (IWGs)—on Strategic Partnerships, Interdisciplinary STEM, Computational Literacy, Operational Transparency and Accountability, Inclusion in STEM, and Supporting Veterans in STEM Careers Act—that work together to carry out a Five-Year Federal STEM Education Strategic Plan, the most recent of which is for 2018–2023. The IWGs pursue three shared goals: foundational STEM literacy, broadening participation in STEM, and STEM workforce preparation. None of the IWGs have a rural-specific focus, although each goal can be taken up at the community level.

Implications for Federal Policy

The federal government funds an abundance of programs related to preK–12 STEM education and workforce development in rural areas. While numerous high-quality programs support preK–12 STEM education and workforce development, relatively fewer focus on rural STEM, and by and large they rely on the distributed choices of grantees to support high-quality STEM education and workforce development in rural communities.

Two possibilities emerge from the analyses conducted for this chapter. First, strategic prioritization could move programs like 21CCLC, PN, and FSCS toward consistent and widespread rural STEM education and workforce projects. Although some programs discuss STEM achievement, generally in the form of student performance on state mathematics assessments, the committee did not identify any that set either an absolute priority on rural STEM education or even a competitive or invitational priority for STEM education and workforce development in rural communities. This one change could have profound effects on the landscape of federal support for rural STEM education and workforce development. Second, the data are abundantly clear that there are almost countless opportunities to expand STEM projects to include education and/or workforce development. These opportunities range from U.S. Department of Interior conservation efforts in national parks to U.S. Department of Transportation engineering projects. In addition, knowledge building at NSF can play an important role in developing new approaches to address rural STEM education and workforce needs, and NASA's OSTEM offers myriad examples of projects that can be adapted for rural communities.

SUPPORTING RURAL EDUCATION THROUGH STATE FUNDING AND POLICY

While federal funding provides some support to schools, it is only about 10 percent of total funding, leaving states and local districts to close the funding gap.[6] Congress appropriates funds annually to 52 state education agencies (in the 50 states, the District of Columbia, and the Commonwealth of Puerto Rico), which in turn award subgrants to local education agencies and other public and private entities such as community-based organizations and educational service agencies. These subgrants are for terms of three to five years. Examples of the priorities that states may include in subgrant competitions include STEM programming and efforts to foster geographic diversity (U.S. Department of Education, 2023). State funding and policies have not traditionally attended to the unique needs of rural districts and schools, but some states have recently enacted legislation to

[6]https://apps.urban.org/features/funding-formulas/

bolster funding for K–12 education in rural communities and to provide innovative exemptions for rural schools, enabling them to provide quality STEM education and workforce development pathways.

Addressing Rural School Funding Formula Limitations

Rural areas tend to "have poverty and lower budgetary revenues than their suburban counterparts" (Johnson & Zoellner, 2016, p. 3). Per-student expenditures are lower in rural school districts and rural schools compared to nonrural school districts and schools (Harris & Hodges, 2018; Showalter et al., 2023). For instance, nonrural school districts "spend an average of $7,685 on the teaching and learning of each student. This figure is over $500 more than the amount spent on the instruction of each rural student" (Showalter et al., 2023, p. 10). But average rural expenditures per student vary across the country, with New York rural districts spending $14,731 per student and Idaho ($4,908) and Mississippi ($5,484) spending the least (Showalter et al., 2023). Furthermore, since 2019, "the state-to-local funding proportions for rural districts have decreased in 27 states, creating more dependency on more inequitable local funding" (Showalter et al., 2023, p. 11).

Because rural school districts are more sparsely populated, they have higher costs related to student transportation (Johnson & Zoellner, 2016). This and other financial and budgetary contextual factors place more constraints on rural school district budgets to offer services and resources for students, such as support for multilingual learners and students with disabilities (Johnson & Zoellner, 2016). And these financial constraints often mean that rural teachers are paid less compared to teachers in nonrural school districts (Harris & Hodges, 2018).

States attempt to address these challenges by increasing the amount of funding that rural schools receive through funding formulas and policies that adjust funding for small school size and isolation. Some states provide extra funds to schools below a certain enrollment threshold; others use teacher-student ratios to make determinations about additional funding for some school districts. Although the state definition of an *isolated* or *small* school varies by state, small schools and districts are typically those with enrollment of fewer than 100 students. In many cases small schools are also isolated, but not necessarily all isolated schools are small (Evans et al., 2020).

States generally identify isolated schools based on one or more of the following criteria:

- large distance between schools,
- distance and time required for students to travel to their school,

- population density of the area surrounding the school,
- total geographical area of the school district, and
- whether geographic barriers are present.

Kolbe et al. (2021) report that at least 13 states adjusted their funding formula to account for their rural districts' geographic location and population density. Others adjusted their funding formula for rural districts based on the driving distances needed to transport students, and 43 states provided supplemental funding for transportation. Some states have attempted to cut costs by encouraging or imposing district consolidation (Lavalley, 2018) and moving to a four-day school week (Anglum & Park, 2021), with mixed results.

To address the needs of small and isolated schools, states may adjust their funding formula to allocate additional funds on a sliding scale or, taking into account the size of the school or district, based on the budgetary discretion of the legislature. In some cases, states use more than one criterion to decide on the provision of additional funding but cap the funds on the school's meeting a minimum threshold in the criteria. Gutierrez and Terrones (2023), summarizing information from different sources, find that 33 states provided additional support to small, sparse, or isolated districts and 10 states provided additional support based on distance (from 7 to 30 miles) to the nearest other district or school.

Some of the largest economic concerns for rural school districts relate to transportation and scarce opportunities for economies of scale. Transportation is important because rural districts generally cover larger geographic areas, and their schools are separated by long distances. Because of their low student population, it is also difficult for rural schools to implement economies of scale to support their needs. On average, for every dollar spent on transportation in rural districts, $10.36 is spent on instruction (most states spend between $9.64 and $12.74). The largest instruction-to-transportation spending ratio is in Alaska ($15.71 on instruction for every dollar on transportation) and the smallest is in West Virginia, which spends $7.46 on instruction for every dollar spent on transportation (Cornman et al., 2021). Rural Alaska districts tend to be small geographically and spend relatively little money on transportation compared to instructional costs, whereas West Virginia's rural districts are consolidated to follow county lines, causing them to spend much more money in transportation relative to instruction.

Innovative State Policies

To provide more accessible STEM learning opportunities to rural students, some states are passing legislation and implementing new policies that directly benefit these students. For example, Texas recently passed legislation to remove barriers and incentivize rural districts to create partnerships known as Districts of Innovation.[7] The legislation provides funding and certain exemptions for rural school districts to partner together, along with local institutions of higher education and industry, to offer students multiple pathways to earn college credit, an associate's degree, and/or industry-based certifications and Level 1 and 2 certificates. The legislation is designed to encourage replication of the state's Rural Schools Innovation Zone, which offers five career pathway–based "academies" through the partnership of three rural school districts with multiple institutions of higher education and industry partners (Pankovits, 2023). Four of the five entities—Ignite Technical Institute, Next Generation Medical Academy, STEM Discovery Zone, and the Grow Your Own educator pipeline initiative—support STEM education and workforce development.

Legislation in Oklahoma aimed at ensuring that all students, including those in rural communities, have access to AP courses went into effect in 2024.[8] Access may be offered at a school or other sites in the district; a technology center in the district; a school or other sites in another district; or through an online learning program offered by the Statewide Charter School Board or one of its vendors. The new law removes barriers that may have prevented access to course offerings and establishes a new program through the Statewide Charter School Board to offer AP coursework online for use by all school districts in the state.

Oklahoma also modified graduation requirements to allow school districts to offer STEM block courses (combining science, technology, engineering, and/or mathematics competencies), and thus enable students to receive high school graduation credit for two subject areas in a single course, as long as the teacher(s) in the block courses have the necessary certifications to provide instruction related to the subject areas.[9] STEM blocks can help rural schools overcome scheduling barriers that often arise because of the schools' more limited staffing compared to their urban or suburban counterparts.

In addition to legislative efforts to promote quality STEM education and workforce development in states, several state education agencies took advantage of opportunities afforded by the Every Student Succeeds Act (ESSA; 2015) to improve their accountability systems and provide incentives to school districts to develop priorities that aligned with their state goals for college and career readiness, including in STEM areas.

[7]https://tea.texas.gov/texas-schools/district-initiatives/districts-of-innovation

[8]https://www.oscn.net/applications/oscn/deliverdocument.asp?id=487131&hits=175+

[9]https://www.oscn.net/applications/oscn/deliverdocument.asp?id=438855&hits=10793+10792+10558+10557+6327+6326+6092+6091+1703+1702+1468+1467+

ESSA offered states more flexibility and authority over their state accountability systems than before, particularly through the indicators for school quality and student success (SQSS) measures, which have been defined as "non-academic measures that must meaningfully differentiate schools from one another and also be comparable across schools" (Kaput, 2018, p. 2). Thirty-six states chose to add SQSS measures incentivizing various aspects of college and career readiness (Kaput, 2018) in their school accountability systems. Several states, including Connecticut and Delaware, include postsecondary study as an SQSS, measuring the percentage of students in each school enrolled in a two- or four-year postsecondary institution anytime during the first year after high school (Erwin et al., 2021). Mississippi and Florida prioritized the passage of AP and International Baccalaureate exams in their new SQSS measures, while Texas, Alabama, and Rhode Island added SQSS measures determining the percentage of students who receive industry credentials (Erwin et al., 2021). Oklahoma, California, and Utah included measures for the number of students enrolled in CTE pathways, and Arkansas and Michigan were two of many states that included measures for dual enrollment in college coursework (Erwin et al., 2021).

None of the SQSS measures are specific to STEM or rural education, but they provide pathways for rural schools to receive credit in state accountability systems for students who complete advanced coursework, CTE programs, dual enrollment in a postsecondary institution, and industry credentials, all of which are important pathways for STEM education and workforce development. Arkansas nodded to STEM in its SQSS measures by stating that it would determine the percentage of students obtaining computer science course credits as part of its accountability system. States are leveraging the new flexibilities under the reauthorization of ESSA to incentivize pathways supportive of STEM education and workforce development. States could further incentivize pathways by considering additional SQSS measures that reflect rural contexts.

Notwithstanding some of the state policy efforts mentioned above, rural educators and education advocates continue to call for policies that give more careful attention to the specific needs of rural educators, students, and families. Surveys and interviews with rural superintendents led to the identification of four priority areas for state legislation to address rural education needs (Arsen et al., 2021):

- teacher recruitment and retention,
- resources for students with mental health problems,
- broadband access, and
- school funding.

The Center on Reinventing Public Education has also recommended four areas for state legislators to address the K–12 education challenges unique to rural communities (Hill, 2015):

- flexibility in funding statutes and categorical programs;
- incentives to share resources, including staff, facilities, and courses;
- unconventional training and career development opportunities; and
- getting the voices of rural leaders heard in the state capitol.

The center also recommended that state legislators increase their presence and familiarity with both the difficulties and the strengths of the state's small, rural school districts.

SUMMARY

The committee considered policy and funding challenges to rural education, including few and sometimes no resources, limited course availability, and/or limited personnel, technical, and logistical support for STEM instruction (e.g., broadband access, adequate transportation). The committee examined federal and state policies that directly impact rural schools and their ability to address these challenges, as well as federal programs and funding (including amounts) for rural students, STEM education, and workforce development. There has been some progress in addressing barriers related to funding, but federal and state entities need to work more closely with rural school districts and provide more adequate support while also recognizing the strengths of these communities. The policies in place have led some educational leaders to generate creative programs, offerings, or initiatives to provide high-quality STEM content to rural students. This development of STEM content is largely attributed to the resilience of rural places and the importance of access to a fair and equitable STEM education.

We present the following major conclusions:

Conclusion 3-1: All states have a significant population of rural students, but federal and state policies do not always attend to the unique needs and strengths of rural communities. Policy decisions and processes often do not take into account potential unintended consequences for rural districts and schools.

Conclusion 3-2: Rural districts and schools in remote areas with low population density and limited access to affordable and reliable broadband face unique challenges for supporting K–12 STEM education and workforce development initiatives, and these challenges are often not adequately addressed by federal and state programs. There is also limited research focused on these remote communities.

Conclusion 3-3: There are many federal programs in K–12 STEM education and workforce development that rural districts, schools, and out-of-school programs can apply to for funding, but few programs target rural districts and schools. In addition, rules for eligibility (including the definition of rurality), program requirements, and the demands of the application process can prevent rural schools, districts, and communities from applying for and receiving funding.

Conclusion 3-4: Some rural communities, districts, and schools lack the capacity (e.g., staffing, time, and expertise) to identify potential funding opportunities to advance STEM education and workforce development opportunities, complete the application process, and meet the reporting requirements if funding is awarded.

Conclusion 3-5: Out-of-school learning opportunities in STEM are an important complement to in-school learning. While many students in rural communities lack access to opportunities in museums or other out-of-school institutions, they often do have access to STEM learning opportunities at home or in nature.

REFERENCES

Advance CTE. (2017). *CTE on the frontier: Providing learners access to diverse career pathways.* https://files.eric.ed.gov/fulltext/ED592018.pdf

Allen, P. J., Lewis-Warner, K., & Noam, G. G. (2020). Partnerships to transform STEM learning: A case study of a STEM learning ecosystem. *Afterschool Matters, 31*, 30–41. https://eric.ed.gov/?id=EJ1249559

Anglum, J. C., & Park, A. (2021). Keeping up with the Joneses: District adoption of the 4-day school week in rural Missouri. *AERA Open, 7*. https://doi.org/10.1177/233285842110028

Apling, R. N. (2007). *Rural education and the Rural Education Achievement Program (REAP): Overview and policy issues.* Congressional Research Service. https://www.policyarchive.org/handle/10207/3073

Arsen, D., Delpier, T., Gensterblum, A., Jacobsen, R., & Stamm, A. (2021). Rural communities need better state education policies. *Phi Delta Kappan, 103*(4), 8–13. https://kappanonline.org/rural-state-education-policies-arsen-delpier-gensterblum-jacobsen-stamm/

Avery, L. M., & Kassam, K. A. (2011). Phronesis: Children's local rural knowledge of science and engineering. *Journal of Research in Rural Education, 26*, 1–18.

Banilower, E. R., Smith, P. S., Malzahn, K. A., Plumley, C. L., Gordon, E. M., & Hayes, M. L. (2018). *Report of the 2018 NSSME+.* Horizon Research.

Barker, B., Valentine, D., Grandgenett, N., Keshwani, J., & Burnett, A. (2018). Using virtual reality and telepresence robotics in making. In *E-Learn: World conference on e-learning in corporate, government, healthcare, and higher education* (pp. 564–568). Association for the Advancement of Computing in Education.

Barrett, B., Bevevino, D., Larkin, A., & Wyner, J. (2023). *Rural community college excellence: A guide to delivering strong opportunity for students and communities*. Aspen Institute.

Beauchamp, A. L., Roberts, S.-J., Aloisio, J. M., Wasserman, D., Heimlich, J. E., Lewis, J. D., Munshi-South, J. Clark, J. A., & Tingley, K. (2022). Effects of research and mentoring on underrepresented youths' STEM persistence into college. *Journal of Experiential Education*, *45*(3), 316–336. https://doi.org/10.1177/10538259211050098

Boynton, M., & Hossain, F. (2010). Improving engineering education outreach in rural counties through engineering risk analysis. *Journal of Professional Issues in Engineering Education and Practice*, *136*(4), 224–232. https://doi.org/10.1061/(ASCE)EI.1943-5541.0000026

Brenner, D. (2016). Rural education and the Every Student Succeeds Act (ESSA). *Rural Educator Policy Brief*. https://digitalcommons.memphis.edu/cgi/viewcontent.cgi?article=1080&context=govpubs-tn-comptroller-office-research-education-accountability

Byker, E. (2014). Sociotechnical narratives in rural, high-poverty elementary schools: Comparative findings from East Texas and South India. *International Journal of Education and Development Using ICT*, *10*(2), 29–40. https://files.eric.ed.gov/fulltext/EJ1071370.pdf

Byun, S. Y., Meece, J. L., & Agger, C. A. (2017). Predictors of college attendance patterns of rural youth. *Research in Higher Education*, *58*, 817–842. https://link.springer.com/article/10.1007/s11162-017-9449-z

Byun, S. Y., Meece, J. L., & Irvin, M. J. (2012). Rural-nonrural disparities in postsecondary educational attainment revisited. *American Educational Research Journal*, *49*(3), 412–437. https://doi.org/10.3102/0002831211416344

Cain, E. J., & Smith, N. L. (2020). Using critical race theory to explore the experiences of college students from rural areas. *Georgia Journal of College Student Affairs*, *36*(1), 3–23. https://eric.ed.gov/?id=EJ1285017

Center for Public Education. (2023). *Educational equity for rural students: Out of the pandemic, but still out of the loop. Part 1: Growing diversity of rural students*. https://www.nsba.org/-/media/CPE-Growing-Diversity-of-Rural-Students.pdf

Chen, X., & Koricich, A. (2014). Reaching out to remote places: A discussion of technology and the future of distance education in rural America. In *E-Learn: World conference on elearning in corporate, government, healthcare, and higher education* (pp. 370–376). Association for the Advancement of Computing in Education.

Cornman, S. Q., Phillips, J. J., Howell, M. R., & Young, J. (2021). *Revenues and expenditures for public elementary and secondary education: FY 19* (NCES No. 2021-302). National Center for Education Statistics, U.S. Department of Education. http://nces.ed.gov/pubsearch

Crain, A., & Webber, K. (2021). Across the urban divide: STEM pipeline engagement among nonmetropolitan students. *Journal for STEM Education Research*, *4*(2), 138–172. https://doi.org/10.1007/s41979-020-00046-8

Culbertson, R., Saw, G. K., Chang, C. N., Hedrick-Roman, K., & Lopez, G. (2023). Deeper learning opportunities and STEM career orientation in out-of-school time (OST) STEM enrichment programs. *Journal of STEM Education: Innovations and Research*, *23*(4).

Dahill-Brown, S. E., & Jochim, A. E. (2018). The power of place in rural schooling. *School Administrator*, *75*(9), 30–35.

De Mars, A., Taken Alive, J., Burns Ortiz, M., Ma, Z., & Wang, M. (2022). Educators' perspectives on factors impacting STEM achievement in rural indigenous student-serving schools. *The Rural Educator*, *43*(1), 24–36.

Erwin, B., Francies, C., Pechota, D., & McCann, M. (2021). *States' school accountability systems: State profiles*. Education Commission of the States. https://www.ecs.org/states-school-accountability-systems-state-profiles/

Eshach, H. (2007). Bridging in-school and out-of-school learning: Formal, non-formal, and informal education. *Journal of Science Education and Technology*, *16*, 171–190.

Evans, A., Syverson, E., & Freemire, L. (2020). *How states allocate funding for rural schools*. Education Commission of the States. https://www.ecs.org/how-states-allocate-funding-for-rural-schools/

Every Student Succeeds Act, 20 U.S.C. § 6301 (2015). https://www.congress.gov/bill/114th-congress/senate-bill/1177

Finkel, L. (2017). Walking the path together from high school to STEM majors and careers: Utilizing community engagement and a focus on teaching to increase opportunities for URM students. *Journal of Science Education and Technology*, *26*, 116–126. https://link.springer.com/article/10.1007/s10956-016-9656-y

García, E., & Weiss, E. (2019a). *The teacher shortage is real, large and growing, and worse than we thought: First report in "The Perfect Storm in the Teacher Labor Market" series*. Economic Policy Institute. https://files.eric.ed.gov/fulltext/ED598211.pdf

———. (2019b). *US schools struggle to hire and retain teachers: Second report in "The Perfect Storm in the Teacher Labor Market" series*. Economic Policy Institute. https://files.eric.ed.gov/fulltext/ED598209.pdf

Goodpaster, K. P., Adedokun, O. A., & Weaver, G. C. (2012). Teachers' perceptions of rural STEM teaching: Implications for rural teacher retention. *The Rural Educator*, *33*(3), 9–22.

Gottfried, A. E., Preston, K. S. J., Gottfried, A. W., Oliver, P. H., Delany, D. E., & Ibrahim, S. M. (2016). Pathways from parental stimulation of children's curiosity to high school science course accomplishments and science career interest and skill. *International Journal of Science Education*, *38*(12), 1972–1995. https://doi.org/10.1080/09500693.2016.1220690

Graham, S. E., & Provost, L. E. (2012). *Mathematics achievement gaps between suburban students and their rural and urban peers increase over time* (Issue Brief No. 52). Carsey Institute. https://eric.ed.gov/?id=ED535962

Griffen, Z. (2020). The 'production' of education: The turn from equity to efficiency in U.S. federal education policy. *Journal of Education Policy*, *37*(1), 69–87. https://doi.org/10.1080/02680939.2020.1751884

Grimes, L. E., Arrastía-Chisholm, M. A., & Bright, S. B. (2019). How can they know what they don't know? The beliefs and experiences of rural school counselors about STEM career advising. *Theory & Practice in Rural Education*, *9*(1), 74–90. https://doi.org/10.3776/tpre.2019.v9n1p74-90

Gutierrez, E., & Terrones, F. (2023). *Small and sparse: Defining rural school districts for K-12 funding*. Urban Institute. https://eric.ed.gov/?id=ED535962

Hanushek, E. A. (1989). Expenditures, efficiency, and equity in education: The federal government's role. *American Economic Review*, *79*(2), 46–51. http://www.jstor.org/stable/1827728

Harris, R. S., & Hodges, C. B. (2018). STEM education in rural schools: Implications of untapped potential. *National Youth-At-Risk Journal*, *3*(1), 3–12.

Hartman, S. L., Hines-Bergmeier, J., & Klein, R. (2017). Informal STEM learning: The state of research, access and equity in rural early childhood settings. *Science Education and Civic Engagement*, *9*(2), 32–39.

Henley, L., & Roberts, P. (2016). Perceived barriers to higher education in STEM among disadvantaged rural students: A case study. *Inquiry: Journal of the Virginia Community Colleges*, *20*(1), Article 4.

Hill, P. T. (2015). States could do more for rural education. *The SEA of the Future: Uncovering the Productivity Promise of Rural Education*, *4*, 4–13.

Hillman, N., Colston, J., Bach-Hanson, J., & Peek, A. (2021). *Mapping rural colleges and their communities*. University of Wisconsin–Madison.

Hirschl, N., & Smith, C. M. (2020). Well-placed: The geography of opportunity and high school effects on college attendance. *Research in Higher Education*, *61*(5), 567–587. https://link.springer.com/article/10.1007/s11162-020-09599-4

Hu, X., & Chan, H. Y. (2024). Preparing for the STEM pathways? Dual enrollment and college major choice in STEM. *Journal of Higher Education*, *95*(5), 607–638.

Ingersoll, R. M., & Tran, H. (2023). Teacher shortages and turnover in rural schools in the US: An organizational analysis. *Educational Administration Quarterly*, *59*(2), 396–431.

Irizarry, Y. (2021). On track or derailed? Race, advanced math, and the transition to high school. *Socius*, 7. https://doi.org/10.1177/2378023120980293

Irvin, M. J., Byun, S. Y., Meece, J. L., Farmer, T. W., & Hutchins, B. C. (2012). Educational barriers of rural youth: Relation of individual and contextual difference variables. *Journal of Career Assessment*, *20*(1), 71–87.

Johnson, J., Showalter, D., Klein, R., & Lester, C. (2014). *Why rural matters 2013-2014: The condition of rural education in the 50 states*. Rural School and Community Trust.

Johnson, J. D., & Zoellner, B. P. (2016). School funding and rural districts. In S. M. Williams & A. A. Grooms (Eds.), *Educational opportunity in rural contexts: The politics of place* (pp. 3–20). Information Age Publishing.

Kaestle, C. (2016). Federalism and inequality in education: What can history tell us? In I. Kirsch & H. Braun (Eds.), *The dynamics of opportunity in America*. Springer. https://doi.org/10.1007/978-3-319-25991-8_3

Kaput, K. (2018). *Briefing memo: Summaries of states' ESSA school quality/student success measures*. Education Evolving. https://www.educationevolving.org/files/Briefing-Memo-States-SQ-SS-Measures.pdf

Kolbe, T., Baker, B. D., Atchison, D., Levin, J., & Harris, P. (2021). The additional cost of operating rural schools: Evidence from Vermont. *AERA Open*, *7*. https://doi.org/10.1177/2332858420988868

Koricich, A., Chen, X., & Hughes, R. P. (2018). Understanding the effects of rurality and socioeconomic status on college attendance and institutional choice in the United States. *Review of Higher Education*, *41*(2), 281–305. https://muse.jhu.edu/article/679334

Koricich, A., Tandberg, D., Bishop, B., & Weeden, D. (2020). Doing the same (or more) with less: The challenges regional public universities face in serving rural populations. *New Directions for Higher Education*, *2020*(190), 59–70.

Kormos, E., & Wisdom, K. (2021). Rural schools and the digital divide: Technology in the learning experience. *Theory & Practice in Rural Education*, *11*(1), 25–39.

Lakin, J. M., Stambaugh, T., Ihrig, L. M., Mahatmya, D., & Assouline, S. G. (2021). Nurturing STEM talent in rural setting. *Phi Delta Kappan*, *103*(4), 24–30.

Lavalley, M. (2018). *Out of the loop: Rural schools are largely left out of research and policy discussions, exacerbating poverty, inequity, and isolation*. Center for Public Education. https://eric.ed.gov/?id=ED608842

Lindsay, J., Hughes, K., Dougherty, S. M., Reese, K., & Joshi, M. (2024). *What we know about the impact of career and technical education: A systematic review of the research*. American Institutes for Research.

Lopez, M. E., Jacobson, L., Caspe, M., & Hanebutt, R. (2019). *Public libraries engage families in STEM*. Global Families Research Project. https://eric.ed.gov/?id=ED592825

Mann, S., Sponsler, B., Welch, M., & Wyatt, J. (2017). *Advanced Placement access and success: How do rural schools stack up?* Education Commission of the States & College Board. https://www.ecs.org/wp-content/uploads/Advanced-Placement-Access-and-Success-How-do-rural-schools-stack-up.pdf

Marksbury, N. (2017). Monitoring the pipeline: STEM education in rural U.S. *Forum on Public Policy Online*, *2017*(2). Oxford Round Table.

McNamee, T. C., & Ganss, K. M. (2023). Rural students in higher education: From college preparation and enrollment to experience and persistence. *Peabody Journal of Education*, *98*(4), 380–395.

Mobley, C., Sharp, J. L., Hammond, C., Withington, C., & Stipanovic, N. (2017). The influence of career-focused education on student career planning and development: A comparison of CTE and non-CTE students. *Career and Technical Education Research*, *42*(1), 57–75.

Muraskin, L., & Lee, J. (2004). *Raising the graduation rates of low-income college students.* Pell Institute for the Study of Opportunity in Higher Education.

National Academies of Sciences, Engineering, and Medicine (NASEM). (2022). *Science and engineering in preschool through elementary grades: The brilliance of children and the strengths of educators.* National Academies Press. https://doi.org/10.17226/26215

National Center for Education Statistics (NCES). (2020). *Dual or concurrent enrollment in public schools in the United States.* Institute of Education Sciences, U.S. Department of Education. https://nces.ed.gov/pubs2020/2020125.pdf

———. (2023). *Enrollment and school choice in rural areas: Condition of education.* Institute of Education Sciences, U.S. Department of Education. https://nces.ed.gov/programs/coe/indicator/lcb

National Research Council (NRC). (2002). *Scientific research in education.* National Academies Press. https://doi.org/10.17226/10236

———. (2009). *Learning science in informal environments: People, places, and pursuits.* National Academies Press.

Nye, B., Swartout, W., Campbell, J., Krishnamachari, M., Kaimakis, N., & Davis, D. (2017). Mentorpal: Interactive virtual mentors based on real-life STEM professionals. *Proceedings of the Interservice/Industry Simulation, Training and Education Conference.*

Office of Management and Budget (OMB). (2024). *Appendix budget of the US government, fiscal year 2025.* The White House. https://www.whitehouse.gov/wp-content/uploads/2024/03/budget_fy2025.pdf

Pankovits, T. (2023). *Reinventing rural education: The rural schools innovation zone. Independent school districts working together to maximize students' college and career pathways.* Progressive Policy Institute.

Peterson, B., Bornemann, G., Lydon, C., & West, K. (2015). Rural students in Washington state: STEM as a strategy for building rigor, postsecondary aspirations, and relevant career opportunities. *Peabody Journal of Education*, *90*(2), 280–293. https://doi.org/10.1080/0161956X.2015.1022397

Pipa, A. F., & Geismar, N. (2022). *Reimagining rural policy: Organizing federal assistance to maximize rural prosperity.* Brookings. https://www.brookings.edu/ research/reimagining-rural-policy-organizing-federal-assistance-to-maximize-rural-prosperity/

Postsecondary National Policy Institute. (2024). *Rural students in higher education factsheet.*

Real, B., & Rose, R. N. (2017). *Rural libraries in the United States: Recent strides, future possibilities, and meeting community needs.* American Library Association.

Rogers, R. R., & Sun, Y. (Eds.). (2019). *Engaging STEM students from rural areas: Emerging research and opportunities.* IGI Global.

Rosenboom, V., & Blagg, K. (2018). *Disconnected from higher education: How geography and internet speed limit access to higher education.* Urban Institute. https://www.urban.org/sites/default/files/publication/96191/disconnected_from_higher_education_1.pdf

Rush-Marlowe, R. (2021). *Strengthening rural community colleges: Innovations and opportunities.* Association of Community College Trustees.

Saw, G. K. (2019). The impact of inclusive STEM high schools on student outcomes: A statewide longitudinal evaluation of Texas STEM academies. *International Journal of Science and Mathematics Education*, *17*(8), 1445–1457. https://link.springer.com/article/10.1007/s10763-018-09942-3

Saw, G. K., & Agger, C. A. (2021). STEM pathways of rural and small-town students: Opportunities to learn, aspirations, preparation, and college enrollment. *Educational Researcher*, *50*(9), 595–606.

Schmitt, J., & DeCourcy, K. (2022). *The pandemic has exacerbated a long-standing national shortage of teachers*. Economic Policy Institute.

Showalter, D., Hartman, S. L., Eppley, K., Johnson, J., & Klein, B. (2023). *Why rural matters 2023: Centering equity and opportunity*. National Rural Education Association. https://wsos-cdn.s3.us-west-2.amazonaws.com/uploads/sites/18/WRMReport2023_DIGITAL.pdf

Showalter, D., Klein, R., Johnson, J., & Hartman, S. L. (2017). *Why rural matters 2015-2016: Understanding the changing landscape*. Rural School and Community Trust.

Steenbergen-Hu, S., & Olszewski-Kubilius, P. (2017). Factors that contributed to gifted students' success on STEM pathways: The role of race, personal interests, and aspects of high school experience. *Journal for the Education of the Gifted*, *40*(2), 99–134.

Stoeger, H., Duan, X., Schirner, S., Greindl, T., & Ziegler, A. (2013). The effectiveness of a one-year online mentoring program for girls in STEM. *Computers & Education*, *69*, 408–418. https://doi.org/10.1016/j.compedu.2013.07.032

Stone III, J. R. (2014). More than one way: The case for high-quality CTE. *American Educator*, *38*(3), 4.

Stringfield, S., & Stone, J. R. (2017). The labor market imperative for CTE: Changes and challenges for the 21st century. *Peabody Journal of Education*, *92*(2), 166–179.

Swan, D. W., Grimes, J., & Owens, T. (2013). *The state of small and rural libraries in the United States* (Research Brief 5). Institute of Museum and Library Services.

Tenenbaum L. S., Anderson, M. K., Ramadorai, S. B., & Yourick, D. L. (2017). High school students' experience with near-peer mentorship and laboratory-based learning: In their own words. *Journal of STEM Education: Innovations and Research*, *18*(3).

Thomas, N., Marken, S., Gray, L., & Lewis, L. (2013). *Dual credit and exam-based courses in U.S. public high schools: 2010–11* (NCES No. 2013-001). National Center for Education Statistics, U.S. Department of Education.

Tyson W., Lee R., Borman K. M., & Hanson M. A. (2007). Science, technology, engineering, and mathematics (STEM) pathways: High school science and math coursework and postsecondary degree attainment. *Journal of Education for Students Placed at Risk*, *12*(3), 243–270.

U.S. Department of Education. (2021). *Informational Document on the Rural Education Achievement Program (REAP)*. Office of Elementary and Secondary Education. https://oese.ed.gov/files/2021/01/19-0043-REAP-Informational-Document-final-OS-Approved-1.pdf

———. (2023). *Guidance on Title VIII of the Elementary and Secondary Education Act*. https://www2.ed.gov/about/inits/ed/non-public-education/files/esea-titleviii-guidance-2023.pdf

U.S. Department of Health and Human Services. (2022). *Community Services Block Grant (CSBG) fact sheet*. Administration for Children and Families, Office of Community Services. https://www.acf.hhs.gov/sites/default/files/documents/ocs/COMM_OCS_CSBG%20FactSheet_FY2022.pdf

U.S. National Science Foundation (NSF). (2013). *Common guidelines for education research and development*. https://www.nsf.gov/pubs/2013/nsf13126/nsf13126.pdf

———. (2024). *Making visible the invisible: STEM talent of rural America: 2024 CEOSE report to congress*. Committee on Equal Opportunities in Science and Engineering.

Vinovskis, M. A. (2022). Federal compensatory education policies from Lyndon B. Johnson to Barack H. Obama. *History of Education Quarterly*, *62*(3), 243–267. https://doi.org/10.1017/heq.2022.21

Wang, X. (2013). Why students choose STEM majors: Motivation, high school learning, and postsecondary context of support. *American Educational Research Journal*, *50*(5), 1081–1121. https://doi.org/10.3102/0002831213488622

Wells, R. S., Chen, L., Bettencourt, G. M., & Haas, S. (2023). Reconsidering rural-nonrural college enrollment gaps: The role of socioeconomic status in geographies of opportunity. *Researcher in Higher Education*, *64*, 1089–1112. https://doi.org/10.1007/s11162-023-09737-8

Wells, R. S., Manly, C. A., Kommers, S., & Kimball, E. (2019). Narrowed gaps and persistent challenges: Examining rural-nonrural disparities in postsecondary outcomes over time. *American Journal of Education, 126*. https://www.researchgate.net/publication/336395419_Narrowed_Gaps_and_Persistent_Challenges_Examining_Rural-Nonrural_Disparities_in_Postsecondary_Outcomes_over_Time/citation/download

Williams, S. M., & Grooms, A. A. (Eds.). (2016). *Educational opportunity in rural contexts: The politics of place*. Information Age.

Wolfe, R. L., Steiner, E. D., & Schweig, J. (2023). *Getting students to (and through) advanced math: Where course offerings and content are not adding up* (American Educator Panels Research Report No. RR-A827-10). RAND Corporation. https://doi.org/10.7249/RRA827-10

Yettick, H., Baker, R., Wickersham, M., & Hupfeld, K. (2014). Rural districts left behind? Rural districts and the challenges of administering the Elementary and Secondary Education Act. *Journal of Research in Rural Education, 29*(13), 1–15.

Zinth, J. D. (2014). *Dual enrollment: A strategy to improve college-going and college completion among rural students*. Education Commission of the States.

4

National Trends in Rural STEM Education and Workforce Development

The previous chapter outlined policies related to rural science, technology, engineering, and mathematics (STEM) education, including students' access to K–12 STEM courses. Rural students generally have less awareness of and access to STEM programming and courses than their urban or suburban peers, and these opportunity gaps translate into disparities in achievement and aspiration as these students move through STEM education and workforce development pathways. However, there are a multitude of unrecognized assets in rural communities that can support STEM education in rural places. In this chapter, we examine the consequences for rural students of having less access to quality STEM education in K–12 schools, as well as some inherent local assets that should be recognized and nurtured to help them move beyond the challenges.

STEM ACHIEVEMENT AND ASPIRATIONS AMONG RURAL STUDENTS

Inequities in formal preK–12 STEM education structures, including fewer STEM teachers and learning opportunities, lead to gaps in both achievement and aspiration between rural and nonrural students enrolled in STEM and among rural students in different subpopulations. Differences emerge as early as kindergarten.

Achievement

Geographical gaps in STEM abilities and achievement, as measured by standardized testing, by rurality and remoteness can be observed in children as young as kindergarten age, and the gaps grow as students progress through the K–12 education system (Graham & Provost, 2012; Johnson et al., 2021; Saw & Agger, 2021). For example, a working paper analyzing National Assessment of Educational Progress (NAEP) data from 2007 to 2022 reports that, while there were generally no significant differences in mathematics scores at grades 4 and 8 between students who attended a school in rural-fringe areas and their peers in large suburban areas, those who attended school in rural-distant and rural-remote areas consistently scored lower in math than their counterparts in large suburban areas (Saw & Longstreet, 2024). The paper similarly reports that in the NAEP science assessment for 4th and 8th graders from 2009 to 2019, geographical gaps were primarily observed between rural-remote and large suburban groups, and that achievement gaps in math and science scores between rural and suburban students appeared to be wider at grade 12. These patterns of geographical achievement gaps largely reflect gaps in opportunity to learn and can also explain rural-nonrural disparities in STEM college enrollment (Saw & Agger, 2021).

Rural students outperform their town and urban peers in NAEP 8th grade math scores (Gagnon, 2022), but by 9th and 11th grade they score lower on math assessment tests compared to their suburban peers (Saw & Agger, 2021). Researchers also find U.S. regional and sociodemographic differences in assessment results (Drescher et al., 2022; Gagnon, 2022). For example, achievement on standardized assessments in 8th grade mathematics is higher in rural New England school districts compared to other U.S. regions; rural students who receive a free or reduced-price lunch perform worse on the math NAEP assessment than their rural peers who do not receive this lunch; and rural White students perform better on the NAEP math assessment than their Black, Latine, and American Indian/Alaska Native peers (Drescher et al., 2022). These disparities may reflect structural inequities rather than individual achievement deficiencies (Drescher et al., 2022).

Using data from the Early Childhood Longitudinal Study, researchers found that rural kindergarten students have lower math scores than their suburban peers but perform at the same level as students from urban school locales. The gap is larger for Asian and Native American students at rural schools, less pronounced for Black, Latine, and White students. The gap between rural and nonrural students increases over time: mathematics achievement for nonrural students improves at a faster rate than for rural students as they move from kindergarten to 8th grade (Graham & Provost, 2012). The discrepancies were not fully explainable by socioeconomic status (SES) or other observed factors in the study. This widening achievement gap continued into high school, indicating that 9th grade students from rural and town locales scored "0.094 and 0.247 standard deviations lower than their suburban counterparts on math assessment tests" (Saw & Agger, 2021, p. 599) and that this gap widened by the end of 11th grade to 0.134 and 0.283 standard deviations.

A study of 4th grade NAEP assessments in science and math that also disaggregated students by English-language learner (ELL) status found that rural students score slightly lower than their suburban peers in math and science, and these gaps followed similar patterns for ELL and non-ELL students (Showalter et al., 2017). Interestingly, the report also found that, while averages were similar, math scores were more evenly distributed in rural communities. In nonrural areas there was more variability, with many high and low scores, whereas in rural communities scores tended to be clustered around the average. While some might interpret this to mean that rural areas are more homogeneous in terms of population characteristics such as race or SES (which in some instances may be true), research indicates that the socioeconomic achievement gap is smaller at rural schools (Stanford, 2023).

To further examine NAEP scores across different student subpopulations and locales, Rush-Marlowe (2024) looked at the percentage of students scoring "below basic" in the grade 4 math NAEP based on data from 2022. In addition to looking at performance based on student locale, Rush-Marlowe disaggregated the data by ELL status, disability status, race, and gender. The percentage of students performing below basic varied by locale,[1] with rural-remote students showing the lowest scores and large suburban areas showing the highest across almost all subgroups. Other locales fell in between on a spectrum between these two groups, with those in more rural areas trending toward lower performance, suburbs performing the best, and mixed results in urban locales.

Figure 4-1 shows the data for rural-remote and large suburban locales across the aforementioned disaggregated groups. In all instances the numbers of rural students performing "below basic" in grade 4 math are significantly greater than in large suburban areas, with the exception of Hispanic/Latine students, where a slightly lower percentage of students in rural-remote locales scored "below basic" compared to their peers in large suburban areas.

The 2022 NAEP tests showed no difference in average math scores between 4th grade students attending school in a rural-fringe area and their peers in large suburban areas (240 for both), whereas students who attended school in a rural-distant (236) or rural-remote (233) area scored somewhat lower (Saw & Longstreet, 2024). A similar pattern was observed

[1]Throughout this chapter, Rush-Marlowe's analysis uses the expanded National Center for Education Statistics (NCES) categories for locale, available at https://nces.ed.gov/programs/edge/Geographic/LocaleBoundaries.

FIGURE 4-1 Percentage of students who scored "below basic" on the grade 4 math NAEP, 2022.
NOTE: ELL = English-language learner.
SOURCE: Rush-Marlowe (2024).

in the 2022 NAEP 8th grade math assessment: There was no significant difference in average math scores between 8th grade students attending school in a rural-fringe area and their peers in large suburban areas (277 vs. 279), but those who attended school in a rural-distant (272) or rural-remote (268) area scored lower than their counterparts in large suburban areas. The gaps in math scores between rural and suburban students are wider among high school seniors: In the 2019 NAEP math test, 12th grade students attending a rural school, whether in fringe (148), distant (146), or remote (146) areas, scored lower than their counterparts attending school in a large suburban area (154; Saw & Longstreet, 2024).

Aspirations

Rural communities have lower rates of college enrollment, which may be part of the reason that rural students are less likely than their peers in urban and suburban areas to have family members or neighbors who pursued careers in STEM fields (Lakin et al., 2021). Rural schools also receive less outreach (relative to suburban and urban schools) from organizations and businesses that can provide students with exposure to STEM career options and mentorship (Harris & Hodges, 2018), and this may negatively affect students' perceptions of the accessibility of STEM careers. One study of rural students' perceptions of STEM found that, even among students who believed that math and science skills were needed "everywhere," when one student was asked where in his rural community he could study calculus he responded, "you [have] to go to a big city to find calculus" (Showalter et al., 2017, p. 40). This is problematic because barriers, real or perceived, can hamper student aspirations. Research shows that "people are less likely to translate their career interests into goals, and their goals into actions, when they perceive their efforts to be impeded by adverse environmental factors" (Lent et al., 2000, p. 38).

Motivational factors such as STEM identity and career aspirations are important individual aspects of a STEM pathway and can be strong predictors of future behavior and success. "Intent to major in STEM while in high school—a proxy of STEM career aspirations—has a larger effect on STEM major enrollment than achievement scores" (Saw & Agger, 2021, p. 596). It is important that these aspirations be formed and nurtured early in educational pathways, as studies show that exposure to STEM experiences before high school increase both student interest in STEM pathways and the likelihood that students will form intentions to pursue further education in STEM fields (Kaggwa et al., 2023). Children can recognize science as a career area and be motivated toward it as early as preschool (Dilek et al., 2020). An emerging body of evidence indicates that preK and elementary school–aged children benefit from early exposure to and engagement in STEM activities, such as engineering design applications and robotics programs, that can cultivate curiosity in scientific discovery and stimulate interest in STEM careers (Akpinar & Akgunduz, 2022; Caspi et al., 2023; Ha et al., 2023).

Few studies have examined geographical differences in STEM identity and career interest among young children, although one found that rural students have a lower science identity compared to urban students (Alhadabi, 2023). Research on STEM aspirations among rural youth is very limited and sometimes contradictory, and studies of subpopulations of rural youth are even more limited, though a case study in rural Appalachia found that young women were more likely than young men to have STEM career aspirations, at 73 percent and 54 percent, respectively (Rosecrance et al., 2019).

Two 2021 studies used the High School Longitudinal Study (HSLS) 2009 data, but defined student groups differently. Crain and Webber (2021) separated students into two categories, metropolitan and nonmetropolitan, while Saw and Agger (2021) used NCES school locales classified in the traditional four categories. Both studies found that rural students have interest in STEM careers at the same rate as their nonrural peers when they enter high school, but Saw and Agger found that a "rural-suburban gap in STEM career aspirations emerged by the end of 11th grade" (p. 598).

Crain and Webber (2021) also examined the percentage of students who expected to have a job in a STEM field by age 30. Surveys were distributed to respondents in 9th grade and again in 11th grade. The results showed that nonmetropolitan students' belief that they would be employed in STEM grew faster than that of their peers from metropolitan areas. This seems to demonstrate that, despite barriers, rural students are interested in STEM fields and aspire to STEM careers.

HSLS data also show that 9th grade students reported their favorite subject as math or science at relatively the same rates in rural, town, urban, and suburban locales (Rush-Marlowe, 2024), although female students in rural and town locales were slightly less likely to say they were interested in pursuing STEM compared to their female peers in urban and suburban locales, with town locales being the lowest, at 10 percent, followed by rural at 14 percent, urban at 15 percent, and suburban at 16 percent. Male students in rural and town locales were also somewhat less likely to pursue STEM than their counterparts in urban and suburban locales: 29 percent of those in rural locales reported interest in a STEM major compared to 31 percent in town locales, 34 percent in suburban, and 36 percent in urban locales. Additionally, the gap between men and women is slightly more pronounced in town locales compared to urban locales: In the latter men are 2.4 times as likely to say they are interested in pursuing STEM compared to women, and in town locales men are 3.1 times as likely. In suburban and rural locales men are 2.1 times as likely to report interest in pursuing STEM compared to women (Rush-Marlowe, 2024).

Analysis of the data disaggregated by race showed that the standard error represented more than 30 percent of the estimate for Black, Latine, Native Hawaiian or Other Pacific Islander, and American Indian or Alaska Native students. This meant it was not possible to graphically show these demographics in Figure 4-2. For Asian students, the *n* size was too small to be reported for rural locales, but in town locales 19 percent reported an interest in pursuing a STEM major, compared to 38 percent in urban locales and 42 percent in suburban locales. Among multiracial students, 18 percent in rural locales reported interest in pursuing a STEM major, compared to 17 percent in town, 23 percent suburban, and 25 percent urban. For White students, 21 percent in rural locales reported interest compared to 23 percent in town, 27 percent in suburban, and 30 percent in urban locales. The data also indicate that White students in rural and town locales are more likely than their Asian or multiracial peers to be interested in pursuing STEM majors. Aspirations are important predictors of future student behavior and success, but are not the only important factor, and may be less predictive in rural contexts where students face unique barriers to pursue their dreams (Rush-Marlowe, 2024).

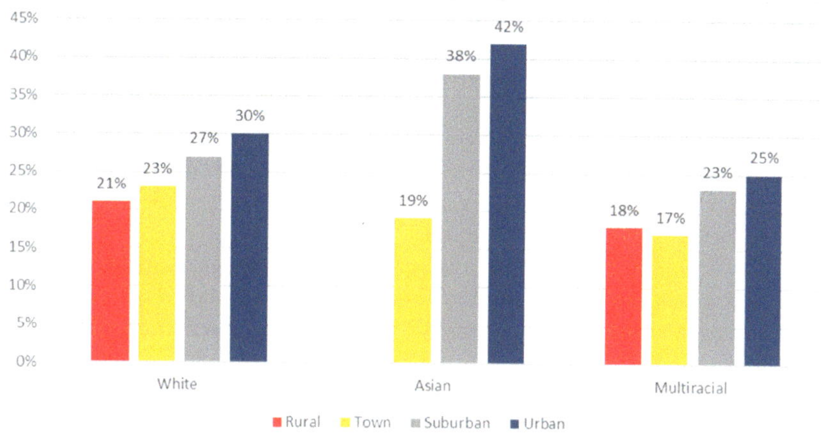

FIGURE 4-2 High school student interest in pursuing a STEM major, by race and locale, 2019.
SOURCE: Rush-Marlowe (2024).

COURSE TAKING AND PERSISTENCE INTO POSTSECONDARY STEM EDUCATION

Given the lower numbers of advanced math, science, and other STEM courses offered in rural schools, it is unsurprising that rural students enroll in STEM courses at lower rates than their nonrural peers. These differences begin as early as kindergarten and continue through the end of high school (Graham & Provost, 2012). In addition, adults in rural communities tend to have lower education levels, nearly half of students in rural communities are in the low socioeconomic status category, and the community culture can discourage students from moving away from home for postsecondary educational opportunities (Peterson et al., 2015). All of these factors affect enrollment and persistence in STEM educational pathways.

STEM Course Taking in K–12

A postsecondary degree is one route to STEM workforce development, but high school graduates who attend school in a rural area earn fewer credits in STEM subjects overall and in advanced STEM courses specifically than their peers in suburban or urban locales (National Center for Education Statistics [NCES], 2024). Multiple studies have focused on rural and nonrural enrollment in STEM courses (mostly mathematics) and across grade levels. Findings show that rural students are less likely to be enrolled in an advanced science or math course in 8th grade compared to their suburban peers (Saw & Agger, 2021) and more likely than their nonrural peers to enroll in lower-level math courses beginning in 9th grade, and that more than a third of rural students do not take a math course in their senior year, a rate much lower than their suburban peers (Anderson & Chang, 2011). Further, although students at rural, urban, and suburban schools tend to have similar enrollment rates in algebra II, fewer rural students go on to take precalculus and calculus (NCES, 2022; Table 4-1).

While much of the research discussed focuses on math, there are also gaps in the number of rural high school students enrolled in advanced science and engineering (S&E) courses (NCES, 2022). Rates of enrollment in any advanced S&E course are comparable among students in rural, urban, and suburban schools, although more students in rural areas (38.8%) enroll in advanced biology courses compared to urban (33.7%) and suburban (34.8%) schools. Table 4-2 shows gaps for rural student enrollment in chemistry, earth science, and physics.

Table 4-3 shows that enrollment rates for high school students in technology courses are fairly comparable across courses, with slightly higher enrollment in some courses for rural compared to urban students. While this may seem promising for rural students, one important factor not shown in the data is the general lack of technology courses available in different types of schools. As technology courses gain in popularity and importance for students, there should be greater effort to ensure that rural students are considered in efforts to provide more courses, especially given the known gaps in availability of broadband and other technological resources.

Rural high school students complete calculus and the combination of biology, chemistry, and physics courses at lower rates than students in

TABLE 4-1 Percentage of High School Students Enrolled in Advanced Mathematics Courses, by Locale, 2019

Locale	Any Advanced Math Course	Algebra II	Precalculus/ Analysis	Calculus	Other Advanced Mathematics
City	90.7 (0.51)	84.6 (0.78)	40.7 (1.17)	16.1 (0.72)	26.4 (0.97)
Suburban	89.5 (0.48)	85.4 (0.62)	41.5 (0.85)	18.8 (0.62)	26.5 (0.90)
Town	87.4 (1.03)	85.0 (1.19)	32.1 (2.08)	11.6 (0.91)	22.9 (1.84)
Rural	88.3 (0.93)	84.8 (1.16)	33.4 (1.29)	11.6 (0.68)	26.2 (1.59)

NOTE: Standard deviations in parentheses.
SOURCE: Data from U.S. Department of Education, National Center for Education Statistics, National Assessment of Educational Progress, 2019 High School Transcript Study. Table prepared in May 2022.

TABLE 4-2 Percentage of High School Students Enrolled in Science and Engineering (S&E) Courses, by Locale, 2019

Locale	Any Advanced S&E Course	Advanced Biology	Chemistry	Advanced Environmental/ Earth Science	Physics	Engineering
City	89.8 (0.65)	33.7 (0.93)	76.8 (1.07)	15.8 (0.74)	45.5 (1.32)	10.7 (0.71)
Suburban	89.8 (0.48)	34.8 (0.81)	77.8 (0.69)	19.3 (0.75)	39.4 (1.03)	12.5 (0.67)
Town	83.3 (1.21)	32.7 (1.58)	69.5 (1.76)	9.3 (1.48)	25.5 (1.88)	11.8 (1.26)
Rural	85.7 (1.22)	38.8 (1.73)	69.6 (1.62)	12.7 (1.30)	31.7 (2.05)	12.1 (1.07)

NOTE: Standard deviations in parentheses.
SOURCE: Data from U.S. Department of Education, National Center for Education Statistics, National Assessment of Educational Progress (NAEP), 2019 High School Transcript Study. Table prepared in May 2022.

urban and suburban schools (NCES, 2022). They also earn fewer Advanced Placement (AP) and International Baccalaureate math and science credits compared to suburban students (Saw & Agger, 2021). In middle school, fewer rural students take algebra compared to their urban and suburban peers, and fewer take geometry compared to suburban middle school students (Banilower et al., 2018).

TABLE 4-3 Percentage of High School Students Enrolled in Technology Courses, by Locale, 2019

Locale	Any Technology Course	Engineering/Science Technologies	Health Science and Technology	Computer Science
City	37.8 (1.24)	5.1 (0.50)	16.2 (0.81)	20.5 (0.98)
Suburban	38.0 (0.91)	7.1 (0.50)	15.7 (0.58)	20.0 (0.77)
Town	39.8 (2.13)	8.9 (1.64)	20.5 (1.12)	15.4 (1.45)
Rural	41.5 (1.75)	8.3 (1.05)	17.6 (0.98)	20.9 (1.56)

NOTE: Standard deviations in parentheses.
SOURCE: Data from U.S. Department of Education, National Center for Education Statistics, National Assessment of Educational Progress (NAEP), 2019 High School Transcript Study. Table prepared in May 2022.

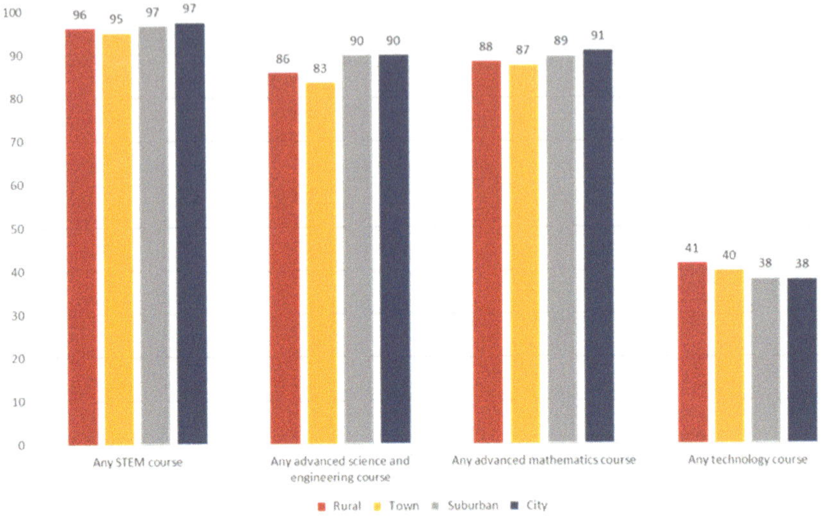

FIGURE 4-3 Percentage of K–12 students enrolled in STEM courses, by school locale, 2019.
SOURCE: Rush-Marlowe (2024).

Using 2019 data from the High School Transcript Study (HSTS), Rush-Marlowe (2024) examined the percentage of K–12 students enrolled in STEM courses (any STEM course, any advanced science or engineering course, any advanced mathematics course, or any technology course) disaggregated by school locale. The rates of enrollment were fairly consistent across locales, with students in town locales marginally less likely to be enrolled in any of the first three categories and rural and town schools showing slightly higher enrollment in "any technology course" than urban and suburban locales (Figure 4-3).

Rush-Marlowe (2024) also compared the percentage of rural students enrolled in five STEM courses with the highest enrollment levels. The data reveal the largest gaps between rural-remote and large suburban locales, with the former enrolling at significantly lower rates in the five most common STEM courses: chemistry, precalculus/analysis, physics, advanced environmental/earth science, and calculus (Figure 4-4). Of the 12 STEM courses in the HSTS data, rural students had lower enrollment levels in 10 (the exceptions were advanced biology and health).

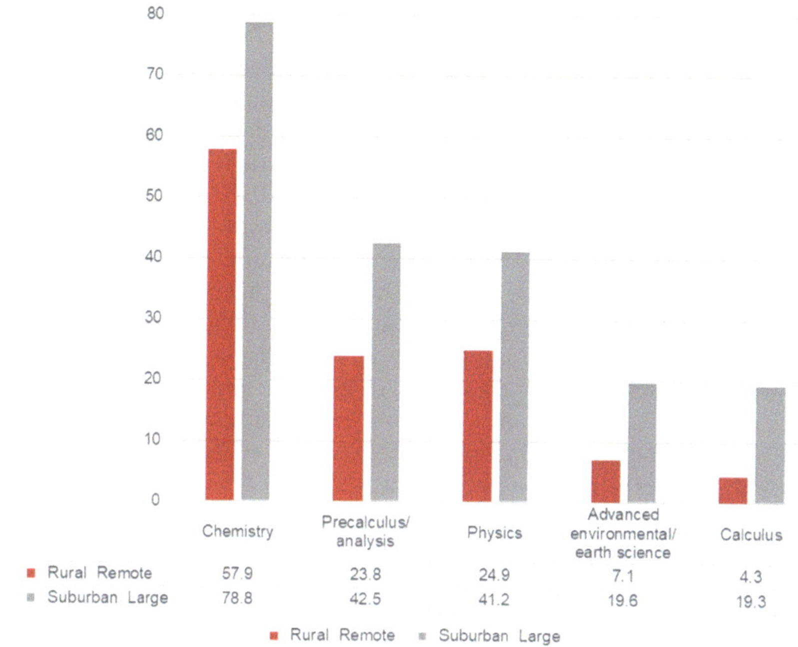

FIGURE 4-4 Percentage of high school students enrolled in selected STEM course, by locale, 2019.
SOURCE: Rush-Marlowe (2024).

Dual Enrollment, Advanced Placement, and Career and Technical Education

Dual enrollment, AP courses, and Career and Technical Education (CTE) all offer rural students opportunities to pursue STEM courses at similar rates to urban and suburban students, but there are unique challenges for rural students in terms of access to and completion of these courses. Dual enrollment programs enable high school students to earn postsecondary credit and are available in about 90 percent of all rural high schools (NCES, 2020). Rural high school juniors and seniors are more likely to take dual enrollment courses than students in other locales (Showalter et al., 2019). This is despite the fact that rural districts face greater challenges than their counterparts in other locales in finding qualified dual enrollment instructors and providing transportation for students enrolled in such programs (Zinth, 2014). In most states, dual enrollment instructors need to meet requirements such as a master's degree or the same qualifications as faculty in the partner postsecondary institution. In most cases, dual enrollment courses are offered online or at the postsecondary institution campuses (Thomas et al., 2013).

As noted in Chapter 3, rural schools offer fewer AP courses than those in urban and suburban areas (Mann et al., 2017): 73 percent of rural schools offer at least one AP course in any subject, compared to more than 92 percent of suburban and urban schools. Further, only 62 percent of students in rural schools had access to AP STEM courses and just 11 percent of them took the corresponding exam, a marked difference between both urban and suburban schools (Mann et al., 2017).

Although rural students had fewer opportunities to take STEM courses and engage in STEM out-of-school learning opportunities, data from NCES (2023) indicate that they were more likely to take CTE courses compared to urban and suburban students. CTE programs are designed to help students develop technical, academic, and workforce skills that can be applied to employment and postsecondary education. In 2019, 91.6 percent of rural high school graduates had taken any CTE courses, higher than students in towns (91.3%), suburban areas (83%), and cities (79.6%; NCES, 2023; Table 4-4). The rural students were more likely to earn CTE credits in information technology (34% compared with 29% nationally) and agriculture, food, and natural resources (25% compared with 11% nationally; NCES, 2023).

One common way rural students attend CTE courses is through area technical centers, which serve students from multiple institutions at the same time (Advance CTE, 2017), provide diverse course offerings, and can make up for limited availability at a student's home institution. While these centers are not available in all states, they have the potential to build strong partnerships with business and industry, which could ultimately lead to more STEM-related courses and work in rural communities. Partnerships that provide experiential learning, including internships, are discussed in Chapter 5.

Another component critical to STEM education and workforce pathways is ensuring that students graduate academically ready for both college and careers (Southern Regional Education Board, 2015). This is a challenge on multiple levels, including in terms of expectations, availability of quality teachers and counselors, limited resources, and course offerings (Peterson et al., 2015). In advising rural students about STEM college and career pathways, school counselors are hampered by limited STEM career advising resources, a lack of local STEM role models (i.e., individuals known to the students who engage in STEM disciplines in life and work in ways that inspire and inform those students), and inadequate financial resources and learning activities for students to explore STEM college majors and careers (Grimes et al., 2019).

Enrollment and Persistence in Postsecondary Education

Rural students graduate from high school at higher rates than their peers from nonrural areas, but they are less likely to pursue postsecondary education (Koricich et al., 2018); in 2022 54.6 percent of rural high school

TABLE 4-4 Percentage of Public and Private High School Graduates Who Earned at Least One Credit in Selected Career/Technical Education Courses in High School, by Locale, 2019

Locale	Any Career/ Technical Education Courses	Agriculture, Food, and Natural Resources	Architecture and Construction	Engineering and Technology	Healthcare Sciences	Information Technology	Manufacturing
City	79.6	4.7	4.0	11.9	11.3	28.0	2.3
	(0.93)	(0.45)	(0.27)	(0.74)	(0.63)	(1.44)	(0.23)
Suburban	83.0	5.6	5.6	15.3	11.0	26.2	3.3
	(0.70)	(0.38)	(0.43)	(0.70)	(0.48)	(0.76)	(0.33)
Town	91.3	21.4	10.1	12.3	14.1	30.2	7.4
	(1.71)	(1.63)	(1.08)	(1.14)	(0.81)	(2.54)	(0.88)
Rural	91.6	25.0	10.0	13.3	12.9	33.9	7.7
	(0.88)	(1.29)	(0.98)	(1.08)	(0.75)	(1.71)	(0.81)

NOTE: Standard deviations in parentheses.
SOURCE: Data from U.S. Department of Education, National Center for Education Statistics, National Assessment of Educational Progress (NAEP), 2019 High School Transcript Study. Table prepared in May 2022.

graduates immediately enrolled in college compared to 63.7 percent of suburban and 58.6 percent of urban high school graduates (Postsecondary National Policy Institute, 2024). Many rural students who do decide to attend college are first-generation students who did not receive sufficient college preparation in high school and are unfamiliar with key tasks like the application process and how to finance a college education (Bright, 2018; Scott et al., 2016). In rural communities, only 21 percent of residents have a bachelor's degree, which, combined with fewer rural teachers and school counselors, can contribute to misunderstandings about the benefits and expectations of pursuing higher education (Chambers & Freeman, 2020; McNamee, 2019).

A minority—between one fourth and one third—of rural students attending two-year colleges transfer to a four-year institution, and almost half (49%) of rural community college students who transfer ultimately earn a bachelor's degree[2] (McNamee & Ganss, 2023).

For the class of 2022, the immediate college enrollment rate of rural high school graduates was 54.6 percent, which was lower compared to their counterparts from urban (58.6%) and suburban (63.7%) high schools (National Student Clearinghouse, 2023). Rural students also enroll in postsecondary STEM degree programs at lower rates than suburban students (12.6% vs. 16.6%; Saw & Agger, 2021).

Two case studies (Felder et al., 1994; Versypt & Versypt, 2013) focused on rural student enrollment in chemical engineering programs. The first, conducted at North Carolina State University, found that students from rural high schools had lower GPAs and persisted and graduated from chemical engineering programs at significantly lower rates than their urban and suburban peers (Felder et al., 1994). The second case study looked at enrollment in chemical engineering majors at six universities in Illinois and Kansas and found that none of the six institutions met or exceeded proportional parity based on students' geographic background, and three of the six did not have a single student from a rural high school enrolled in a chemical engineering program (Versypt & Versypt, 2013).

An additional case study (Darrah et al., 2023) took a unique approach to defining rurality to examine how many rural and nonrural students declared STEM majors and graduated with a STEM degree within five years from an (unnamed) large public university in West Virginia. To define rurality the authors created county-level classifications that included high school enrollment, percentage of rural high schools (based on NCES locale codes), median high school size, number of libraries, and number of museums, among other factors. This allowed them to reclassify their area of study into three locale codes, of which locale code 3 was the "most rural:" defined as having the fewest resources, smallest high schools, and highest percentage of rural high schools. As shown in other research, locale code 3 had the highest high school

[2]https://nscresearchcenter.org/tracking-transfer/

graduation rates but the lowest college attendance rates. This study also found that these students had the highest percentage of STEM majors but the lowest levels of STEM graduation within five years (Darrah et al., 2023).

At the national level, Saw and Agger (2021) found geographic disparities in STEM enrollment between rural and nonrural students, with 16.6 percent of suburban students reported enrolling in a postsecondary STEM degree program at either a 2- or 4-year college, as opposed to 12.6 percent and 13.1 percent of rural and small-town students, respectively. Other research looked at nonmetropolitan student persistence in STEM programs and found that nonmetropolitan locale was not a significant factor in whether a student persisted in a STEM major (Crain & Webber, 2021), indicating that the definitions used in rural educational research can affect both the results found and their implications.

Disaggregated by locale and no other student characteristics, enrollment data for postsecondary STEM majors differ somewhat (Rush-Marlowe, 2024). Rural locales actually had the highest rates of STEM enrollment, at 47.9 percent, followed by suburban at 45.4 percent and urban at 43.5 percent; students from high schools in towns had the lowest rates of STEM majors, at 37.7 percent. It is unclear why rural locales are so high in this instance and why there is such a large discrepancy between outcomes for rural and town students. Examination of the most common STEM majors by locale showed that students from rural high schools pursued almost every specific STEM major at equivalent or lower rates than their peers from other locales, with the exception of healthcare fields. It is possible that the large number of students from rural locales pursuing health care are skewing the rest of the data, as can be seen in Figure 4-5.

To better understand postsecondary STEM attainment among rural students, Rush-Marlowe (2024) used the 2015–2016 Baccalaureate and Beyond data to examine the percentage of students who attained a bachelor's degree in a STEM field within six years of enrolling in an undergraduate degree program, disaggregated by high school locale and with locale data broken out into the 12 locale groups rather than the condensed four groups. As shown in Figure 4-6 and Table 4-5, students in all three town locales have the lowest attainment rates after enrolling, followed by rural-distant and then urban. Students from suburban, rural-remote, and rural-fringe locales had similar levels of attainment. Students from town fringe locales had the lowest levels of attainment, at just over 20 percent, and midsize suburban locales had the highest levels, just over 60 percent. Thus, while the rate of enrolling in postsecondary STEM degree programs is lower for rural students (Saw & Agger, 2021), persistence to degree after enrolling is similar across some rural, suburban, and urban populations (Rush-Marlowe, 2024).[3]

[3]Because of small cell size limitations and error size in estimates, the data could not be disaggregated by gender, race/ethnicity, or other student characteristics.

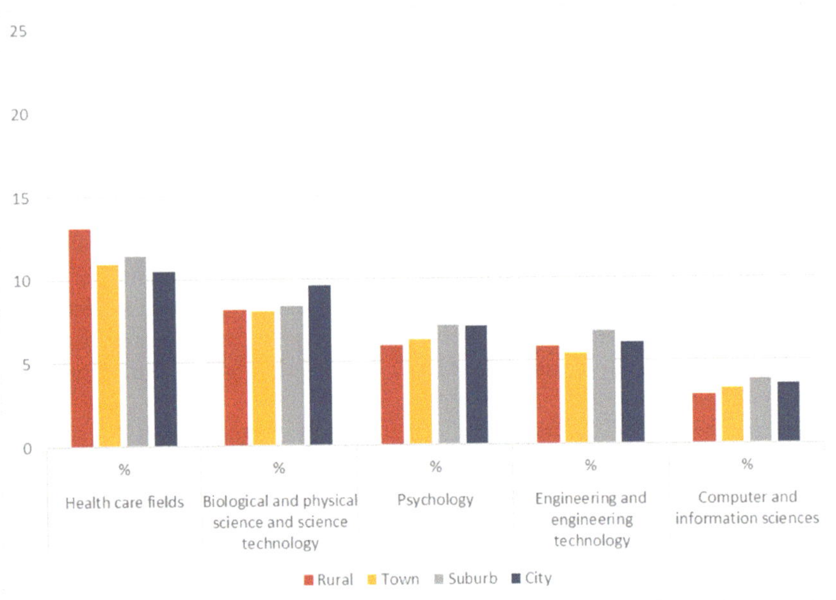

FIGURE 4-5 Most common STEM majors by high school locale.
SOURCE: Rush-Marlowe (2024).

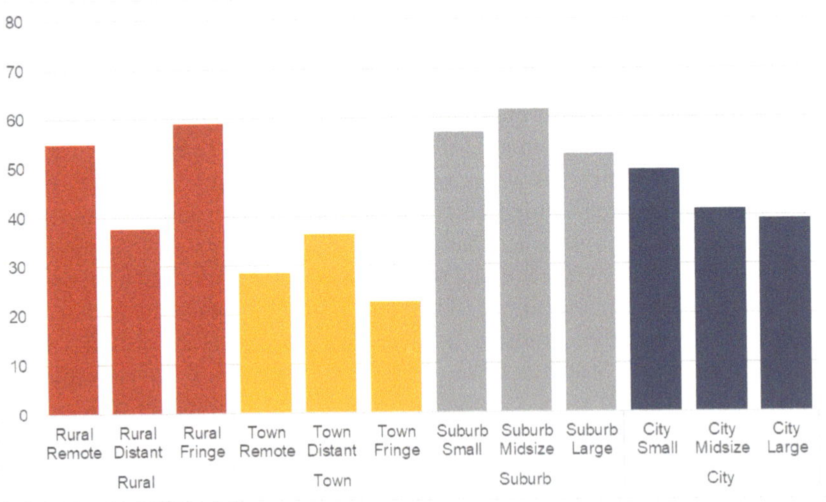

FIGURE 4-6 Bachelor's degree attainment in a STEM field within six years of enrollment, by locale (percent).
SOURCE: Rush-Marlowe (2024).

TABLE 4-5 Bachelor's Degree Attainment in a STEM or Non-STEM Field within Six Years of Enrollment, by Locale (percent)

	Math/Computer/Sciences/ Engineering/Technologies	Social/Behavioral Sciences	Non-STEM
City, Large	17.63%	14.93%	67.44%
City, Midsize	24.43%	14.86%	60.71%
City, Small	25.55%	12.23%	62.21%
Suburb, Large	19.64%	13.36%	67.00%
Suburb, Midsize	20.50%	17.96%	61.55%
Suburb, Small	26.41%	17.50%	56.09%
Town, Fringe	14.19%	9.13%	76.68%
Town, Distant	17.51%	11.76%	70.73%
Town, Remote	22.87%	9.65%	67.48%
Rural, Fringe	19.79%	13.11%	67.11%
Rural, Distant	22.37%	10.48%	67.15%
Rural, Remote	25.86%	5.11%	69.04%
Total	**21.01%**	**13.39%**	**65.60%**

SOURCE: Committee generated using Baccalaureate and Beyond (B&B:16/20) data (Henderson et al., 2022).

The data and analyses paint a fairly complex picture and show that additional research is needed to better understand the experiences and outcomes of rural students in postsecondary STEM fields. Although it seems clear that rural students face barriers to enrolling or matriculating in STEM fields at the same rates as their nonrural peers, research is needed to gain a more comprehensive and nuanced understanding of these patterns.

Entering the STEM Workforce

While research on rural students' aspirations in STEM fields and progression to STEM majors and matriculation is minimal, there is even less on rural students in the STEM workforce. A study published in 2021 examines the mechanisms that likely contribute to rural individuals' exclusion from careers in STEM and academia, but does not provide substantial empirical evidence of this exclusion (O'Neal & Perkins, 2021). The article primarily points to other studies on the postsecondary enrollment patterns of rural students and NCES data showing that urban students are about three times as likely as rural students to be enrolled in graduate or professional programs. Because many STEM careers require advanced credentials, and rural students are less likely to enroll in these advanced programs, they are less likely to be represented in STEM careers. A recent National Science Foundation report looks at the geographic distribution of the STEM workforce by education background, but data are displayed only at the state level (Taylor & Arbeit, 2024). All states have at least some rural areas and some have higher levels of rural population than others, so discussing state-level data is not particularly meaningful in this context.

To develop a preliminary understanding of the available data on rural students in the STEM workforce, Rush-Marlowe (2024) analyzed the HSLS, which includes data on employment in STEM fields in students' first job after high school. Looking at the data by locale alone did not reveal significant differences between rural and other areas. When disaggregated by race and ethnicity, some groups (Native Hawaiian or Other Pacific Islander, American Indian or Alaska Native, and multiracial students) did not have large enough *n* sizes to be reliable, but the data demonstrated gaps between Asian, Black, Latine, and White students across locales. Estimates for Asian students from rural locales were too small to be reliable, but Asian students from town locale high schools were much less likely to be employed in STEM in their first jobs compared to their peers from suburban and urban locales: 96 percent of Asian students from a town high school were *not* employed in STEM after high school, compared to 85 percent in suburbs and 87 percent in urban locales. For Black students, rates were similar for rural, town, and suburban locales: 97 percent were *not* employed in STEM, compared to 93 percent of their peers from urban locales. For Latine students, 96 percent of those from rural locales were *not* in STEM jobs, compared to 99 percent from town locales, 93 percent from suburban, and 92 percent from urban locales. Among White students, 96 percent of those from rural locales were *not* employed in STEM fields, compared to 95 percent in town and suburban locales and 93 percent in urban locales. These data show that, across many racial groups, students from rural high schools are less likely to be employed in STEM than their peers in urban and suburban locales after high school graduation.

Because many STEM professions require more than a high school diploma, Rush-Marlowe (2024) also examined data from the Baccalaureate and Beyond survey, which asks students if their most recent job within four years of their bachelor's degree was in a STEM field. Disaggregating by both locale and race/ethnicity produced unreliable estimates, but students from "town-distant" high schools were the least likely to be employed in a STEM job (22.9%), rural-remote students were slightly more likely to be employed in STEM (23.8%), and students from midsize suburban locales were the most likely (29.2%). Table 4-6 shows the percentage of students employed in a STEM occupation within four years of earning their bachelor's degree, broken out by locale. However, these analyses do not account for STEM jobs that require more than a high school diploma but less than a bachelor's degree (as described in Chapter 1).

TABLE 4-6 Percentage of College Graduates Employed in STEM, by Locale, 2016

	Most recent job, within 4 yrs of BA: Occupation in STEM	
	No	Yes
City, Large	73.56	26.44
City, Midsize	71.79	28.21
City, Small	71.84	28.16
Suburb, Large	72.36	27.64
Suburb, Midsize	70.83	29.17
Suburb, Small	72.10	27.90
Town, Fringe	70.37	29.63
Town, Distant	77.09	22.91
Town, Remote	73.65	26.35
Rural, Fringe	73.14	26.86
Rural, Distant	73.39	26.61
Rural, Remote	76.16	23.84
Total	**72.54**	**27.46**

SOURCE: Committee generated from Baccalaureate and Beyond (B&B:16/20) data (Henderson et al., 2022).

ASSETS OF RURAL COMMUNITIES RELATED TO STEM EDUCATION AND WORKFORCE DEVELOPMENT

While data indicate that rural communities face many challenges in providing STEM education and workforce development opportunities, leading to achievement and aspiration gaps, these communities also have assets that can enrich and promote STEM learning, such as place-based learning and strong community ties, as will be elaborated in Chapter 5. For example, many rural communities have strong historical and current ties to specific industries such as agriculture, fishing, timber, or mining. From a young age, children growing up in these communities often gain firsthand experiences in these trades, which can give them deep applied knowledge in science, technology, math, and engineering and promote interest in pursuing STEM-related careers. They can also gain knowledge and skills relevant to natural resources. The lived experiences and accumulated insight of rural residents, including those from Indigenous and tribal communities, are untapped assets of expertise that can advance natural resource preservation and conservation work.

The central social, cultural, and economic role that rural schools often hold in their communities (Schafft, 2016) helps students see the relevance of science and engineering to their own lives and futures, by fostering a stronger connection to the subject matter. In addition, due to small class sizes and increased interactions with families, rural teachers can be seen as the "faces" of their rural school (Hammack et al., 2023) and develop close relationships with their students that result in more individualized instruction and improved student behavior (Tran et al., 2020). In addition, school-community partnerships are often enhanced in rural areas (Schafft, 2016), and community-based programs can leverage local expertise and environmental features such as farms, forests, and rivers to create meaningful learning experiences (Avery, 2013).

Thus, rural areas provide a rich context for learning science and engineering, and with access to the outdoors or work in agricultural industries such as farming or fishing many rural students naturally develop their engineering and science skills in their daily lives (Avery, 2013). Given connections to STEM content in these forms, opportunities for place-based education in rural areas abound and such learning can increase students' access, engagement, and achievement in science content (Avery, 2013). Moreover, using place to educate creates an informed citizenry ready to advocate for their rural home and its relationship in a global context (Eppley, 2017) and prepares rural youth for local STEM employment opportunities (Starrett et al., 2022).

SUMMARY AND CONCLUSION

This chapter has examined the consequences for rural students of less access to quality STEM education in K–12 schools. Because of opportunity gaps in this education, students in rural areas overall have lower achievement in STEM courses and fewer aspirations to enter a STEM career or college major. They are also less likely to enroll and persist in STEM courses throughout their educational pathway. Despite these challenges, the assets of rural communities support STEM education and workforce development.

> *Conclusion 4-1: Many rural students lack access to STEM coursework (e.g., computer science classes, Advanced Placement and International Baccalaureate courses in math) and programs (e.g., Talented and Gifted and Career and Technical Education [CTE] programs, dual enrollment, and third- and fourth-year CTE courses) that can better prepare them to pursue diverse STEM-related education and careers. These disparities in STEM learning opportunities translate into STEM achievement and aspiration gaps between rural and nonrural students, and these gaps grow as students move through K–12 schooling.*

Chapter 5 further explains how the assets of rural communities can be leveraged to provide engaging and effective STEM learning experiences.

REFERENCES

Advance CTE. (2017). *CTE on the frontier: Catalyzing local efforts to improve program quality.* https://careertech.org/wp-content/uploads/2023/01/CTE_Frontier_Program_Quality_2017_0.pdf

Akpinar, B., & Akgunduz, D. (2022). The effect of STEM applications in preschool on students' career goals and perceptions of engineering. *International Journal of Early Childhood, 54*, 249–269. https://doi.org/10.1007/s13158-022-00330-1

Alhadabi, A. (2023). Individual and contextual effects on science identity among American ninth-grade students (HSLS: 09): Hierarchical linear modeling. *Research in Science & Technological Education, 41*(3), 886–905. https://doi.org/10.1080/02635143.2021.1972959

Anderson, R., & Chang, B. (2011). Mathematics course-taking in rural high schools. *Journal of Research in Rural Education, 26.* https://jrre.psu.edu/sites/default/files/2019-08/26-1.pdf

Avery, L. M. (2013). Rural science education: Valuing local knowledge. *Theory into Practice, 52*(1), 28–35.

Banilower, E. R., Smith, P. S., Malzahn, K. A., Plumley, C. L., Gordon, E. M., & Hayes, M. L. (2018). *Report of the 2018 NSSME+.* Horizon Research. https://eric.ed.gov/?id=ED598121

Bright, D. J. (2018). The rural gap: The need for exploration and intervention. *Journal of School Counseling, 16*(21), n21.

Caspi, A., Gorsky, P., Nitzani-Hendel, R., & Shildhouse, B. (2023). STEM-oriented primary school children: Participation in informal STEM programmes and career aspirations. *International Journal of Science Education, 45(*11), 923–945. https://doi.org/10.1080/09500693.2023.2177977

Chambers, C. R., & Freeman, S., Jr. (2020). To be young, gifted, and Black: The relationship between age and race in earning full professorships. *Review of Higher Education, 43(*3), 811–836. https://doi.org/10.1353/rhe.2020.0008

Crain, A., & Webber, K. (2021). Across the urban divide: STEM pipeline engagement among nonmetropolitan students. *Journal for STEM Education Research*, 4(2), 138–172. https://doi.org/10.1007/s41979-020-00046-8

Darrah, M., Humbert, R., & Howley, C. (2023). Differentiating rural locale factors related to students choosing and persisting in STEM. *Research in Higher Education Journal, 42.* https://files.eric.ed.gov/fulltext/EJ1347536.pdf

Dilek, H., Tasdemir, A., Konca, A. S., & Baltaci, S. (2020). Preschool children's science motivation and process skills during inquiry-based stem activities. *Journal of Education in Science, Environment and Health*, 6(2), 92–104. https://doi.org/10.21891/jeseh.673901

Drescher, J., Podolsky, A., Reardon, S. F., & Torrance, G. (2022). The geography of rural educational opportunity. *Russell Sage Foundation Journal of the Social Sciences, 8*(3), 123–149. https://doi.org/10.7758/RSF.2022.8.3.05

Eppley, K. (2017). Rural science education as social justice. *Cultural Studies of Science Education, 12,* 45–52. https://link.springer.com/content/pdf/10.1007/s11422-016-9751-7.pdf

Felder, R. M., Mohr, P. H., Dietz, E. J., & Baker–Ward, L. (1994). A longitudinal study of engineering student performance and retention II. Rural/urban student differences. *Journal of Engineering Education, 83*(3), 209–217. https://doi.org/10.1002/j.2168-9830.1994.tb01106.x

Gagnon, D. J. (2022). Student achievement in rural America. In A. P. Azano, K. Eppley, & C. Biddle (Eds.), *The Bloomsbury handbook of rural education in the United States* (pp. 215–224). Bloomsbury.

Graham, S., & Provost, L. (2012). *Mathematics achievement gaps between suburban students and their rural and urban peers increase over time.* Carsey Institute. https://doi.org/10.34051/p/2020.172

Grimes, L. E., Arrastía-Chisholm, M. A., & Bright, S. B. (2019). How can they know what they don't know? The beliefs and experiences of rural school counselors about STEM career advising. *Theory & Practice in Rural Education*, *9*(1), 74–90. https://doi.org/10.3776/tpre.2019.v9n1p74-90

Ha, V. T., Hai, B. M., Mai, D. T. T., & Van Hanh, N. (2023). Preschool STEM activities and associated outcomes: A scoping review. *International Journal of Engineering Pedagogy*, *13*(8). https://online-journals.org/index.php/i-jep/issue/view/1041

Hammack, R., Stanton, C. R., & Boyle, J. (2023). "Step outside": A portrait of an exemplary rural K-8 science educator. *Journal of Research in Science Teaching*, *60*(3), 544–567. https://scholarworks.montana.edu/server/api/core/bitstreams/69125d4c-f310-471b-a133-e0b39438ea02/content

Harris, R. S., & Hodges, C. (2018). STEM education in rural schools: Implications of untapped potential. *National Youth-At-Risk Journal*, *3*(1). https://doi.org/10.20429/nyarj.2018.030102

Henderson, M., Drummond, M., Thomsen, E., Yates, S., & Cooney, J. (2022). *Baccalaureate and beyond (B&B:16/20): A first look at the 2020 employment and education experiences of 2015–16 college graduates* (NCES 2022-241). National Center for Education Statistics, U.S. Department of Education. https://nces.ed.gov/pubsearch/pubsinfo.asp?pubid=2022241.

Johnson, A., Kuhfeld, M., & Soland, J. (2021). The forgotten 20%: Achievement and growth in rural schools across the nation. *AERA Open*, *7*, 23328584211052046.

Kaggwa, R. J., Blevins, A., Wester, E., Arango-Caro, S., Woodford-Thomas, T., & Callis-Duehl, K. (2023). STEM outreach to underresourced schools: A model for inclusive student engagement. *Journal of STEM Outreach*, *6*(1). https://doi.org/10.15695/jstem/v6i1.04

Koricich, A., Chen, X., & Hughes, R. P. (2018). Understanding the effects of rurality and socioeconomic status on college attendance and institutional choice in the United States. *Review of Higher Education*, *41*(2), 281–305. https://doi.org/10.1353/rhe.2018.0004

Lakin, J. M., Stambaugh, T., Ihrig, L. M., Mahatmya, D., & Assouline, S. G. (2021). Nurturing STEM talent in rural settings. *Kappan Online*, *103*(4), 24–30. https://kappanonline.org/stem-talent-rural-lakin-stambaugh-ihrig-mahatmya-assouline/

Lent, R. W., Brown, S.D., & Hackett, G. (2000). Contextual supports and barriers to career choice: A social cognitive analysis. *Journal of Counseling Psychology*, *47*(1), 36–49. https://doi.org/10.1037/0022-0167.47.1.36

Mann, S., Sponsler, B., Welch, M., & Wyatt, J. (2017). *Advanced Placement access and success: How do rural schools stack up?* https://www.ecs.org/wp-content/uploads/Advanced-Placement-Access-and-Success-How-do-rural-schools-stack-up.pdf. Education Commission of the States & College Board.

McNamee, T. (2019). Social capital in the rural United States and its impact on educational attainment. In R. D. Bartee, & P. George (Eds.), *Contemporary perspectives on social capital in educational contexts* (pp. 201–220). Information Age Publishing.

McNamee, T. C., & Ganss, K. M. (2023). Rural students in higher education: From college preparation and enrollment to experiences and persistence. *Peabody Journal of Education*, *98*(4), 380–395. http://dx.doi.org/10.1080/0161956X.2023.2238508

National Center for Education Statistics (NCES). (2020). *Dual or concurrent enrollment in public schools in the United States*. Institute of Education Sciences, U.S. Department of Education. https://nces.ed.gov/pubs2020/2020125.pdf

———. (2022). *High school mathematics and science course completion: Condition of education*. Institute of Education Sciences, U.S. Department of Education. https://nces.ed.gov/programs/coe/indicator/sod

———. (2023). *Career and technical education programs in rural high schools: Condition of education*. Institute of Education Sciences, U.S. Department of Education. https://nces.ed.gov/programs/coe/indicator/lce

———. (2024). *College preparatory coursework in rural high schools: Condition of education.* Institute of Education Sciences, U.S. Department of Education. https://nces.ed.gov/programs/coe/indicator/lcd

National Student Clearinghouse Research Center. (2023). *High school benchmarks 2023.* https://public.tableau.com/app/profile/researchcenter/viz/HighSchoolBenchmarks2023/HSBDraftDashboard

O'Neal, L., & Perkins, A. (2021). Rural exclusion from science and academia. *Trends in Microbiology, 29*(11), 953–956.

Peterson, B., Bornemann, G., Lydon, C., & West, K. (2015). Rural students in Washington state: STEM as a strategy for building rigor, postsecondary aspirations, and relevant career opportunities. *Peabody Journal of Education*, *90*(2), 280–293. https://doi.org/10.1080/0161956X.2015.1022397

Postsecondary National Policy Institute. (2024). *Rural students in higher education factsheet.* https://pnpi.org/wp-content/uploads/2024/02/RuralStudents_FactSheet_Feb24.pdf

Rosecrance, P. H., Graham, D., Manring, S., Cook, K. D., Hardin, E. E., & Gibbons, M. M. (2019). Rural Appalachian high school students' college-going and STEMM perceptions. *Career Development Quarterly*, *67*(4), 327–342. https://doi.org/10.1002/cdq.12202

Rush-Marlowe, R. (2024). [Rural students as an underserved population in STEM education and workforce]. Paper commissioned for the Committee on K–12 STEM Education and Workforce Development in Rural Areas.

Saw, G. K., & Agger, C. A. (2021). STEM pathways of rural and small-town students: Opportunities to learn, aspirations, preparation, and college enrollment. *Educational Researcher*, *50*(9), 595–606. https://doi.org/10.3102/0013189X211027528

Saw, G. K., & Longstreet, C. (2024, October 26). Trends in mathematics and science achievement gaps by rurality and remoteness in the United States, 2007-2022 [Conference presentation]. The 6th International Emerging Rural Scholars Summit (Virtual).

Schafft, K. A. (2016). Rural education as rural development: Understanding the rural school–community well-being linkage in a 21st-century policy context. *Peabody Journal of Education*, *91*(2), 137–154. https://doi.org/10.1080/0161956X.2016.1151734

Scott, S., Miller, M. T., & Morris, A. A. (2016). Rural community college student perceptions of barriers to college enrollment. *Academic Leadership Journal in Student Research*, *4*.

Showalter, D., Hartman, S. L., Johnson, J., & Klein, B. (2019). *Why rural matters 2018-2019: The time is now.* Rural School and Community Trust. https://files.eric.ed.gov/fulltext/ED604580.pdf

Showalter, D., Klein, R., Johnson, J., & Hartman, S. L. (2017). *Why rural matters 2015-2016: Understanding the changing landscape.* Rural School and Community Trust. https://eric.ed.gov/?id=ED590169

Southern Regional Education Board. (2015). *Benchmarking state implementation of college- and career-readiness standards, aligned assessments and related reforms.* https://www.sreb.org/sites/main/files/file-attachments/crossstatefindings_sreb.pdf?1464014058

Stanford, L. (2023). The state of rural schools, in charts: Funding, graduation rates, performance, and more. *Education Week*. https://www.edweek.org/leadership/the-state-of-rural-schools-in-charts-funding-graduation-rates-performance-and-more/2023/11

Starrett, A., Irvin, M. J., Lotter, C., & Yow, J. A. (2022). Understanding the relationship of science and mathematics place-based workforce development on adolescents' motivation and rural aspirations. *American Educational Research Journal*, *59*(6), 1090–1121. https://doi.org/10.3102/00028312221099009

Taylor, D., & Arbeit, C. A. (2024). *Geographic distribution of the STEM workforce.* National Science Foundation. https://ncses.nsf.gov/pubs/nsb20245/geographic-distribution-of-the-stem-workforce

Thomas, N., Marken, S., Gray, L., & Lewis, L. (2013). *Dual credit and exam-based courses in US public high schools: 2010–11* (NCES No. 2013-001). National Center for Education Statistics, U.S. Department of Education. https://nces.ed.gov/pubs2013/2013001.pdf

Tran, H., Hardie, S., Gause, S., Moyi, P., & Ylimaki, R. (2020). Leveraging the perspectives of rural educators to develop realistic job previews for rural teacher recruitment and retention. *The Rural Educator*, *41*(2), 31–46. https://files.eric.ed.gov/fulltext/EJ1277657.pdf

Versypt, J. J., & Versypt, A. N. F. (2013). Mapping rural students' STEM involvement: Case studies of chemical engineering undergraduate enrollment in the states of Illinois and Kansas. *2013 ASEE Annual Conference & Exposition Proceedings*. https://www.asee.org/public/conferences/20/papers/7257/download

Zinth, J. D. (2014). *Dual enrollment: A strategy to improve college-going and college completion among rural students*. Education Commission of the States. https://files.eric.ed.gov/fulltext/ED561909.pdf

5

Effective STEM Learning Experiences and Pathways

Over the last several decades, research has provided insights into effective approaches to science, technology, engineering, and mathematics (STEM) learning and teaching and these are guiding improvements in STEM education. The evidence shows that learning is not simply transmission of knowledge about a discipline. Rather, people learn through actively making sense of the world and their learning is shaped by social and cultural contexts. This viewpoint differs significantly from the view of learning as knowledge transmission that organized formal schooling, including STEM education, in the United States in the 20th century. Current evidence-based approaches to STEM education that emphasize the importance of relevant phenomena, problems, and engagement in authentic STEM tasks offer opportunities to design STEM education that is more responsive to the priorities and needs of rural settings.

In this chapter we summarize key insights from research on STEM learning and teaching and describe the elements of productive STEM learning experiences. We then discuss strategies for designing STEM education and workforce development that leverage rural assets, including place-based approaches, local rural knowledge, and culturally responsive and sustaining pedagogy. Finally, we present approaches and models for workforce development that can begin as early as middle school and provide rural students with supportive pathways that connect them with opportunities in their community.

Throughout the chapter, when we refer to STEM we mean both the individual disciplines—science, technology, engineering, and mathematics—and efforts to support interdisciplinary learning experiences that emphasize the connections between them. Effective STEM education combines both discipline-focused and interdisciplinary learning experiences (National Academy of Engineering [NAE] & National Research Council [NRC], 2014).

WHAT DO PRODUCTIVE LEARNING EXPERIENCES IN STEM LOOK LIKE?

Learners' experiences as they interact with educators and peers in classrooms and other learning environments in and out of school are the heart of STEM education. In this section we briefly review current understandings of how people learn in the STEM disciplines and what they mean for the design of effective STEM learning environments in rural settings. A full discussion of all the recent advances in research on STEM learning is beyond the scope of this chapter; for such discussions see *How People Learn II* (National Academies of Sciences, Engineering, and Medicine [NASEM], 2018), *STEM Integration in K–12 Education* (NAE & NRC, 2014), and Nasir et al. (2020, 2021).

How People Learn in STEM

Research on learning over the past several decades upends some traditional views of learners as passive receivers of knowledge, recognizing learners as actively working to make sense of the world (NASEM, 2018; NRC, 2000). These insights also emphasize that learning does not happen only while individuals are in school. Rather, it is a cultural, social, and historical process that takes place over time and across the multiple settings of learners' lives, including in their families, the natural world, community settings, and schools (NASEM, 2024a). Starting from the very beginning of their life, children work to make sense of the world around them and find solutions to problems that present themselves in daily life. Their varied learning experiences and contexts are important for shaping how people know and understand the world, but they are not always acknowledged or leveraged in formal STEM learning contexts.

Learning is a fundamentally social process. Through interactions and discussions with adults and peers in different environments, learners ask questions, test their ideas, refine their skills, and revise their understanding. Even when a learner is engaging in an individual task they are using tools or engaging with ideas developed by other people. The knowledge and practices of the STEM disciplines themselves have been developed by people participating in disciplinary communities over centuries. When students learn in STEM, they are learning to participate in these communities, becoming familiar with core disciplinary ideas and engaging in disciplinary practices such as designing investigations in science (NRC, 2012), modeling with mathematics (see Common Core Standards in Mathematics), or applying systems thinking in engineering (see ITEEA standards); information about the mathematics standards and ITEEA standards is presented in Box 5-1.

Learning in the STEM disciplines also involves the development of interest, identity, and sense of belonging (NASEM, 2018; NRC, 2012). Initial interest in a problem or phenomenon might drive initial engagement, but for learners to continue to pursue learning opportunities in science or mathematics or computer science, they need to continue to see the relevance of the learning for themselves. Increasingly, researchers are finding that identity and belonging—feeling welcome, capable of learning in a discipline and of being successful—are important not only for long-term persistence in STEM but also for how learners engage in each learning opportunity (NASEM, 2018, 2024b). This is particularly important for learners who may face barriers to entering STEM disciplines, including women, Black, Latine, and Indigenous people, and people experiencing poverty (NASEM, 2024b).

Decades of research make clear that young children are fully capable of engaging in STEM learning (NASEM, 2022, 2024a; NRC, 2007, 2012). In fact, their curiosity about the world around them is an important asset that can be leveraged in the classroom. In addition, the foundation set during the preschool and elementary grades is critical to children's success in later grades, in terms of both proficiency with disciplinary concepts and practices, and interest and sense of competence (NASEM, 2022, 2024a). In preschool and across the elementary grades, learners need opportunities to participate in STEM in caring contexts where they can explore, engage in dialogue, and pursue their curiosity and interests (NASEM, 2022, 2024a).

As noted, STEM learning in later grades relies heavily on the foundation set in prekindergarten and elementary grades, as well as on continuing formal and informal learning outside of school (NASEM, 2019, 2022, 2024a). It is most effective with a coherent and carefully chosen sequence of learning experiences in which students revisit topics, are supported in making connections, and revise their thinking based on new information both within and across grades (NASEM, 2022). Yet despite the importance of foundational learning, science and engineering are often short-changed during the elementary grades, with much less time devoted to science instruction than to mathematics (Horizon Research, 2019; NASEM, 2022).

The research on learning and teaching in STEM has informed the standards for curriculum and assessment adopted by states across the country.

BOX 5-1
Standards of K–12 STEM Education

Evidence produced over the past 30–40 years from research on learning and teaching has informed the development of national curricular frameworks and standards introduced during the past decade, including the Common Core Standards in Mathematics (CCSM), *Framework for K–12 Science Education* (NRC, 2012), Standards for Technological and Engineering Literacy, and K–12 Computer Science Framework. These have informed the development of state-level standards across the United States.

One of the major advances across these frameworks and standards is an emphasis on moving away from simply knowing content or mastering algorithms. Instead, they call for students to put their knowledge to use while engaging in disciplinary practices—that is, the skills and strategies used by experts in a given discipline.

The standards documents above outline both concepts to be learned in a discipline and disciplinary practices. For example, the CCSM identifies the following standards for mathematical practice:

- make sense of problems and persevere in solving them,
- reason abstractly and quantitatively,
- construct viable arguments and critique the reasoning of others,
- model with mathematics,
- use appropriate tools strategically,
- attend to precision,
- look for and make use of structure, and
- look for and express regularity in repeated reasoning.

The *Framework for K–12 Science Education* outlines the following science and engineering practices:

- ask questions (for science) and define problems (for engineering);
- develop and use models;
- plan and carry out investigations;
- analyze and interpret data;
- use mathematics and computational thinking;
- construct explanations (for science) and design solutions (for engineering);
- engage in argument from evidence; and
- obtain, evaluate, and communicate information.

This shift to recognizing that learning in the STEM disciplines involves using one's knowledge of key concepts to engage in disciplinary practices has profound implications for the design of curricula and instruction. To develop proficiency of the sort described in these standards, learners need opportunities to engage in real-world problem solving and investigations, to discuss their emerging understanding with others, and to reflect on and refine their knowledge and skills over time.

These standards in mathematics, science, engineering, and computer science differ from previous standards and are catalyzing changes to instruction at the classroom level including in rural districts (see Box 5-1).

Effective Instruction

The insights about learning described above have tremendous implications for the design of learning experiences and instruction. In productive STEM learning environments, students engage independently and collaboratively in a caring community and through meaningful investigation, problem solving, and/or design experiences. As the students refine their explanations and/or solutions over time, educators monitor learning to inform instruction. In these classrooms, STEM teachers scaffold and facilitate individual and small- and large-group problem solving in a supportive classroom environment that foregrounds culturally sustaining, authentic STEM learning, celebrates mistakes, promotes reflection and revision, and allows for the emotions that accompany their students' deep learning. Monitoring the progress of all students in order to adjust moment-to-moment instructional moves as well as to plan for future instruction based on varied evidence of student learning enables productive experiences for the students.

This approach to design of learning experiences and instruction differs markedly from more traditional approaches that often emphasized transmission of knowledge with limited opportunities for students to engage in discussion with each other or to explore how what they are learning in school is connected to their local communities or contexts. The shift in instructional approach for science and engineering is captured in Figure 5-1 (NASEM, 2019). Some of the major changes illustrated also apply to the other STEM disciplines. For example, syntheses of research in mathematics education produced by the Institute of Education Sciences and guidance from the National Council of Teachers of Mathematics emphasize instructional practices such as helping students identify mathematics in the everyday world, promoting discourse about mathematics, engaging students in small-group problem solving, articulating and comparing different approaches to solving problems, and encouraging time for reflection (Frye et al., 2013; National Council of Teachers of Mathematics, 2014; Star et al., 2015; Woodward et al., 2012). These shifts—to allowing more time for discussion, connecting more clearly to students' everyday experience outside of school, and promoting shared sense making and problem solving—open up numerous opportunities for designing learning experiences that connect to and leverage the assets of rural communities and settings.

Several instructional approaches or models reflect these shifts. We describe some of these in the following sections together with ways they can be tailored to or used in rural settings.

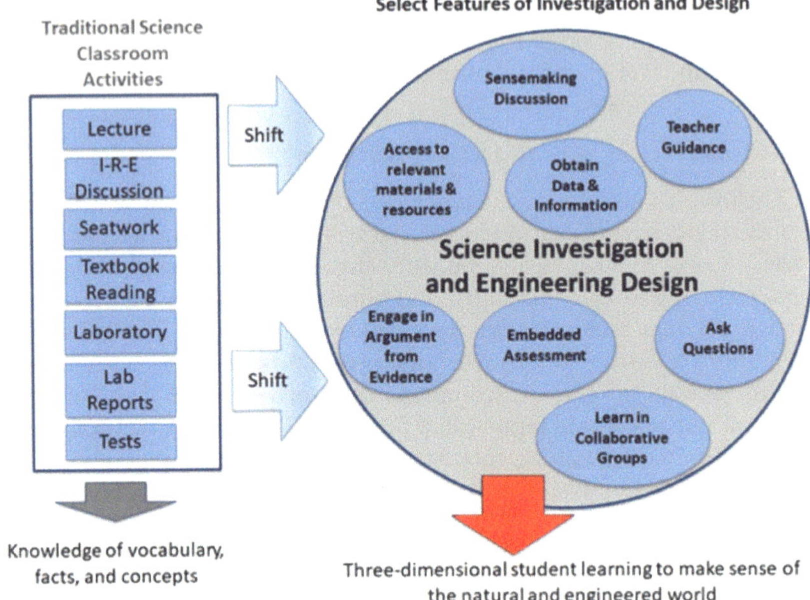

FIGURE 5-1 Shifts in STEM instructional approaches.
NOTE: I-R-E = initiation-reply-evaluation.
SOURCE: National Academies (2019).

Centering Instruction on Meaningful Phenomena and Problems

Anchoring instructional experiences in problems and phenomena linked to learners' previous experiences, knowledge, interests, and identities promotes engagement in disciplinary practices and understanding, and emphasizes the relevance of the STEM disciplines to learners' daily lives (NAE & NRC, 2014; NASEM, 2019, 2022). In science and engineering, educators can leverage students' curiosity by choosing locally and/or culturally relevant phenomena and design challenges (NASEM, 2019). Allowing learners to then pose and pursue their own questions and/or develop their own solutions supports students' sense of competence and sustains their interest. In mathematics, educators can ground problems in real-world situations and support students in seeing mathematics in their everyday lives.

The Working Together Project (WTP), implemented in 11 rural middle schools in Colorado, is an example of centering meaningful, local issues. The three-year curriculum, codeveloped with community members, uses evidence-based pedagogical practices and takes place during the school day (often through elective courses). Through a service learning process called *AIM* (Assess, Identify, Make It Happen), students pursue academic learning goals while meeting school needs using disciplinary knowledge and practices to influence changes in policy and social practices to solve a problem. A qualitative case study found that students who completed the courses associated with the WTP were exposed to evidence-based pedagogical practices and showed growth in personal responsibility, collaborative and professional skills, connectedness to school, and program planning skills (Ingman et al., 2022).

Project-based learning (PBL) is another promising strategy for engaging rural students in STEM education. It allows students to work on real-world problems and projects, fostering critical thinking and problem-solving skills. Research indicates that PBL can significantly improve student engagement and achievement in STEM subjects (Holmes, 2012). One exemplary PBL initiative is the Eco-Schools USA program. Implemented in various school districts across the country, it engages students in hands-on, inquiry-based projects focused on environmental sustainability. Students participate in activities such as energy audits, waste management, and water conservation projects, all aimed at making their schools more environmentally sustainable. The program not only enhances students' understanding of environmental issues but also fosters a sense of responsibility and leadership.[1]

Makerspaces and Dream Labs

Emerging STEM programs often incorporate the latest technological tools and pedagogical approaches to create dynamic and engaging learning environments. One such strategy is the use of makerspaces and dream labs, which are collaborative workspaces equipped with tools like 3D printers, laser cutters, and robotics kits, allowing students to design, prototype, and create projects. These spaces encourage creativity, innovation, and hands-on learning (Kurti et al., 2014). For example, the Fab Lab network, supported by MIT's Center for Bits and Atoms, has established makerspaces in schools worldwide, providing students with access to advanced fabrication technologies and fostering a culture of invention and exploration (Gershenfeld, 2005).

Virtual and Augmented Reality

Another innovative strategy is the integration of virtual and/or augmented reality (VR/AR) in STEM education. VR/AR offers immersive experiences that can make abstract concepts more concrete and engaging. Programs such as zSpace and Google Expeditions provide virtual field trips, interactive simulations, and 3D modeling experiences that enhance

[1]EcoSchools US, National Wildlife Federation, https://www.nwf.org/eco-schools-us

student understanding and interest in STEM subjects. These technologies are particularly beneficial in rural or underserved areas where access to traditional STEM resources may be limited (Lindgren & Johnson-Glenberg, 2013). STEM industries are also using VR/AR for workforce training and workplace simulations for student and employee development in various STEM careers.[2]

Role of Instructional Materials

Use of high-quality instructional materials is critical for advancing effective STEM education. Research has shown that their use has positive effects on students' outcomes (Chingos & Whitehurst, 2012; Koedel & Polikoff, 2017; Steiner, 2017). In science and engineering, high-quality materials facilitate careful sequencing of phenomena and design challenges across units and grade levels to increase coherence as students become increasingly sophisticated S&E learners (NASEM, 2019).

The use of high-quality instructional materials can also save teachers time. In addition, with the shift to more complex instructional approaches such as those outlined above, good instructional materials provide guidance on selection of phenomena and problems, scaffolds for students, and approaches to classroom assessment. At the same time, to ensure that STEM learning experiences are relevant to local rural contexts, the instructional materials chosen need to be somewhat flexible so that teachers can tailor them to their own contexts and students.

Results from the 2018 National Survey of Science & Mathematics Education indicate that in both these subjects teachers in rural districts and schools felt that they had more autonomy over pedagogical and curricular decisions than their peers in urban and suburban settings (Banilower et al., 2018). This finding is encouraging as it suggests that rural teachers may have opportunities to modify instruction and curricula to incorporate phenomena, problems, and issues relevant to the local context (see Chapter 6 for further discussion of teachers' autonomy).

Instructional resources are most effective when they are accompanied by professional learning for teachers, along with assessment activities (Roschelle et al., 2010). Professional learning that helps teachers understand the underlying purposes and structures of the instructional resources is particularly important. This understanding allows them to select and adapt resources in ways that are coherent and maintain the integrity of the resources as originally intended (Davis & Varma, 2008). (Chapter 6 further discusses educators and professional learning.) Emerging work is exploring how instructional resources can be modified for use in rural contexts.

[2]https://www.acteonline.org/tech-changes-how-we-learn/

For example, the Maine Mathematics and Science Alliance is working in collaboration with BSCS Science Learning to test a model to support 3rd through 5th grade teachers in incorporating locally or culturally relevant place-based phenomena into rigorously tested curricular units that are aligned to the Next Generation Science Standards.[3]

LEVERAGING ASSETS OF RURAL COMMUNITIES FOR STEM LEARNING

As noted in Chapter 2, rural communities have many assets that can be leveraged for STEM education. While classrooms in all communities are connected to the ecological, cultural, historical, geographical, and political contexts in which schooling takes place (Aguirre et al., 2024; Goffney et al., 2018; Greer et al., 2009), rural communities particularly benefit from assets such as deeply rooted values-based education, strengths in community and familial networks, relationship to place, and the resilience and centrality of schools (Carr & Kefalas, 2009; Kastelein et al., 2018; KewalRamani et al., 2018).

Most research at the intersection of STEM and rural education is in the form of small-scale case studies on pilot programs that enhance STEM offerings in rural places or focuses exclusively on the challenges rural students face without empirically examining how the challenges affect the students' outcomes. Exceptions include studies that have analyzed national datasets to look at rural students in STEM fields, but these are few and far between. Beyond the general dearth of research in this area, there is an important framework missing from most rural STEM research: With few exceptions, studies do not acknowledge rural communities' assets that make their communities vibrant and strong and can support improvements in STEM education and workforce outcomes if they are better acknowledged, understood, and supported.

Rural communities are often small, and this frequently translates to small class size, which means better student-teacher ratios. These can foster stronger relationships and mean that teachers are likely to be very familiar with a student's family and interests, which can in turn help teachers work with students to explore burgeoning interests in STEM. Small, often tight-knit communities also mean that students often have very strong ties: "a deep sense of place and pride in their community [. . .] can serve as a powerful incentive to study STEM-related topics that are relevant to real-world challenges and opportunities in the local area" (Lakin et al., 2021, pp. 24–25).

Rural communities can also be rich environments for students to learn about STEM from their natural environment. Because they are often

[3]https://sites.google.com/mmsa.org/pebles2/home

surrounded by nature, tying STEM learning to the local flora and fauna can be an effective way to promote STEM education. "Rural school districts are positioned well, literally, to take advantage of an interdisciplinary [STEM] approach. The rich connection with the local land, culture, and community has been leveraged by numerous rural districts, to varying degrees, in the form of place-based education" (Showalter et al., 2017, p. 39).

There is a substantial body of research on the benefits of place-based education, inquiry-based learning, and culturally informed pedagogy such as culturally responsive and culturally sustaining approaches (Marlowe & Page, 1998), but there has not been sufficient research on how these intersect with the integration of STEM lessons in rural environments. In 2019 the National Indian Education Study found that Indigenous students who attended schools where teaching incorporated knowledge from Native Americans or Alaska Natives were more likely to be high achieving in math and science (De Mars et al., 2022). Another study also found that students in courses that connected science to their everyday lives were able to connect the science they learn inside and outside school, and this enhanced their success in science (Avery & Kassam, 2011).

The following sections highlight three strategies for leveraging rural assets to provide STEM learning experiences that can promote the success of rural students across K–12 and into postsecondary education.

Leveraging Local Rural Knowledge

Students do not come into the classroom as empty vessels waiting to be filled with knowledge from the teacher. Rather, they come to school possessing a vast range of knowledge and skills learned through their daily lives and cultural experiences. These funds of knowledge are "historically accumulated and culturally developed bodies of knowledge and skills essential for household or individual functioning and well-being" (Moll et al., 1992, p. 133). Drawing on the *funds of knowledge* concept, Avery (2013) coined the term local rural knowledge (LRK) to describe the things rural children learn while interacting with their families and environment.

Just by engaging in the day-to-day practices and agricultural activities that are common in rural places, children can gain STEM knowledge across several disciplines (Avery & Kassam, 2011). Activities such as raising and caring for crops and livestock, tinkering on equipment, building and maintaining structures, and exploring local forests, prairies, or wetlands all provide opportunities for deep and thoughtful observation and hands-on learning in the physical, life, and earth sciences, engineering, and mathematics. Unfortunately, the funds of knowledge that children possess are not often recognized or drawn on in formal school classroom settings, despite research showing that connecting such knowledge to teaching practices can increase student engagement in and understanding of science and engineering in both urban and rural contexts (e.g., Barton, 2002; Mejia et al., 2014; Morris et al., 2021; Rincón & Rodriguez, 2021).

As noted, many rural places are characterized by strong kinship ties and shared values, as well as local schools that serve as hubs for social, cultural, and recreational activities (Miller & Goodnow, 1995; Seal & Harmon, 1995). The deep social and familial ties and sense of place in rural communities can offer powerful opportunities for transforming STEM instruction in schools, particularly by connecting local rural knowledge with formal classroom teaching (Avery, 2013; Goodpaster et al., 2012). To do this, Avery (2013) recommended providing teachers with professional development programs on how to identify LRK, providing students with concrete examples of how their LRK connects to STEM concepts taught in school, and connecting classroom learning to local community experts and elders.

Place-Based Learning Experiences

Place-based education leverages the local community and environment—the physical places where learners and educators live—for learning concepts and practices of a discipline (Yemini et al., 2023). This approach increases academic achievement, helps strengthen students' ties to their community, and enhances students' appreciation for the natural world (Sobel, 2004). And by involving community partners and assets in school activities, it also contributes to community vitality and environmental health (Sobel, 2004).

Innovative examples of place-based education can be found in the Teton Science Schools in Jackson, Wyoming, and the Gulf Shores City Schools in Alabama. The former uses the unique natural environment of the Teton Range and Yellowstone ecosystem as a living laboratory for students. Through field expeditions, students engage in ecological research, wildlife tracking, and environmental monitoring. They learn about local flora and fauna, geological formations, and conservation efforts in their community and natural surroundings.[4] This hands-on approach not only enhances students' understanding of scientific concepts but also instills a sense of stewardship and connection to their local environment. By collaborating with local scientists, park rangers, and conservationists, the Teton Science Schools provide a rich, immersive educational experience that extends beyond the classroom and deeply roots students in their rural community and environment.

The Gulf Shores City Schools' place-based Sustainability Initiative offers preK–12 students immersive learning experiences that use local natural and community resources. The initiative includes the Gulf Coast

[4]https://www.tetonscience.org/

Sustainability Academy at Gulf Shores High School, which features hands-on STEAM[5] education that focuses on environmental sustainability. Students engage in projects like oyster gardening, in which they grow and maintain oysters for restoration in Mobile Bay and participate in field experiences and research at sites such as Gulf State Park and Little Lagoon. The program also integrates scuba diving in the marine and environmental science Summer Weekly Accelerated Vocational Experiences curriculum, allowing students to explore underwater ecosystems firsthand.[6]

The Gulf Coast Sustainability Academy further integrates work-based learning through internships and local career exploration, preparing students for careers in marine biology, environmental science, and related STEM fields. The district supports vertical alignment and professional development for educators and has created a team to integrate sustainability practices across the curriculum. This comprehensive strategy enhances academic achievement, fosters environmental stewardship, and promotes community engagement, providing students with valuable experiences and practical skills directly applicable to a future career.

Similarly, the University of Iowa's STEM Excellence Center and Leadership Project took a place-based approach to supporting out-of-school-time STEM learning with eight rural middle schools in a research practice partnership (RPP; Lakin et al., 2021). Teachers adapted curricula to center community issues and interests: Student projects include creation of a local butterfly garden, an ongoing prairie restoration project, and design of flood-safe buildings with 3D design software in a community affected by recent flood damage. The results from the RPP revealed four keys to successful STEM development in these rural districts:

- The STEM Excellence programs with the most staying power provide agency to students to choose and design their own solutions to problems.
- Teachers actively recruit as many students as possible to participate in out-of-school STEM opportunities.
- Connecting with STEM professionals both in and beyond (but near) the rural community supports students in their STEM identity and pursuit of learning and career goals, and positively reinforces sense of community. For example, teachers worked with local hobby groups to bring horticulture experts to meet with the students and also facilitated virtual meetings with STEM professionals or field trips to university labs to see STEM research.

[5]STEAM = science, technology, engineering, art, and mathematics.

[6]www.gsboe.org

- Near-peer mentors support participants in developing more complicated projects, and students mentored by near-peers volunteer to mentor elementary students in their robotics program (Lakin et al., 2021).

Importantly, place-based learning activities that connect to local phenomena and problems can both bolster STEM degree attainment and counter the idea that students must leave rural communities to seek employment in STEM fields (Harris & Hodges, 2018). For example, Humboldt State University, described as "one of the most isolated of the 23 campuses of the California State University system and one of the most northerly Hispanic Serving Institutions on the West Coast" (Sprowles et al., 2019, para. 1), has implemented first-year, place-based learning communities that integrate diverse aspects of their location into the curriculum and student affairs to provide a cross-cultural, validating environment that supports students in their STEM studies. The rural university's greatest strength—and challenge—is its remote location, which includes redwood forests and beaches. Sprowles et al. (2019) sought to connect the STEM students with each other and with the local environment by emphasizing both a connection to place and various disciplines such as environmental resource engineering, physical and life sciences, natural resource management, and Native American studies. The authors found that students who participated in the program had an increased sense of belonging and were more likely to persevere and to find academic success in their STEM coursework (Sprowles et al., 2019). This example shows the benefits of place-based education for postsecondary student outcomes and opportunities, and the role of rural regional institutions in educating the future STEM workforce in rural locales.

Culturally Competent Instruction

Effective instructional approaches make connections to and honor students' cultural heritage and cultural ways of knowing. Such approaches include culturally relevant (Ladson-Billings, 1995), culturally responsive (Gay, 2018, 2021), and culturally sustaining (Paris, 2012; Paris & Alim, 2017) models of instruction. These models combine support for the development of competencies in the concepts and practices of the disciplines with support for development of learners' agency, leveraging students' cultural and linguistic assets and centering their competence as sense makers (NASEM, 2024b). The models assume that a key goal in teaching is to relate disciplinary ideas to ways of knowing, speaking, and being that are part of students' everyday practices in their families and communities (NASEM, 2024b).

With increases in racial, ethnic, and linguistic diversity in rural communities, these approaches are essential in rural regions in all states.

For example, in migrant communities in rural areas where students and families speak multiple languages, teachers might leverage languages other than English to support students in their learning. Teachers can support students in solidifying their STEM thinking by prioritizing the use of students' home language, drawing attention to the intellectual contributions students make, and reinforcing STEM learning as making sense of the world both in and out of the classroom through engaging in disciplinary practice (NASEM, 2024b).

These approaches are particularly important for rural districts and schools that serve Indigenous communities. Indigenous knowledge systems are integrated epistemological systems taught through Indigenous pedagogies that support an understanding of an interconnected world and people's place in it. These systems integrate ideas that are commonly referred to as *science knowledge* (Barnhardt & Kawagley, 2005; Cajete, 2000; Michell, 2005) and may be interchangeable with other terms such as *ethnoscience*, *Indigenous science*, and *minobimaatiwiiwin*, an Ojibway expression meaning "the path to the good life" (McGregor, 2009).

Barnhardt and Kawagley (2005) use a two-way street metaphor that calls for western scientists and educators to understand Indigenous epistemologies as knowledge systems rather than relying on the more typical approach of requiring Indigenous students to learn western science and to carry the burden of integrating it with their Indigenous science knowledge. The authors point out that, "although Native people may need to understand western society, this should not be at the expense of what they already know and the ways they have come to know it. Non-Native people also need to recognize the coexistence of multiple worldviews and knowledge systems, and find ways to understand and relate to the world in its multiple dimensions and varied perspectives" (Barnhardt & Kawagley, 2005, p. 3).

Recognizing the need for deeply collaborative work that centers indigenous knowledge, the Native Earth | Native Sky program builds culturally relevant earth-sky STEM programming for middle schoolers in three Oklahoma Native American nations through coconstruction of the curriculum.[7] The project seeks to create a holistic curriculum that interweaves Native American stories and language with STEM principles. Lessons are combined with art, culture, and social studies to celebrate each nation's unique heritage.

---

[7]Oklahoma State University in cooperation with NASA, https://www.nativeearthnativesky.org/

STEM PATHWAYS AND WORKFORCE DEVELOPMENT

Throughout their academic careers, students may engage in numerous STEM-related learning experiences across a tapestry of contexts including formal preK–12 school settings, community colleges and universities, career technology centers, and informal experiences that often take place outside traditional school settings. Cumulatively, these various experiences influence what students do with their STEM learning and can shape the decisions they make about their future (NASEM, 2024b). The term *STEM pathways* refers to the diverse formal and informal educational and occupational routes that individuals can take in STEM fields; pathways can vary in how coherent they are and how well they connect to particular careers (Tyson et al., 2007). The term *pathways* is used instead of *pipeline* to acknowledge the numerous ways that students can navigate into and through STEM careers, and to signal that choosing to not pursue a STEM career is a valid option rather than a "loss" (NASEM, 2024b).

Theoretical perspectives from economics, sociology, and psychology are useful for understanding and characterizing the STEM pathways of rural students. In human capital theory (Becker, 1962; Heckman, 2000), advanced or rigorous training is an important way to increase a student's ability to succeed in their academic and future career pursuits. A key component of human capital for advanced studies and career development in STEM is academic preparation in STEM subjects. According to the status attainment model (Blau & Duncan, 1967; Sewell et al., 1969), entering a particular occupation (e.g., agricultural scientist or computer support specialist) involves two major developmental processes: (a) formation of educational and occupational aspirations, and (b) specialized training and (possibly) certificate or degree attainment. For rural students, each of these developmental processes is shaped by their local knowledge, connections to people, and belonging to place. In addition, place-based opportunities (e.g., local job prospects, school-industry partnerships) and barriers (e.g., lack of work-based learning sites, distance to postsecondary institutions) and an individual's choices about those opportunities and barriers affect these two developmental processes (Pedersen & Gram, 2018; Tieken, 2016).

At least two psychology-based perspectives are helpful in this context. Building on work associated with identity formation, achievement theory, and attribution theory, situated expectancy-value theory (SEVT; Eccles & Wigfield, 2020) posits that STEM pathways are determined by a series of choices and achievements, which are influenced by local contexts and social or cultural norms, from early childhood to adolescence and into adulthood. According to SEVT, achievement-related choices, such as STEM college majors and career choices, are most directly determined by expectancy beliefs (i.e., beliefs about how well one can complete a task) and task values (i.e., perceptions about the worth of a certain task; Eccles & Wigfield, 2020; Eccles et al., 1983). From the perspective of social cognitive career theory (SCCT), self-efficacy beliefs, outcome expectations, personal goals and interests, and environmental influences and barriers are central to career development (Lent & Sheu, 2010; Lent et al., 1994). Both SEVT and SCCT have been shown to be useful in understanding rural students' STEM learning experiences and pathways (Blanchard et al., 2023; Crain & Webber, 2021; Gutierrez et al., 2022; Meador, 2018; Saw & Agger, 2021; Starrett et al., 2022).

Collectively, these economic, sociological, and psychological theories suggest that STEM achievement, motivational factors (particularly STEM identity and career aspirations), academic and career preparation, and educational attainment, shaped by changing norms and local contexts across various developmental stages, are important for understanding STEM educational and career pathways of preK–12 students in rural areas.

Building Pathways

Preparing students for the careers of the future requires multifaceted strategies that transcend traditional educational methods. This shift is supported by federal and state policies aimed at enhancing STEM learning, teacher recruitment and retention, and equity and inclusion, such as the Every Student Succeeds Act, Alabama's TEAMS Act, and the Strengthening Career and Technical Education for the 21st Century Act (Perkins V). The rapid technological advances and growing complexity of the global job market necessitate the development of a robust STEM foundation from an early age.

An example of translating the diversity and complexity of career pathways is seen in the work of the Southern Regional Education Board's (SREB's) 2015 Commission on Career and Technical Education, made up of policymakers, practitioners, and industry leaders from across the United States. The commission's task was to develop recommendations for career pathways that lead to credentials and degrees in high-wage, high-skill, high-demand careers. The resulting paper, *Credentials for All: An Imperative for SREB States*, identified eight actions particularly pertinent to the rural context to support the goal of doubling the number of young adults with a relevant credential or degree by the age of 25. According to the report, a rigorous and relevant career pathway

- combines a college-ready academic core with challenging technical studies and requires students to complete real-world assignments;
- aligns secondary, postsecondary, and workplace learning using strategies like dual enrollment and work-based learning;

- creates guidance systems that include career information, exploration, and ongoing career and college counseling beginning in the middle grades; and
- allows students to choose accelerated learning options in settings that provide the extended time needed to earn advanced industry credentials.

Career and Technical Education Pathways

Career and Technical Education (CTE) programs that incorporate career exploration, awareness, and academic preparation play a crucial role in helping students grasp the vast array of STEM-related careers and the various paths to reach them. Through courses in aviation, aerospace, IT, audiovisual, engineering, biomedical, game design, health care, nanotechnology, or robotics, students are introduced to exciting fields they might not have considered previously, opening a world of possibilities, sparking interest, and guiding them toward fulfilling STEM careers and credentialing opportunities.

STEM-intensive courses are integrated in CTE through career clusters, which offer students a comprehensive look at various career fields. Out of 16 career clusters, with 81 unique career pathways, 6 are STEM focused: Agriculture, Food, and Natural Resources; Health Science; Information Technology; Manufacturing; Science, Technology, Engineering, and Mathematics; and Transportation, Distribution, and Logistics (Advance CTE, 2024). Students can explore different career options, take personalized career assessments, and understand the advanced math and science courses necessary for STEM careers.

Work-Based Learning/Workforce Development

One of the most effective strategies for enhancing STEM education is through work-based learning (WBL) and workforce development programs, which connect classroom learning with real-world applications to prepare students for careers in STEM fields. WBL is a critical component of workforce development, and WBL-related opportunities can be implemented as early as elementary school and increase in depth through high school.

A broad definition of WBL was developed by a workforce development task force (representing education, industry, government) in Alabama to align efforts: "Sustained interactions with industry or community professionals in real workplace settings, to the extent practicable, or simulated environments at an educational institution that foster in-depth, first-hand engagement with the tasks required of a given career field, that are aligned to curriculum and instruction" (Alabama State Department of Education, 2023). This definition informed the development of a WBL continuum (see Figure 5-2) that includes

- *Career Awareness: Learning about Work*. Potential activities: job shadowing, career day, career expo/fair, industry tours, guest speakers
- *Career Exploration: Learning for Work*. Potential activities: simulated workplace, employability/skill training, externship, cooperative education
- *Career Preparation: Learning through Work*. Potential activities: field experience, internship, clinical/practicum, registered apprenticeship, on-the-job training/learning

Each year an inventory of WBL opportunities based on the WBL continuum and best practices is published in the *Alabama Work-Based Learning Handbook* and celebrated with the Governor's WBL Seal of Excellence.

AT A GLANCE WBL INVENTORY

WBL TYPE	IS THE WORKPLACE ACTIVITY ALIGNED WITH THE JOB SPECIFIC COURSEWORK?	WHAT IS THE TYPICAL DURATION?	IS THERE A PAID OPTION?	IS THERE AN OPPORTUNITY TO EARN CREDIT?	TYPE OF ACTIVITY?	DOES MY ORGANIZATION OR PROGRAM OFFER THIS?
JOB SHADOWING	NO	1 DAY	NO	NO	A	
CARRER FAIR/EXPO	NO	1 DAY	NO	NO	A	
EMPLOYABILITY SKILLS TRAINING	SOMETIMES	VARIES	NO	YES	A/E	
INDUSTRY TOURS	NO	1 DAY	NO	NO	A	
SIMULATED WORKPLACE	YES	1-2 SEMESTERS	NO	YES	A/E	
EXTERNSHIP	NO	1-2 WEEKS	MAYBE	NO	A/E	
SCHOOL-BASED ENTERPRISE	SOMETIMES	VARIES	MAYBE	MAYBE	A/E/P	
INTERNSHIP	SOMETIMES	VARIES	MAYBE	MAYBE	A/E/P	
CLINICAL/PRACTICUM FIELD EXPERIENCE	YES	1-2 SEMESTERS	MAYBE	YES	E/P	
COOPERATIVE EDUCATION	NO	VARIES	YES	MAYBE	E/P	
ON-THE-JOB LEARNING	YES	VARIES	MAYBE	YES	P	
PRE-APPRENTICESHIP	YES	VARIES	MAYBE	YES	A/E/P	
REGISTERED APPRENTICESHIP	YES	1-4 YEARS	YES	YES	P	

FIGURE 5-2 At-a-glance work-based learning (WBL) inventory.
NOTE: A = awareness; E = exploration; P = preparation.
SOURCE: Alabama Office of Apprenticeship (2024, p. 36).

Developing and Leveraging Partnerships and Networks

One of the most promising strategies for developing robust pathways in STEM involves bridging preK–12 STEM education initiatives, industry, and nonprofits while also taking advantage of STEM-related regional, state, and federal programs. These strategic partnerships are crucial in providing the necessary resources, expertise, and real-world learning opportunities that enhance STEM education (Means & Neisler, 2021).

Partnering with Industry

Across the nation, a growing number of partnerships between K–12 schools, STEM industries, and/or postsecondary institutions seek to better align curriculum and training and offer opportunities for experiential and work-based learning, including internships/externships and apprenticeships for students (Ainslie & Huffman, 2019; Alfeld et al., 2013). For rural students who typically have limited access to informal learning spaces (e.g., science museums) and programs (e.g., STEM fairs, afterschool programs; Saw & Agger, 2021), school-industry partnerships have been shown to enhance STEM career identity, exploration, and preparation, especially in relation to regional workforce opportunities and postsecondary education (Avery, 2013; Nixon et al., 2021).

In Iowa, the STEM Business Engaging Students and Teachers program connects rural schools with local businesses to develop curriculum and projects that address real-world problems.[8] For example, the Northeast Iowa STEM Hub collaborates with local agricultural companies to integrate agricultural technology in the classroom. Students engage in hands-on learning through projects like drone-based crop monitoring and soil health assessments, preparing them for careers in modern agriculture.

Many rural school districts have successfully created strategic partnerships based on community needs. Putnam County Schools in rural Tennessee have partnered with local manufacturing companies to offer a robust work-based learning program. Students participate in internships, apprenticeships, and job shadowing in various manufacturing settings.[9]

These partnerships illustrate the power of collaboration between schools and industries in enhancing STEM education and providing students with valuable skills and experiences. By leveraging local resources and industry expertise, they help bridge the gap between education and the workforce, ensuring that students are well prepared for STEM-related careers in rural areas and beyond.

---

[8] https://educate.iowa.gov/iowa-stem/stem-best

[9] Putnam County Schools Work-Based Learning Program, https://www.putnamcountyesc.org/work-based-learning

State and Regional STEM and Workforce Development Hubs and Councils

Regional STEM hubs and organizations in the western United States offer a promising emerging strategy for enhancing preK–12 STEM education by fostering collaboration, providing resources, and creating networks that support both educators and students. They link schools with industry partners, higher education institutions, and community organizations to create a cohesive and supportive STEM learning environment.

The Oregon STEM Hub Network, which has multiple regional hubs (e.g., the South Metro-Salem STEM Partnership, the Lane STEM Hub), works collaboratively to connect schools with industry partners, higher education institutions, and community organizations. These hubs aim to provide hands-on, real-world STEM learning experiences and professional development opportunities for educators. For example, the South Metro-Salem STEM Partnership has developed programs that engage students in STEM fields through project-based learning and mentorship from industry professionals, preparing them for future STEM careers.

STEM East, in eastern North Carolina, was founded to address the lack of both awareness of jobs that exist in the region and understanding of the education and skills required for those jobs.[10] Founders of the program recognized that there are quite a few industries and industry clusters in the regions, but many people, including educators, were unaware of them. The goal is to build awareness to retain young people in the region. STEM East is a cooperative program across economic development, local employers, school districts, and community colleges. Their work includes improving the quality of STEM education in the local schools, engaging with industry, conducting job fairs and promoting early credentialing, and helping community colleges achieve U.S. National Science Foundation Advanced Technology Education grants. The program also holds workshops for teachers to increase their awareness of local industries, which include aviation, smart agriculture, health sciences, green energy, blue economy (sustainable use of ocean resources), and biopharma.

Regional STEM hubs not only enhance educational experiences but also build stronger communities by aligning educational outcomes with local workforce needs. By leveraging local resources and expertise, they ensure that students are better prepared for future STEM careers and that educators have the tools and support needed to deliver high-quality STEM education.

Regional workforce development councils also play a crucial role in aligning education with local economic needs to ensure that students have

[10]STEM East was described by Patrick Miller, of the North Carolina East Alliance, in a presentation to the committee.

the skills required for the jobs of today and tomorrow. These councils foster partnerships between education, industry, government, and community organizations to develop strategies and programs that address workforce shortages and enhance career readiness.

For example, in Washington, a Workforce Training and Education Coordinating Board oversees the state's 12 Workforce Development Areas, each governed by a local workforce development council.[11] The councils work with local industries, educational institutions, and community organizations to create training programs that meet the specific needs of regional employers. Initiatives include career pathways in high-demand fields such as health care, advanced manufacturing, and information technology, as well as efforts to integrate CTE with work-based learning opportunities.

STEM Learning Ecosystems and Alliances

Recognizing the power of partnerships across different sectors in a community, the STEM Learning Ecosystems initiative, established in 2015, has worked to support communities and regions in creating partnerships among diverse organizations and stakeholders to support STEM learning.[12] A STEM learning ecosystem can include many different kinds of partners, including schools, afterschool and summer programs, colleges and universities, businesses, government, and community-based organizations. Ecosystems are intended to help to connect learning pathways for young people, close opportunity gaps, stimulate economic growth, and address talent shortages. There are currently over 100 STEM ecosystems across the country, some of which are centered in rural areas. For example, in Maine a cadre of STEM guides helped students identify and take advantage of STEM learning opportunities across five small communities (Mokros et al., 2017). Other examples include Learning Ecosystems Northeast, which is working to create climate and data learning experiences for youth, and Engine of Central PA, which connects 12 counties in Pennsylvania.

Building on the successes of the STEM Learning Ecosystems approach, a National Academies report called on states and regions to "establish local and regional alliances for STEM opportunity" (NASEM, 2021, p. 47) that would develop an evidence-based vision and plan for improving STEM education. Each plan would include attention to providing high-quality learning experiences and instructional materials, building a robust and diverse educator workforce, and creating pathways for students interested in pursuing STEM-related careers.

---

[11]https://wtb.wa.gov/

[12]stemecosystems.org

SUMMARY AND CONCLUSIONS

This chapter describes effective STEM learning experiences based on new insights in this area. Instructional models include phenomenon, problem, and project-based learning experiences that leverage the places, issues, knowledge, culture, and communities of rural areas. High-quality instructional materials expertly adapted by educators to local contexts support both STEM teaching and learning. States and districts can reinforce the continuous and active nature of learning by supporting students as they navigate their educational pathways, which include formal, informal, and in-school and out-of-school learning experiences, ideally supported by local business and industry partners, institutions of higher education, or other local entities. Experiences in these pathways often influence how students perceive the usefulness of STEM in their lives, how they see themselves in STEM, and the degree to which students interested in STEM enter the local workforce.

The ongoing development of STEM pathways and of integrated strategies and approaches in STEM education are essential for preparing students to succeed in the workforce. Continued research and investment in promising and emerging strategies will ensure that students are well equipped to navigate and succeed in future STEM careers. By embracing multifaceted strategies, educators, industry, organizations, and policymakers can create a robust and dynamic STEM education system that meets the evolving needs of an increasingly complex and technology-driven world.

Conclusion 5-1: Rural students' competencies in STEM build over time beginning in the early grades (preK–2). Learning experiences in the core STEM subjects throughout the elementary grades are essential for building the knowledge, skills, and dispositions that develop STEM literacy and lead to later success including in STEM and related careers.

Conclusion 5-2: STEM learning experiences that connect to and leverage rural students' local experiences and knowledge are important components of effective K–12 STEM education in rural settings. Place-based learning experiences, often through local partnerships and the adaptation of instructional materials for local relevance, can be especially productive for building rural students' competence and motivation (e.g., interest, identity) in STEM.

Conclusion 5-3: High-quality instructional materials with connected professional development that can be adapted for local relevance are important for supporting effective K–12 STEM education in rural areas.

Conclusion 5-4: Pathways to and through STEM education in rural communities are enriched by STEM learning opportunities through schools, afterschool programs, summer camps and programs, public libraries, museums, local businesses, and virtual platforms. But these learning opportunities are sometimes constrained by limited funding and availability in rural communities.

Conclusion 5-5: Promising models for designing STEM enrichment education and workforce development programs in rural areas (i) involve partnerships between K–12, local higher education institutions, Tribal Nations and other tribal leaders, and local government and business; (ii) provide students with job-relevant experiences (i.e., internships, apprenticeships); and (iii) target flexible and transferable knowledge and skills that are relevant to STEM education and local job opportunities.

In the next chapter we turn our attention to rural educators and their recruitment, retention, and professional development.

REFERENCES

Advance CTE. (2024). *Career clusters: Pathways to college & career readiness.* https://careertech.org/career-clusters/

Aguirre, H. C. C., Delgado, P. N., & Carrillo, L. R. G. (2024). *Asset-based approaches to transformative learning: Community and culture in an undergraduate engineering research program at a Hispanic Serving Institution.* 2024 ASEE Annual Conference & Exposition. https://peer.asee.org/asset-based-approaches-to-transformative-learning-community-and-culture-in-an-undergraduate-engineering-research-program-at-a-hispanic-serving-institution.pdf

Ainslie, P. J., & Huffman, S. L. (2019). Human resource development and expanding STEM career learning opportunities: Exploration, internships, and externships. *Advances in Developing Human Resources*, *21*(1), 35–48. https://doi.org/10.1177/1523422318814487

Alabama Office of Apprenticeship. (2024). *Alabama work-based learning handbook* (3rd ed.).

Alabama State Department of Education. (2023). *Alabama work-based learning handbook.* https://www.alabamaachieves.org/wp-content/uploads/2023/10/CTE_20231018_Alabama-Work-Based-Learning-Handbook_V1.0.pdf

Alfeld, C., Charner, I., Johnson, L., & Watts, E. (2013). *Work-based learning opportunities for high school students.* National Research Center for Career and Technical Education. https://files.eric.ed.gov/fulltext/ED574519.pdf

Avery, L. M. (2013). Rural science education: Valuing local knowledge. *Theory into Practice*, *52*(1), 28–35.

Avery, L. M., & Kassam, K.-A. (2011). Children's local rural knowledge of science and engineering. *Journal of Research in Rural Education*, *26*(2).

Banilower, E. R., Smith, P. S., Malzahn, K. A., Plumley, C. L., Gordon, E. M., & Hayes, M. L. (2018). *Report of the 2018 NSSME+*. Horizon Research.

Barnhardt, R., & Kawagley, A. O. (2005). Indigenous knowledge systems and Alaska Native ways of knowing. *Anthropology & Education Quarterly*, *36*(1), 8–23. https://doi.org/10.1525/aeq.2005.36.1.008

Barton, A. C. (2002). Urban science education studies: A commitment to equity, social justice and a sense of place. *Studies in Science Education*, *38*(1), 1–37. https://doi.org/10.1080/03057260208560186

Becker, G. (1962). Investment in human capital: A theoretical analysis. *Journal of Political Economy, 70*(5). http://www.jstor.org/stable/1829103

Blanchard, M. R., Gutierrez, K. S., Swanson, K. J., & Collier, K. M. (2023). Why do students attend STEM clubs, what do they get out of it, and where are they heading? *Education Sciences, 13*(5), 1–26. https://doi.org/10.3390/educsci13050480

Blau, P. M., & Duncan, O. D. (1967). *The American occupational structure.* Wiley.

Cajete, G. (2000). *Native science: Natural laws of interdependence.* Clear Light Publishers.

Carr, P. J., & Kefalas, M. J. (2009). *Hollowing out the middle: The rural brain drain and what it means for America.* Beacon Press.

Chingos, M. M., & Whitehurst, G. J. (2012). *Choosing blindly: Instructional materials, teacher effectiveness, and the Common Core.* Brookings Institution.

Crain, A., & Webber, K. (2021). Across the urban divide: STEM pipeline engagement among nonmetropolitan students. *Journal for STEM Education Research*, *4*(2), 138–172. https://doi.org/10.1007/s41979-020-00046-8

Davis, E. A., & Varma, K. (2008). Supporting teachers in productive adaptation. In Y. Kali, M. C. Linn, & J. E. Roseman (Eds.), *Designing coherent science education* (pp. 94–122). Teachers College Press.

De Mars, A., Taken Alive, J., Ortiz, M. B., Ma, Z., & Wang, M. (2022). Educators' perspectives on factors impacting STEM achievement in rural Indigenous student-serving schools. *The Rural Educator*, *43*(1), 24–36. https://scholarsjunction.msstate.edu/cgi/viewcontent.cgi?article=1001&context=ruraleducator

Eccles, J. S., Adler, T. F., Futterman, R., Goff, S. B., Kaczala, C. M., Meece, J. L., & Midgley, C. (1983). Expectancies, values, and academic behaviors. In J. T. Spence (Ed.), *Achievement and achievement motives: Psychological and sociological approaches* (pp. 75–146). W. H. Freeman and Company.

Eccles, J. S., & Wigfield, A. (2020). From expectancy-value theory to situated expectancy-value theory: A developmental, social cognitive, and sociocultural perspective on motivation. *Contemporary Educational Psychology*, *61*, 101859. https://doi.org/10.1016/j.cedpsych.2020.101859

Frye, D., Baroody, A. J., Burchinal, M., Carver, S. M., Jordan, N. C., & McDowell, J. (2013). *Teaching math to young children: Educator's practice guide* (NCEE No. 2014-4005). National Center for Education Evaluation and Regional Assistance, Institute of Education Sciences, U.S. Department of Education. https://eric.ed.gov/?id=ED544376

Gay, G. (2018). *Culturally responsive teaching: Theory, research, and practice.* Teachers College Press.

———. (2021). Culturally responsive teaching: Ideas, actions, and effects. In H. R. Milner IV, & K. Lomotey (Eds.), *Handbook of urban education* (pp. 212–233). Routledge.

Gershenfeld, N. A. (2005). *Fab: The coming revolution on your desktop—from personal computers to personal fabrication.* Basic Books.

Goffney, I., Gutiérrez, R., & Boston, M. (2018). *Rehumanizing mathematics for Black, Indigenous, and Latinx students.* National Council of Teachers of Mathematics. https://math.oregonstate.edu/sites/math.oregonstate.edu/files/2022-03/Rochelle%20Gutierrez%20-%20The%20Need%20to%20Rehumanize%20Mathematics.pdf

Goodpaster, K. P., Adedokun, O. A., & Weaver, G. C. (2012). Teachers' perceptions of rural STEM teaching: Implications for rural teacher retention. *The Rural Educator*, *33*(3), 9–22. https://files.eric.ed.gov/fulltext/EJ987621.pdf

Greer, B., Mukhopadhyay, S., Powell, A. B., & Nelson-Barber, S. (Eds.). (2009). *Culturally responsive mathematics education.* Routledge. https://api.pageplace.de/preview/DT0400.9781135593346_A24927984/preview-9781135593346_A24927984.pdf

Gutierrez, K. S., Blanchard, M. R., & Busch, K. C. (2022). What effective design strategies do rural, underserved students in STEM clubs value while learning about climate change? *Environmental Education Research, 28*(7), 1043–1069. https://doi.org/10.1080/13504622.2022.2032611

Harris, R. S., & Hodges, C. B. (2018). STEM education in rural schools: Implications of untapped potential. *National Youth-At-Risk Journal, 3*(1), 3–12. https://files.eric.ed.gov/fulltext/EJ1269639.pdf

Heckman, J. J. (2000). Policies to foster human capital. *Research in Economics, 54*(1), 3–56. https://doi.org/10.1006/reec.1999.0225

Holmes, L. M. (2012). *The effects of project-based learning on 21st century skills and No Child Left Behind accountability standards.* University of Florida.

Horizon Research. (2019). *Highlights from the 2018 NSSME+.* https://horizon-research.com/NSSME/wp-content/uploads/2019/01/Highlights-from-2018-NSSME.pdf

Ingman, B., Lohmiller, K., Cutforth, N., & Belansky, E. (2022). The potential of service learning in rural schools: The case of the Working Together Project. *The Rural Educator, 43*(2), 1–15. https://files.eric.ed.gov/fulltext/EJ1362125.pdf

Kastelein, K., Allen, S., Keller, T. E., & Mokros, J. (2018). *The 2018 Rural Informal STEM Conference: Final report.* Maine Mathematics and Science Alliance. https://www.mmsa.org/projects/RuralConference2018

KewalRamani, A., Zhang, J., Wang, X., Rathbun, A., Corcoran, L., Diliberti, M., & Zhang, J. (2018). *Student access to digital learning resources outside of the classroom.* National Center for Education Statistics. https://doi.org/10.1177/0031721720956841

Koedel, C., & Polikoff, M. (2017). Big bang for just a few bucks: The impact of math textbooks in California. *Evidence Speaks Reports, 2*(5), 1–7. https://www.schoolinfosystem.org/pdf/2017/01/es_20170105_polikoff_evidence_speaks.pdf

Kurti, R. S., Kurti, D. L., & Fleming, L. (2014). The philosophy of educational makerspaces: Part 1 of making an educational makerspace. *Teacher Librarian, 41*(5), 8. https://www.newblankets.org/worth_a_look/philosophy_of_makerspace.pdf

Ladson-Billings, G. (1995). Toward a theory of culturally relevant pedagogy. *American Educational Research Journal, 32*(3), 465–491. https://www.jstor.org/stable/1163320

Lakin, J. M., Stambaugh, T., Ihrig, L. M., Mahatmya, D., & Assouline, S. G. (2021). Nurturing STEM talent in rural setting. *Phi Delta Kappan, 103*(4), 24–30.

Lent, R. W., Brown, S. D., & Hackett, G. (1994). Toward a unifying social cognitive theory of career and academic interest, choice, and performance. *Journal of Vocational Behavior, 45*(1), 79–122.

Lent, R. W., & Sheu, H.-B. (2010). Applying social cognitive career theory across cultures: Empirical status. In J. G. Ponterotto, J. M. Casas, L. A. Suzuki, & C. M. Alexander (Eds.), *Handbook of multicultural counseling* (3rd ed., pp. 691–701). Sage Publications.

Lindgren, R., & Johnson-Glenberg, M. (2013). Emboldened by embodiment: Six precepts for research on embodied learning and mixed reality. *Educational Researcher, 42*(8), 445–452. https://doi.org/10.3102/0013189X13511661

Marlowe, B. A., & Page, M. L. (1998). *Creating and sustaining the constructivist classroom.* Corwin Press.

McGregor, D. (2009). Honouring our relations: An Anishnaabe perspective on environmental justice. In J. Agyeman, P. Cole, R. Haluza-DeLay, & P. O'Riley (Eds.), *Speaking for ourselves: Environmental justice in Canada* (pp. 27–41). University of British Columbia Press. https://doi.org/10.59962/9780774816205-004

Meador, A. (2018). Examining recruitment and retention factors for minority STEM majors through a stereotype threat lens. *School Science and Mathematics, 118*(1–2), 61–69. https://doi.org/10.1111/ssm.12260

Means, B., & Neisler, J. (2021). Teaching and learning in the time of COVID: The student perspective. *Online Learning, 25*(1). https://files.eric.ed.gov/fulltext/EJ1287125.pdf

Mejia, J. A., Wilson-Lopez, A., Hailey, C., Hasbun, I., & Householder, D. (2014). Funds of knowledge in Hispanic students' communities and households that enhance engineering design thinking. *2014 ASEE Annual Conference & Exposition Proceedings*. https://www.asee.org/public/conferences/32/papers/9703/download

Michell, H. (2005). Nēhîthâwâk of Reindeer Lake, Canada: Worldview, epistemology and relationships with the natural world. *Australian Journal of Indigenous Education, 34*, 33–43.

Miller, P. J., & Goodnow, J. J. (1995). Cultural practices: Toward an integration of culture and development. *New Directions for Child and Adolescent Development*. https://doi.org/10.1002/cd.23219956703

Mokros, J., Atkinson, J., Allen, S., Saunders, A., & Kastelein, K. (2017). Facilitating formal–informal connections in rural STEM ecosystems. *Connected Science Learning, 1*(3). https://doi.org/10.1080/24758779.2017.12420473

Moll, L., Amanti, C., Neff, D., & Gonzalez, N. (1992). Funds of knowledge for teaching: Using a qualitative approach to connect homes and classrooms. *Theory into Practice, XXXI*(2). https://education.ucsc.edu/ellisa/pdfs/Moll_Amanti_1992_Funds_of_Knowledge.pdf

Morris, J., Slater, E., Fitzgerald, M. T., Lummis, G. W., & van Etten, E. (2021). Using local rural knowledge to enhance STEM learning for gifted and talented students in Australia. *Research in Science Education, 51*, 61–79. https://doi.org/10.1007/s11165-019-9823-2

Nasir, N. S., Lee, C. D., Pea, R., & McKinney de Royston, M. (2020). *Handbook of the cultural foundations of learning*. Taylor & Francis. https://doi.org/10.4324/9780203774977

———. (2021). Rethinking learning: What the interdisciplinary science tells us. *Educational Researcher, 50*(8), 557–565. https://doi.org/10.3102/0013189X211047251

National Academies of Sciences, Engineering, and Medicine (NASEM). (2018). *How people learn II: Learners, contexts, and cultures*. National Academies Press. https://doi.org/10.17226/24783

———. (2019). *Science and engineering for grades 6–12: Investigation and design at the center*. National Academies Press. https://doi.org/10.17226/25216

———. (2022). *Science and engineering in preschool through elementary grades: The brilliance of children and the strengths of educators*. National Academies Press. https://doi.org/10.17226/26215

———. (2024a). *A new vision for high-quality preschool curriculum*. National Academies Press. https://doi.org/10.17226/27429

———. (2024b). *Equity in K–12 STEM education: Framing decisions for the future*. National Academies Press.

National Academy of Engineering & National Research Council (NAE & NRC). (2014). *STEM integration in K–12 education: Status, prospects, and an agenda for research*. National Academies Press.

National Council of Teachers of Mathematics. (2014). *Principles to actions: Ensuring mathematical success for all*. www.nctm.org/principlestoactions

National Research Council (NRC). (2000). *How people learn: Brain, mind, experience, and school: Expanded edition*. National Academies Press. http://nap.nationalacademies.org/9853

———. (2007). *Taking science to school: Learning and teaching science in grades K-8*. National Academies Press.

———. (2012). *A framework for K–12 science education: Practices, crosscutting concepts, and core ideas*. National Academies Press.

Nixon, J., Stoiber, A., Halverson, E., & Dando, M. (2021). Making makers: Tracing STEM identity in rural communities. *Journal of Pre-College Engineering Education Research, 11*(1), 12. https://docs.lib.purdue.edu/jpeer/vol11/iss1/12/

Paris, D. (2012). Culturally sustaining pedagogy: A needed change in stance, terminology, and practice. *Educational Researcher, 41*(3), 93–97. https://doi.org/10.3102/0013189X12441244

Paris, D., & Alim, H. S. (Eds.). (2017). *Culturally sustaining pedagogies: Teaching and learning for justice in a changing world*. Teachers College Press.

Pedersen, H. D., & Gram, M. (2018). The brainy ones are leaving: The subtlety of (un)cool places through the eyes of rural youth. *Journal of Youth Studies, 21*, 620–635. https://doi.org/10.1080/13676261.2017.1406071

Rincón, B. E., & Rodriguez, S. (2021). Latinx students charting their own STEM pathways: How community cultural wealth informs their STEM identities. *Journal of Hispanic Higher Education, 20*(2), 149–163. https://doi.org/10.1177/1538192720968276

Roschelle, J., Shechtman, N., Tatar, D., Hegedus, S., Hopkins, B., Empson, S., Knudsen, J., & Gallagher, L. P. (2010). Integration of technology, curriculum, and professional development for advancing middle school mathematics: Three large-scale studies. *American Educational Research Journal, 47*(4), 833–878. https://www.jstor.org/stable/40928357

Saw, G. K., & Agger, C. A. (2021). STEM pathways of rural and small-town students: Opportunities to learn, aspirations, preparation, and college enrollment. *Educational Researcher, 50*(9), 595–606. https://doi.org/10.3102/0013189X211027528

Seal, K. R., & Harmon, H. L. (1995). *Realities of rural school reform.* https://files.eric.ed.gov/fulltext/ED384454.pdf

Sewell, W. H., Haller, A. O., & Portes, A. (1969). The educational and early occupational attainment process. *American Sociological Review, 34*(1), 82–92. https://doi.org/10.2307/2092789

Showalter, D., Klein, R., Johnson, J., & Hartman, S. L. (2017). *Why rural matters 2015-2016: Understanding the changing landscape.* Rural School and Community Trust.

Sobel, D. (2004). Place-based education: Connecting classrooms and communities. *Education for Meaning and Social Justice, 17*(3), 63–64.

Southern Regional Education Board. (2015). *Credentials for all: An imperative for SREB states.* Southern Regional Education Board. https://www.sreb.org/publication/credentials-all-imperative-sreb-states

Sprowles, A., Goldenberg, K., Goley, P. D., Ladwig, S., & Shaughnessy, F. J. (2019). Place-based learning communities on a rural campus: Turning challenges into assets. *Learning Communities: Research & Practice, 7*(1), 6. https://files.eric.ed.gov/fulltext/EJ1218557.pdf

Star, J. R., Caronongan, P., Foegen, A., Furgeson, J., Keating, B., Larson, M. R., Lyskawa, J., McCallum, W. G., Porath, J., & Zbiek, R. M. (2015). *Teaching strategies for improving algebra knowledge in middle and high school students* (NCEE No. 2014-4333). National Center for Education Evaluation and Regional Assistance, Institute of Education Sciences, U.S. Department of Education. https://ies.ed.gov/ncee/wwc/docs/practiceguide/wwc_algebra_040715.pdf

Starrett, A., Irvin, M. J., Lotter, C., & Yow, J. A. (2022). Understanding the relationship of science and mathematics place-based workforce development on adolescents' motivation and rural aspirations. *American Educational Research Journal, 59*(6), 1090–1121. https://doi.org/10.3102/00028312221099009

Steiner, D. M. (2017). *Curriculum research: What we know and where we need to go.* StandardsWork.

Tieken, M. C. (2016). College talk and the rural economy: Shaping the educational aspirations of rural, first-generation students. *Peabody Journal of Education, 91*(2), 203–223. https://doi.org/10.1080/0161956X.2016.1151741

Tyson, W., Lee, R., Borman, K. M., & Hanson, M. A. (2007). Science, technology, engineering, and mathematics (STEM) pathways: High school science and math coursework and postsecondary degree attainment. *Journal of Education for Students Placed at Risk, 12*(3), 243–270. https://doi.org/10.1080/10824660701601266

Woodward, J., Beckmann, S., Driscoll, M., Franke, M., Herzig, P., Jitendra, A., Koedinger, K. R., & Ogbuehi, P. (2012). *Improving mathematical problem solving in grades 4 through 8: A practice guide* (NCEE No. 2012-4055). National Center for Education Evaluation and Regional Assistance, Institute of Education Sciences, U.S. Department of Education. http://ies.ed.gov/ncee/wwc/publications_reviews.aspx#pubsearch/

Yemini, M., Engel, L., & Ben Simon, A. (2023). Place-based education: A systematic review of literature. *Educational Review*, 1–21. https://doi.org/10.1080/00131911.2023.2177260

6

Educator Recruitment, Retention, and Professional Learning

Earlier chapters reviewed trends in rural science, technology, engineering, and mathematics (STEM) education and workforce development, and Chapter 5 discussed effective STEM learning experiences for rural students. Given the importance of a quality STEM education to individual, community, and national outcomes, the development and retention of a STEM educator workforce is critical. This chapter considers the challenges and assets associated with teaching in rural communities and presents some promising practices for recruitment, retention, and ongoing professional learning opportunities for rural educators.

CHALLENGES IN RECRUITING, HIRING, AND RETAINING RURAL EDUCATORS

Access to highly qualified educators is paramount to the development of rural youth and their outcomes. Teachers have a tremendous impact on student learning and achievement (Darling-Hammond, 2000; Goe & Stickler, 2008) and the lack of qualified STEM educators will hinder the preparation of rural students for participating both in the STEM workforce and as engaged citizens. However, rural schools have difficulty hiring for STEM positions (National Center for Education Statistics, 2012), which often means that these positions are filled by educators without adequate training.

Teachers affect student achievement, high school graduation rates, college attendance, and employment earnings (Opper, 2019). They also impact their students' exposure to and interest in STEM-related careers as well as their ability to engage with STEM ideas and make decisions about important topics such as energy use and health care. Without access to knowledgeable, skilled educators, rural children are missing out on opportunities to engage with STEM concepts. And as noted in previous chapters, a lack of quality STEM education in elementary and secondary school can hamper students' ability both to develop the STEM literacy skills to improve their decision making and everyday lives and to pursue STEM majors or careers.

One study found that female elementary teachers' anxiety about mathematics education negatively affected their female students' interest, confidence, and achievement in math (Beilock et al., 2011). Teachers who are not prepared in other STEM areas may similarly be more likely to display anxiety about teaching the subject. Yet, despite the importance of teachers to student outcomes, relatively little is known about teachers' specific knowledge (Filgona et al., 2020) or attitudes about the subjects they teach.

Although much is known about designing effective teacher learning experiences generally (e.g., Darling-Hammond et al., 2017) and in science (e.g., the Council of State Science Supervisors' Science Professional Learning Standards[1]), there are fewer well-developed theories related to the ways teachers incorporate and implement in their classrooms what they learn through professional development activities (Kennedy, 2016). There is also limited research examining the long-term effects on student achievement of teachers' participation in professional learning: research often examines the impacts while the teachers are engaged in the professional learning intervention but do not follow them to see if they continue practicing program suggestions or revert to prior practices and curriculum (Kennedy, 2016).

Within the school walls, counselors are also some of the most important individuals that students interact with. In rural schools more than 50 percent of juniors and seniors who reported getting information about college and career options said they got it from their school counselor (Grimes et al., 2019). However, when disaggregating based on race, the same study found that rural students of color were much less likely than their White peers to get information from a counselor, and instead got their information from adults outside of the school setting (Grimes et al., 2019). This points to an important potentially compounding inequity. Although the study does not offer an explanation for this pattern, bias and perceptions—both self-perceptions and those of the counselors—about which students are likely to go to college may play a role. The study also found that, while rural school counselors are often told it is important to provide counseling specific to STEM, they are not provided with either training on how to do so or "concrete strategies, tools or interventions" (Grimes et al., 2019, p. 82) to implement such guidance.

Schools throughout the United States have for decades struggled to recruit and retain staff (Malkus et al., 2015; Monk, 2007; Showalter et al., 2019),

[1]https://cosss.wildapricot.org/Professional-Learning

and the pandemic exacerbated the problem (Schmitt & deCourcy, 2022). Several aspects of rurality and rural teaching make this challenge unique. Geographic isolation, onerous workload, limited access to professional development, and inadequate salaries are all potential deterrents for teachers. And for districts, a limited supply of candidates makes it difficult to fill vacancies (Goodpaster et al., 2012; Monk, 2007; Rhinesmith et al., 2023).

Teacher preparation programs generally do not incorporate rural-specific coursework or offer field placements in rural communities, limiting preservice teachers' exposure to rural schools (Mitchell et al., 2019). For both these reasons rural schools frequently have fewer candidates to choose from, resulting in a reliance on less experienced or less qualified teachers (Hammer et al., 2005). Remote schools appear to have particular difficulty filling teaching vacancies (Player, 2015). Vacancies are especially challenging for small programs, which may be staffed by only one or two teachers; when a teacher leaves, the entire program might need to shut down. In some regions, these hiring struggles may reflect larger trends of rural out-migration; research in rural Appalachia, for example, indicates that teachers are much more likely to leave the region than transfer to it (Cowen et al., 2012).

Rural schools also struggle to hire school counselors (American School Counselor Association, 2023). The schools are disproportionately likely to have no counselor on staff (Gagnon & Mattingly, 2016) or to employ counselors with little training in guidance for STEM study and STEM careers (Grimes et al., 2019). Rural students have less access to school counselors and psychologists than their nonrural peers (Showalter et al., 2023).

Many rural Career and Technical Education (CTE) programs also face hiring challenges (Fischer, 2024). However, states can implement policies to provide avenues for teachers to gain a CTE teacher or license. Common pathways include completion of a high school diploma or equivalent, a postsecondary degree, postsecondary-level CTE coursework, a specified number of hours or years of work or apprenticeship experience in a CTE occupational area, an industry-recognized license or certification, teacher certification exams, and/or professional development or training required in the CTE field or a specific occupation area (Education Commission of the States, 2023). Perkins V funding has been used by several states to develop teacher preparation programs that address their needs, and it can also be used to provide professional development for CTE teachers and higher education faculty. Such development could be designed to enhance knowledge and skills related to different aspects of the industries represented in the CTE programs.[2]

Retention of teachers in rural schools is another critical issue. High turnover rates are common, driven by professional isolation, limited career

[2]https://www2.ed.gov/about/offices/list/ovae/pi/cte/perkins-educator-prep.pdf

advancement opportunities, and the demanding nature of teaching in multigrade or multisubject settings (Kannapel & DeYoung, 1999). The challenges of recruiting and retaining high-quality rural teachers are even more pronounced in specialty fields, including STEM (Ingersoll & Tran, 2023; Monk, 2007; Yoon et al., 2019). The nature of rural STEM teaching may exacerbate the challenge of recruiting and retaining strong STEM teachers. Given the small size of many rural schools, rural STEM teachers might need to cover many different subjects (Marder et al., 2017); for example, a single high school science teacher may be responsible for teaching all the science classes (e.g., biology, chemistry, and physical science; Monk, 2007). Research also indicates that rural science teachers may be challenged to meet the needs of a classroom with a diverse range of abilities and may chafe under a reluctance to change among administrators (Goodpaster et al., 2012). These pressures reduce the pool of strong candidates and force districts to hire less qualified candidates—rural STEM teachers are less likely than their urban counterparts to have majored in science or earned a graduate degree (Marder et al., 2017).

While the turnover rate for rural teachers (15%) is the same as for suburban teachers and slightly less than for urban teachers (18%), the rate for rural high-poverty schools (28%) is 9 percentage points greater than for urban high-poverty schools (19%), and the difference widens to 12 percentage points for schools serving a high percentage of students of color (32% for rural and 28% for urban). Rural teacher retention rates vary from state to state and even within states. For example, in Alaska, teacher turnover rates average 14 percent in urban districts, 22 percent for rural hubs, and 31 percent for remote rural communities (DeFeo & Tran, 2019), and some rural Alaskan communities experience annual turnover rates as high as 85 percent (Adams & Woods, 2015).

Although many factors likely contribute to the difficulty of rural schools in recruiting and retaining STEM educators, two in particular are geographic isolation and salaries.

Geographic Isolation

Rural schools often struggle to attract qualified candidates because of their remoteness and lack of amenities that urban or suburban settings offer (Monk, 2007). This cultural, social, and professional isolation is especially pronounced for teachers who are in more geographically isolated districts. In large western states, schools may be several hours' drive to the next nearest population center, which can make it difficult for teachers to build social networks with near-age peers (Oyen & Schweinle, 2021). For young teachers just out of college, the importance of finding a romantic partner may be a primary barrier to living and working in a rural community (Rooks, 2018).

And many rural schools are in high-poverty areas with limited access to cultural activities such as theater and recreation (Tran et al., 2020).

Large geographic distances between schools and small populations can also lead to professional isolation—rural teachers may be the only person teaching their grade or discipline for many miles. This isolation can lead to dissatisfaction and prompt teachers to relocate to more urban districts (Goodpaster et al., 2012; Oyen & Schweinle, 2021). Indeed, teachers are twice as likely to leave rural schools to take jobs in nonrural locations as they are to leave nonrural jobs to take a rural position (Ingersoll & Tran, 2023).

Finally, cultural exchange barriers can be problematic for teachers who are not from the area or one similar to where the school is located. This can be especially challenging for teachers from the U.S. mainland who take positions in the Alaskan bush (DeFeo & Tran, 2019) or those recruited from foreign countries—a practice in hard-to-staff rural schools in multiple states (Tran et al., 2020; Versland et al., 2020).

Salaries

Geographic isolation is compounded by lower salaries compared to urban districts, which also make rural positions less attractive to potential candidates (Showalter et al., 2017). This issue is not limited to rural areas, but most rural districts struggle to pay teachers at the same rates as nonrural districts. According to the latest *Why Rural Matters* report (Showalter et al., 2023), the average adjusted salary for U.S. rural teachers was $5,271 less than for teachers at nonrural schools. Although these reported salaries are adjusted for the local area, it is important to address the assumed acceptability of lower salaries in areas with a lower cost of living. It is not true that the cost of living is lower in all rural areas than in nonrural areas—for example, it is higher in Alaska. And although the cost of housing in some rural areas may be less expensive than in urban or suburban areas, rural residents purchase goods and services in a global economy and may have to order and ship items because of a lack of local shopping options. Thus, lower salaries may not provide rural teachers with the financial capacity to live comfortably.

In addition to being paid less, rural teachers often have extended workloads that include responsibilities beyond student instruction, such as facilitating multiple extracurricular activities, monitoring students during nonclass times, even driving bus routes and serving in custodial roles. These fiscal and workload challenges prevent some qualified applicants from applying for rural teaching positions. Many of the preservice teachers in one study expressed a desire to work in rural South Dakota but financial barriers prevented them from doing so (Moeller et al., 2016).

Another study found that salary was a major factor influencing whether undergraduate students in South Carolina would consider teaching in a rural school; participants were willing to accept a lower salary to become teachers, when compared to the starting salaries for their majors, as long as the salary was not too much lower (Tran & Smith, 2019). This means that students majoring in fields that tend to pay higher salaries, such as STEM fields, were not willing to accept the rural teaching salaries because they were much lower than they could earn in industry. Low salaries have also led teachers to leave rural districts to work in higher-paying nonrural districts (Leech et al., 2022).

PROFESSIONAL LEARNING OPPORTUNITIES

Teachers in rural areas generally have fewer opportunities for professional growth and collaboration, and this exacerbates challenges to rural educator retention (Glover et al., 2016). The lack of professional support and development can lead to burnout and dissatisfaction, prompting teachers to leave for more favorable conditions elsewhere.

Several metrics also suggest spatial inequities in preparation for a teaching career: rural teachers tend to come to the classroom with a weaker educational background than their urban and suburban peers. Information collected by the 2020–2021 National Teacher and Principal Survey indicates that rural teachers tend to have lower educational attainment than their counterparts in suburban areas and cities, and they graduate from less selective colleges than teachers in other areas (Player & Katz, 2016). Research in rural Appalachia found that rural districts tend to hire the least qualified new teachers (Fowles et al., 2014).

Professional development must be continuous and context specific, and for rural teachers it should be relevant to their particular teaching contexts and address the needs of their students (Barley & Beesley, 2007). But for rural teachers, accessing any kind of professional development is a challenge, as distance from universities and other outside providers creates significant barriers. In addition, the type or content of the professional development offered may not be relevant to the needs of rural school teachers, administrators, and other school staff (Johnson & Howley, 2015).

Compared to their urban counterparts, rural STEM teachers have traditionally had fewer opportunities for subject-related professional development (Hossain & Robinson, 2012). For example, results from the National Survey of Science and Mathematics Education in both 2012 and 2018 (Banilower et al., 2013, 2018) indicated that rural schools were generally less likely than suburban or urban schools to offer science- or mathematics-focused one-on-one coaching, although both surveys showed that study groups were similar across community settings (see Table 6-1). In addition,

TABLE 6-1 Professional Development Opportunities for Teachers of Science and Mathematics, Across Locales

	Science				Mathematics			
	Study Groups		One-on-One Coaching		Study Groups		One-on-One Coaching	
	2012	2018	2012	2018	2012	2018	2012	2018
Percentage of Rural Schools	42	32	11	20	48	56	18	25
Percentage of Suburban Schools	38	40	20	27	47	62	25	43
Percentage of Urban Schools	38	36	30	38	54	53	47	51

SOURCE: Committee generated from Banilower et al. (2013, 2018).

the 2018 results showed that rural schools were less likely to offer professional learning workshops in science (37% compared to 53% of suburban and 59% of urban schools), mathematics (62% vs. 63% of suburban and 75% of urban schools), or computer science (24% compared to 33% of suburban and 39% of urban schools; Banilower et al., 2018). Rural schools are less likely to require teacher professional development in how students learn science or math concepts (Saw & Agger, 2021). Another challenge related to professional development is that rural schools often lack an adequate supply of substitute teachers to cover for teachers who wish to travel to and attend professional learning opportunities during the school day (Skyhar, 2020).

The availability of online professional learning experiences for teachers has increased in the last few years, with virtual summer institutes (e.g., Thompson et al., 2022) and other virtual professional learning experiences (Lo, 2024; Thiele & Bogdon, 2022); although the research base is limited, some have found online professional learning to be effective for teachers (Lo, 2024).[3]

ASSETS FOR RURAL EDUCATOR RECRUITMENT, RETENTION, AND PROFESSIONAL LEARNING

Despite the aforementioned challenges, rural contexts offer unique benefits for STEM teaching. A rural lifestyle characterized by relaxed pace, low crime, family-oriented culture, and proximity to the outdoors draws some teachers to rural schools (Tran et al., 2020). While not all rural areas

[3]This paragraph was changed and a citation was added after release of the report to accurately reflect information that was presented to the committee.

are characterized by clean environments and beautiful landscapes, outdoor recreation opportunities are a great asset of many (Leech et al., 2022; Tran et al., 2020).

Informal learning plays a crucial role in rural science education, bridging gaps in formal education systems and fostering inquiry and lifelong learning. This form of education includes activities and experiences outside the traditional classroom setting, such as community science programs, museums, 4-H clubs, and environmental education centers, all of which are especially vital in rural areas with limited resources and access to advanced science facilities (Falk & Dierking, 2010).

The importance of informal education in rural science instruction extends to its role in professional development for educators. Informal education settings often serve as venues for teachers to gain new skills and knowledge, which they can then integrate into their classroom teaching (Bevan et al., 2010). By providing opportunities for collaboration and professional growth, informal education supports the broader educational ecosystem in rural areas.

Goodpaster et al. (2012) worked with rural high school teachers to identify what they considered benefits of teaching science in their schools. The teachers reported trust between school officials and community members, community members' willingness to serve as guest science content experts, opportunities to connect classroom science content to local rural life, such as through agriculture, and autonomy over what is taught in the classroom.

Teachers in rural schools tend to have greater autonomy to make choices about their teaching than their peers in urban and suburban schools, though education policy is becoming increasingly restrictive in some rural districts, such that teachers in some schools have little control over curriculum choices (Inouye et al., 2024). But there is evidence that rural teachers have the control to customize their teaching to connect to their local contexts, and more choice in what to teach and when and how to teach it (Hammack et al., 2023; Tran et al., 2020). Greater autonomy means that rural teachers have the flexibility to abandon the traditional views of teaching STEM subjects as discrete disciplinary areas, and instead leverage local resources to implement a more interdisciplinary approach to STEM teaching (Hammack et al., 2023).

Box 6-1 highlights a rural teacher whose story exemplifies the assets of teaching STEM in rural schools (see Hammack et al., 2023, for additional details about this teacher).

The way Judy leveraged the assets of her rural community enabled her to sustain a rural teaching career that spanned more than three decades, suggesting that support for teachers to leverage local assets could help with rural teacher retention and career-long professional learning. Further, Judy

BOX 6-1
A Rural STEM Teacher's Experience

Judy Boyle has over 30 years of rural classroom teaching experience, 22 of which have been in one-room schools in New Hampshire and Montana. When she accepted her first teaching job in a K–8 combined classroom, Judy was provided with a science textbook to use as her sole curriculum. She recognized that "that book isn't where science is. Science is *outside*," and because of the autonomy her rural school provided, Judy discarded the book and began teaching science through experiential inquiry-oriented methods in outdoor settings. She began taking students on field studies, which she emphasized were not "field trips" but field-based science learning experiences filled with question generation, data collection, and student sense making around phenomena.

When Judy relocated across the country a few years later, to the rural community of Divide, Montana, she found herself in a completely new environment. She recognized that she could not engage her students in authentic, place-connected field studies without first building her knowledge of the area and relationships with community members. After several years of relationship building, she launched the Big Hole Watershed (BHW) project with the help of Montana Fish, Wildlife, and Parks, the Big Hole Watershed Committee, and other community members such as parents and school alumni. Through the BHW project, Judy's students have been collecting and analyzing water quality data along the Big Hole River for more than a decade. They present their findings to the Big Hole Watershed Committee members, who use the data in their decision making. Judy also uses the BHW project to teach other disciplines such as history, geography, and economics, as the river holds important historic and contemporary economic and cultural significance for the communities in the watershed. Judy says, "The river is close to my heart because it is close to my students. It's their river. The river makes science *real*."

The school board and community of Divide trust Judy with the education of their children because she took the time to learn about what was important to the community and designed curriculum around it. If Judy's students ask a question about a local phenomenon, she has the autonomy to "just go" and engage the students in a field study while their curiosity is fresh. This autonomy was afforded because Judy made an effort to dismantle the walls between her classroom and the community, and the results are evident in community members' participation in the field studies and turnout for the 8th grade Divide School graduating class of one student.

Judy's approach to teaching recognizes and leverages the assets of her community. The relationships she cultivated with local and statewide stakeholders alike support not only her students' learning but also her own professional growth. Judy's story highlights some ways that rural teachers can combat the isolation they may feel in rural areas.

SOURCE: Adapted from Hammack et al. (2023).

used her rural context to provide meaningful opportunities for students to engage in phenomenon-driven investigations that not only enhanced their STEM knowledge and skills but also engaged them as "active and authentic members of the local scientific community" (Hammack et al., 2023, p. 559). Because Judy was learning alongside her student scientists, she was also enriching her own professional growth and strengthening ties with the community.

PROMISING PRACTICES FOR RURAL STEM EDUCATOR RECRUITMENT, RETENTION, AND PROFESSIONAL LEARNING

Given the reported factors and negative stereotypes associated with rural places, it can be challenging to recruit potential STEM teachers, especially those with no experience living in rural areas, as well as retain them and provide adequate professional learning experiences. But programs exist to leverage the assets in rural areas to address the STEM teaching workforce needs of rural schools. Below we highlight examples of successful programs.

Preservice Teacher Training for Rural Areas

An individual's experiences in rural places as well as their perceptions of rurality directly influence teacher preparation for rural places (Walker-Gibbs et al., 2015). While there can be a disconnect between rural community residents and people recruited from elsewhere (Corbett & Gereluk, 2020), teacher preparation programs can lessen the disconnect by purposefully preparing preservice teachers for rural settings (Vernikoff et al., 2019). Unfortunately, few teacher preparation programs offer rural-specific coursework or opportunities for placement in rural schools, and "there is relatively little known about intentional efforts to prepare teachers specifically for rural classrooms" (Azano & Stewart, 2016, p. 108). It is crucial for all teachers to learn about the contexts in which they teach, and providing preservice teachers with coursework that enables them to learn about the rural contexts where they will be placed is one way to prepare them for rural settings (Schulte, 2018).

Just discussing rurality in coursework is not enough. Moffa and McHenry-Sorber (2018) interviewed five first-year rural teachers who grew up in rural Appalachia and attended the same teacher preparation program. Although they were enrolled in the same program, they experienced the coursework differently: some felt that rurality was largely absent from the coursework; others felt that place-based discussions did occur in the coursework and that rurality was mentioned often because most graduates would take jobs in rural schools. Some participants felt that some of the professors equated rurality with poverty and drug use and showed a very limited, homogeneous, and largely negative view of rurality, devoid of the rich diversity present in rural Appalachia. While rurality and place may have been a part of the curriculum, the authors noted that the program used a "stereotyped or generalist approach to teaching about rurality or Appalachia and a deficit-focused model of understanding rural peoples and social space," resulting in tension while navigating complex relationships between the rural upbringing of the participants and their experiences in their teacher preparation program (Moffa & McHenry-Sorber, 2018, p. 36). This approach left some of the participants feeling the need to advocate for rural spaces by becoming representatives for rural ways of living and elevating their lived experiences as examples for their classmates to learn from. The study highlights the importance of *how* rural is framed in teacher preparation programs and not just whether it is represented in coursework.

Most teacher preparation programs are at universities in nonrural communities, which can limit the ability for preservice teachers to participate in rural field experiences. The Rural Schools Collaborative Rural Teacher Corps Network[4] recruits students from rural areas and provides scholarships for education majors, and rural field-based experiences are beginning to surface in the literature.

Rural field-based experiences, though limited in number and diverse across locations, can help to reduce negative stereotypes and promote better understandings of rurality, with longer experiences offering the most benefit (Reagan et al., 2019). Mitchell et al. (2019) shared examples of field-based experiences of various lengths designed to introduce preservice teachers to rural schools in the United States and Australia. One example was a field trip program offered through the University of Colorado Colorado Springs (UCCS), in which preservice teachers participated in five four-hour visits in a rural school (within 40 miles of UCCS) where they observed two different classrooms and spent time with a school administrator learning about the school. The UCCS program is too young to know its long-term impacts on teacher recruitment and retention but many participants indicated that it helped them learn about rural schools and whether they would be interested in rural employment.

At Montana State University (MSU), students in the teacher education program can participate in a rural-intensive practicum program (Mitchell et al., 2019; Versland et al., 2020). They travel to and live in a remote rural community for a week, during which they are engaged at the school site for about nine hours each day. In the evenings, the preservice teachers meet with university faculty for debriefing sessions and plan their lessons for the following day. Exit interviews with the participating preservice teachers

[4]https://ruralschoolscollaborative.org/programs/rural-teacher-corps

showed that the experiences positively changed their perceptions of teaching in rural communities, and many acknowledged that the experience had reversed their preconceived notions about the capabilities of rural students. Like the program at UCCS, the program at MSU has not been in place long enough to determine long-term benefits, but more than half of the participating preservice teachers have specifically requested student rural teaching placements. Teachers and administrators in these schools have responded positively to the practicum program and believe that the model holds promise for rural teacher recruitment and retention (Mitchell et al., 2019; Versland et al., 2020).

The rural field experience programs at UCCS and MSU show promise for rural teacher recruitment, but the numbers of students reached are small. There are costs such as transportation and housing associated with these types of programs. At the time Mitchell et al. (2019) wrote their article, the state of Colorado provided $4,000 stipends to up to 40 participants to complete the rural practicum experience. MSU covered the cost of transportation (practicum sites were 400 miles from campus), housing, and meals for its weeklong program and paid a small stipend for preservice teachers to offset the costs associated with missing a week of work, as many were paying their own way through college (Versland et al., 2020). The costs and capacity of partner schools limit the number of students who can participate in these programs each semester.

Grow Your Own (GYO) and Rural Residency Programs

Research suggests that teachers who are "homegrown" have higher retention rates: those who grew up in rural communities are more likely to be recruited to and remain teaching in rural schools than those who did not grow up in rural environments (Ulferts, 2016). Numerous GYO programs are being implemented across all 50 states with great variability, with pathways for high school student dual enrollment, training and credentialing of paraeducators,[5] and alternative certification pathways for college-educated career changers (Garcia, 2020). The mere creation of such pathways is not sufficient, though: they must be well designed and use effective recruitment strategies (Miller et al., 2019). For research on an alternative licensure program at Mississippi State University, Miller et al. (2019) had to invest significant time and effort in recruiting participants. They determined that the most effective efforts used effective communication strategies, built and maintained community relationships, and targeted appropriate audiences.

[5]Individuals who provide support in schools and classrooms, such as teachers' aides or instructional assistants (https://www.nea.org/about-nea/our-members/education-support-professionals/paraeducator).

The U.S. Department of Education Teacher Quality Partnership (TQP) program at California State University, Chico, was designed specifically to prepare preservice teachers for rural classrooms (Schulte, 2018). Participants engaged in place-based coursework with readings and assignments on rural education research and theories, were placed in a rural classroom for a full academic year and completed university coursework that required them to research the communities where they were placed. Through their research, participants were compelled to confront any preconceived notions they held about the rural communities in which they were placed and they had to identify community assets that could inform their teaching. Data collected after the program ended show that 25 percent of participants who committed to teaching in rural schools indicated that their experiences in the rural TQP program influenced their choice (Schulte, 2018).

The Carolina Transition to Teaching program, funded by a TQP grant, partnered with two school districts in rural South Carolina to implement a 14-month residency model to recruit local community members to the teaching profession (D'Amico et al., 2022). District representatives were directly involved in the program planning process. Program participants were required to have at least a bachelor's degree and would earn a master's of education in teaching as well as a state teaching credential upon successfully completing the program. Participants received a $15,000 living wage stipend during the program. At the start of the program, participants completed an intensive two-week summer institute, engaging with rural youth during the second week. They then completed a year-long residency in a local rural school, coteaching with a mentor teacher, while taking graduate courses (both virtually and in person at the school sites). After completion of the residency, participants were supported through the three-year Carolina Teacher Induction Program. Interviews with participants revealed that support from the residency program staff was essential to participant success, but some expressed concerns about their relationship with the mentor teachers, pointing to a need for program staff to carefully place participants in the right classrooms (D'Amico et al., 2022).

The Montana Rural Teacher Project (MRTP) is a TQP grant program designed to recruit college graduates living in rural Montana to a Master of Arts in Teaching program that would result in teacher licensure (Luebeck & Downey, 2024). Program participants complete three semesters of virtual coursework over a 12-month period that coincides with their field placement in a local community school. During fall semester, participants complete a 100-hour in-school practicum and transition to student teaching in the same school the following spring semester. They also complete a one-week campus-based summer residency. Coursework is designed to be place attentive, highlighting the value of local knowledge and helping participants deepen their understanding of rural education and how to thrive in a rural school.

Through the TQP grant, MRTP is able to offer participants a living stipend during the 12-month program and two years of support during an induction program that includes one-on-one content mentoring from a veteran teacher, virtual professional learning community membership, and professional learning resources (Luebeck & Downey, 2024).

The programs described highlight the importance of centering local community knowledge in coursework and of working with community partners in the development and implementation of program activities. This relationship building requires time and effort before, during, and after the program, and there are limits to the number of participants each program can support (depending on capacity and funding). All of the aforementioned programs required the support of federal funds (i.e., TQP) to provide living stipends to participants during the 12 to 14 months of their residency. These programs show promise, but because they have only been in place a short time their impact on rural teacher retention is yet to be determined.

Teacher Recruitment

As noted, teacher recruitment can be a challenge in rural districts, and some struggle to receive even a single applicant for open positions. When positions go unfilled the schools are left with limited choices: either to not offer the course or to fill it with an unqualified individual. Because highly qualified STEM teachers are often harder to recruit, finding ways to attract STEM talent to rural teaching is of paramount importance.

Students who attended rural schools are 5.5 times more likely to consider teaching in a rural school (Oyen & Schweinle, 2021), but recruiting individuals who grew up in a rural community is only one option. A statewide Washington study found that the location where one accepts their first teaching job is more closely related to the location where they completed their student teaching than the location of the teacher's hometown, and that teachers are nearly 10 times more likely to take a teaching job within a 10-mile radius of their student teaching placement than within a 50-mile radius (Krieg et al., 2016). The same study also found that preservice teachers were more likely to accept employment at districts with student characteristics similar to those of the district where they did their student teaching. This points to the value of rural field placement experiences and coursework for teacher recruitment.

Numerous states have turned to alternative teaching certification pathways to meet teacher workforce needs. Some scholars have noted that alternative programs can be an effective way to increase the numbers of certified teachers (Barley, 2009; Donaldson, 2012). However, it is imperative to note that not all such programs are equally effective at preparing future teachers, and some may be structured in ways that actually promote teacher turnover in high-needs schools (defined in terms of percent of students receiving free or reduced-price lunch). For example, Donaldson (2012) found that, on average, half of Teach for America (TFA) teachers placed in high-needs schools left after two years, and only 20–31 percent of TFA teachers (depending on their age) stayed at their school more than three years. Rooks (2018) found that the structure that TFA used to train and place new teachers in rural schools, especially the cohort model that encourages teachers to socialize with other TFA teachers rather than more permanent residents in the area, undermined long-term retention in those schools and communities.

Teacher Retention

Retention rates vary across contexts and so do the factors that influence them, indicating that there are unlikely to be uniform solutions to the rural teacher retention problem (Rhinesmith et al., 2023). The research literature points to a variety of financial incentives to support teacher retention, such as merit-based raises, pay for extended-day work, and transportation funds (Rosenburg et al., 2015), as well as housing assistance and loan forgiveness (Rooks, 2018). For example, in Alaska the provision of formal induction and mentoring through the Statewide Mentor Project increased retention rates by 10 percent for teachers in rural districts serving Alaska Native students.

The assets and challenges of teaching in rural communities can be perceived differently. While one individual may greatly appreciate a close-knit community where everyone knows each other, another may prefer the anonymity of more populous urban spaces. Some individuals prefer wide open spaces and proximity to nature while others prefer cityscapes and the convenience of nearby shopping venues. Thus recruiting teachers who are the correct fit for the rural school and community is important for retention (DeFeo & Tran, 2019; Tran et al., 2020). For example, teachers from the U.S. mainland who are recruited to the Alaskan bush regions have higher turnover rates than those who completed their teacher preparation program in Alaska,[6] often because they did not understand what the living conditions would be like (DeFeo et al., 2018). Rural Alaskan superintendents therefore invest time and money in orienting potential teaching recruits to the Alaskan bush country and local cultures (DeFeo & Tran, 2019).

Professional Learning Opportunities

Rural teachers often teach multiple subjects to diverse students and may teach a discipline outside of their expertise or professional training.

[6]https://ies.ed.gov/ncee/edlabs/regions/northwest/pdf/ak-educator-retention-infographic-update.pdf

For example, a rural high school STEM teacher may teach courses in Earth science, biology, chemistry, physics, algebra, and/or geometry all in the same day. Graduating from a teacher preparation program with deep expertise in all of these disciplines would be challenging. Further, STEM fields are changing so rapidly that staying abreast of the most recent knowledge and practices in a STEM discipline requires continual professional learning.

Opportunities for professional learning can occur through peer mentorship, professional conferences, or formal learning programming offered by professional development hubs and institutions of higher education. Research shows that participating in STEM-focused professional learning programs can enhance rural teachers' teaching efficacy (Durr et al., 2020; Hammack et al., 2020, 2024) and content knowledge (Maina et al., 2021; Prusaczyk & Baker, 2011), resulting in enhanced student learning of STEM concepts (Barrett et al., 2015). Unfortunately, access to high-quality STEM-focused professional learning opportunities and the costs associated with these opportunities are barriers for rural teachers (Goodpaster et al., 2012; Thiele & Bogdon, 2022).

Because rural school districts may serve students in a large geographical area, their teachers may lack access to nearby peers. A rural high school science teacher might be the only one for dozens of miles and more than an hour's drive (sometimes across rough terrain) from the closest peer, which can lead to professional isolation. Limited opportunities for professional collaboration with colleagues contribute to increased teacher turnover in rural districts (Goodpaster et al., 2012), although more recently virtual and hybrid professional learning opportunities can help rural teachers find professional colleagues for collaborations (Thiele & Bogdon, 2022; Thompson et al., 2022).

Creating professional development opportunities and spaces for rural teachers to collaborate with and receive mentorship from others looks very different in rural districts than in urban or suburban districts. Given the diversity across rural contexts, professional development opportunities and programs targeting rural teacher retention need to be tailored to fit the unique needs of the teachers and communities (Rhinesmith et al., 2023).

Importantly, not all professional development programs are equally effective. A 2016 metasynthesis of literature found that the most effective ones were offered by those who were very familiar with the problems faced by teachers, had much experience working with teachers, and based the programs on their personal experience and expertise (Kennedy, 2016). In contrast, large-scale programs that relied on intermediaries who were less familiar with teachers' experiences were not as effective. Given this finding, providers of professional learning programs for rural teachers should be knowledgeable of rural contexts.

Face-to-Face Professional Learning

Professional learning providers, such as institutions of higher education, are not often located near rural schools (Reagan et al., 2019; Schafft, 2016), and this can make it more challenging for rural teachers to access quality professional learning opportunities (Reagan et al., 2019). Teachers in remote regions may have to drive six or more hours to reach a professional learning hub, requiring days of travel in addition to the time required to attend the events. Programs can be made more accessible to rural teachers by offering financial support to offset travel costs. For teachers in rural Canada, for example, geographic challenges were mitigated by holding professional learning meetings in regions that were centrally located and sending the providers to those locations, and by providing teachers with mileage reimbursement to help offset the costs of attending (Skyhar, 2020).

Providing professional learning opportunities during weekends and summers can also make them more accessible for rural teachers. For example, the U.S. National Science Foundation (NSF)-funded Research Experiences for Teachers (RET) in Engineering and Computer Science program "supports summer research experiences for K-14 educators that foster long-term collaborations between universities, community colleges, school districts and industry partners"[7] and provides extended-duration content-focused learning experiences for teachers. But although RET programs recruit widely and accept rural teachers, few have focused specifically on rural teachers. Three that have done so are described below.

The MSU Western Transportation Institute engaged high school teachers in research projects covering a variety of rural transportation challenges and solutions (Gallagher & Woolard, 2022). These RET participants also engaged in weekly professional development workshops on inquiry-based learning, Next Generation Science Standards (NGSS) Science and Engineering Practices, curriculum development, and assessment. The program provided opportunities to focus on content-specific professional learning, which was not available in the participants' home schools. After completing the six-week summer program, the teachers reported increased knowledge of science and engineering (S&E) content as well as greater confidence and willingness to implement the NGSS in their classrooms. They also commented on the importance of being able to network with other rural teachers during the program as a way to combat professional isolation in their home communities. Gallagher and Woolard recommend identifying ways to support peer-to-peer networks after RET participants leave campus.

In one unnamed upper Midwest rural state, preservice teachers were paired with rural "solitary" middle and high school teachers for a RET

[7]https://new.nsf.gov/funding/opportunities/research-experiences-teachers-engineering-computer

program (Shume et al., 2022). Teachers were considered solitary if they were the only mathematics, science, or technology education teacher in their school who served grades 6–8, 9–12, or 7–12. The research experiences were designed using an agricultural framework that aligned with the large agriculture industry in the rural areas where participants lived (Bowen et al., 2021). Participants developed lesson plans based on their research experiences and received follow-up support during the next academic year when they taught the lessons. Teachers who participated in the RET program reported a more sophisticated understanding of what is involved in conducting engineering research, appreciation for the importance of engaging students in authentic problem solving through engineering design, and greater awareness of the value of student metacognition when engaging in engineering design. They also appreciated being able to network with other rural teachers (Bowen et al., 2021).

A third RET program supported pre- and in-service elementary teachers from rural and American Indian reservation communities in a six-week residential program (Lux et al., 2024). On-campus family housing and travel expenses were provided to reduce barriers for participants from remote areas. In addition to spending time engaged in engineering research laboratories, the participants had weekly cultural and curriculum-specific professional development activities. Topics included Montana's Indian Education for All framework, NGSS, the BSCS Science Learning 5E instructional model, the Universal Design for Learning framework, and Indigenous science knowledge. Participants also made field trips to industry facilities and Indigenous cultural sites connected to the RET theme of energy. Explicit time for community and relationship building was built into the program through communal lunches, talking circles, and evening recreational and cultural activities such as hiking and beading circles. After the program, participants exhibited significant gains in their efficacy for teaching science, mathematics, and engineering, and reported that having time to focus on Indigenous science learning and making cultural connections between the lab and their lesson planning was critical to their professional growth. Like the participants in the RET programs described above, these teachers expressed the importance of interacting with their peers, referring to "hallway" talk in the dorms and in the cafeteria as one of the most influential features of their professional growth. While they appreciated the time built into the formal program activities for reflection, being able to talk informally with other educators was an added benefit that they were not used to having as rural educators.

Remote Professional Learning

Remote learning through virtual platforms can offer rural teachers access to professional learning opportunities not available nearby if they are used effectively (Thiele & Bogdon, 2022). Several organizations have developed resources and information for both teachers and educators in out-of-school-time settings to provide STEM learning for youth. For example, the STAR Net library[8] system supports library staff with networking opportunities and learning materials. Click2Science[9] has offered video-based professional learning opportunities and resources for STEM programs since 2013 and expanded to Click2ComputerScience in 2021 and Click2Engineering in 2022. The Million Girls Moonshot Toolkit[10] also provides resources to help educators engage girls in STEM learning.

Research shows that online professional learning can increase teacher efficacy (Durr et al., 2020; Hammack et al., 2024). In one study, rural STEM teachers engaged in online professional learning communities (PLCs) through which they uploaded videos of themselves teaching (Durr et al., 2020) and the PLC facilitators and peer teachers provided feedback on the videos. The study authors found that online PLCs could be a powerful way to connect rural STEM teachers to one another but reported concerns with technology challenges related to both device and broadband availability. A separate study also engaged rural teachers in online PLCs as well as additional professional learning (PL) activities through an NSF-funded project that the research team refers to as STEM STRONG (Hammack et al., 2024). The program targeted elementary teachers in four western states and began with an intensive five-day online summer PL on NGSS-aligned S&E instruction. The PL team shipped materials to the participants ahead of time so they would have everything needed to engage in hands-on activities from their own locations.[11] Afterward, the research team provided teachers with a menu of electronic supports during the academic year, including access to a shared Google Classroom site, shared resources, and monthly PLC meetings. During PLC meetings teachers worked together in grade-level groups to plan how to implement community-connected engineering tasks as well as NGSS-aligned assessment tasks with their students. The teachers showed significant gains in their teaching efficacy after participation in the online PL program. The team will continue offering fully online modest supports for two years after the initial summer PL to monitor whether teachers retain their initial efficacy gains and to identify which types of supports were most impactful.

Learning to Use Place-Based and Other Rural-Specific Approaches

Using place-based teaching approaches and leveraging funds of knowledge (FoK) and local rural knowledge for classroom instruction can enhance

[8] https://www.starnetlibraries.org/

[9] https://click2sciencepd.org/

[10] https://www.milliongirlsmoonshot.org/toolkit

[11] https://www.wested.org/wested-bulletin/insights-impact/demystifying-science-and-engineering-rural-classrooms/

student learning (see Chapter 5), but doing so requires focused teacher training. A scoping literature review focused on FoK use in STEM education research returned few publications (nine studies) on preparing pre- and in-service teachers to leverage students' funds of knowledge (Denton and Borrego, 2021). Of those nine, seven focused on preservice teachers' learning of FoK in coursework (Aguirre et al., 2012; Ciechanowski et al., 2015; Diaz & Bussert-Webb, 2017; Gallivan, 2017; Graue et al., 2015; McLaughlin & Calabrese-Barton, 2013; Stoehr & Civil, 2019), one on middle school STEM teachers (Kier & Khalil, 2018), and one on STEM camp instructors (Mejia et al., 2019). Only one of these studies described the context as rural (Diaz & Bussert-Webb, 2017): in a Texas-Mexico unincorporated border town with limited services, preservice teachers acted as tutors for youth in the community, designing and implementing math and science lessons that connected youth FoK to geometry, ecology, botany, and entomology. Diaz and Bussert-Webb reported that the preservice teachers, none of whom had heard of FoK before the project, recognized the value of designing math and science lessons connected to students' FoK and planned to use this approach in their future classrooms.

NSF has funded projects that focus on professional development for teachers connecting local knowledge and Indigenous culture to classroom engineering instruction. Hammack et al. (2021) conducted summer online professional development workshops with pre- and in-service teachers in rural and Indigenous serving communities, to help teachers identify students' local knowledge. Teachers learned how to use ethnographic methods to learn about their students and communities, and later used that knowledge in classroom instruction. Over the course of the program, participating teachers developed identities as engineering teachers, showed significant gains in teaching efficacy, and increased the amount of time they spent on inquiry- and design-based classroom instruction (Boz et al., 2023; Lux et al., 2022).

Bowman et al. (2024) developed the Culturally Relevant Engineering Design (CRED) framework as a way for teachers in rural school districts in North Dakota to connect local Indigenous knowledge to classroom S&E instruction. At a summer professional development workshop teachers learned how to work with local community members and elders to identify and apply local knowledge to classroom engineering design tasks; three cohort meetings throughout the academic year provided additional support on implementing lessons in the classroom. Bowman et al. found significant improvements in participants' engineering teaching efficacy and cultural and community understanding. The CRED is also being used by the STEM STRONG team (mentioned above) in their ongoing work. Preliminary findings indicate that when rural elementary teachers implement CRED-aligned engineering lessons, student engagement increases.

A collaboration between the Maine Mathematics and Science Alliance and BSCS Science Learning provides professional learning experiences to support teachers as they incorporate locally or culturally relevant phenomena in curricular units aligned to the NGSS and design their own instructional plans for those units. Teachers are also learning to incorporate their own knowledge and place-based phenomena in existing curricula, allowing them to connect with students.[12]

SUMMARY AND CONCLUSIONS

Recruiting, retaining, and professionally developing rural teachers requires a multifaceted approach that addresses the unique challenges of rural education. Competitive incentives, supportive professional environments, and continuous, context-specific professional development are needed for rural districts to build a stable and effective teaching workforce and to ensure that all students have access to high-quality education. But large research gaps exist related to best practices for developing and sustaining the rural STEM education workforce. Research is needed on best practices for rural STEM educator recruitment, retention, and professional learning.

Technologies and new programs hold significant promise for enhancing education in rural K–12 schools, but substantial challenges must be overcome. Addressing infrastructure deficits, financial limitations, and the need for professional development are essential steps toward ensuring that all students, regardless of geographic location, have equal access to high-quality educational opportunities.

Conclusion 6-1: Teacher preparation programs often use a generalized approach for training and do not adequately prepare future educators for rural spaces. There are limited opportunities to do student teaching in rural areas, and some new educators may not be prepared to deal with issues such as how to identify and leverage local assets and knowledge related to STEM, isolation, lack of access to professional development opportunities, and how to enter and build relationships in tight-knit communities.

Conclusion 6-2: Rural schools, especially in remote locations and on reservations, greatly struggle to fill STEM teacher positions. As a result, a position may go unfilled and a specific course may not be taught or taught by a teacher who does not have the qualifications to teach it.

---

[12]https://sites.google.com/mmsa.org/pebles2/research

Conclusion 6-3: Many rural teachers lack local access to STEM-focused professional learning and mentorship opportunities. Promising strategies for addressing this lack include use of remote and online options (including repositories of resources and online opportunities to collaborate with other teachers), teacher-industry externships, consortia efforts among districts, and regional service centers.

REFERENCES

Adams, B. L., & Woods, A. (2015). A model for recruiting and retaining teachers in Alaska's rural K–12 schools. *Peabody Journal of Education*, *90*(2), 250–262. https://doi.org/10.1080/0161956X.2015.1022115

Aguirre, J. M., Turner, E. E., Bartell, T. G., Kalinec-Craig, C., Foote, M. Q., Roth McDuffie, A., & Drake, C. (2012). Making connections in practice: How prospective elementary teachers connect to children's mathematical thinking and community funds of knowledge in mathematics instruction. *Journal of Teacher Education*, *64*(2), 178–192. https://doi.org/10.1177/0022487112466900

American School Counselor Association. (2023). School counselor shortages. *Current Issues in Education*. https://www.schoolcounselor.org/getmedia/f73304ab-5ac5-4ba5-8342-826a3bc205a2/CIE-Employment-Shortages.pdf

Azano, A. P., & Stewart, T. T. (2016). Confronting challenges at the intersection of rurality, place, and teacher preparation: Improving efforts in teacher education to staff rural schools. *Global Education Review*, *3*(1), 108–128. https://files.eric.ed.gov/fulltext/EJ1090174.pdf

Banilower, E. R., Smith, P. S., Malzahn, K. A., Plumley, C. L., Gordon, E. M., & Hayes, M. L. (2018). *Report of the 2018 NSSME+*. Horizon Research. https://eric.ed.gov/?id=ED598121

Banilower, E. R., Smith, P. S., Weiss, I. R., Malzahn, K. A., Campbell, K. M., & Weis, A. M. (2013). *Report of the 2012 National Survey of Science and Mathematics Education*. Horizon Research. https://files.eric.ed.gov/fulltext/ED541798.pdf

Barley, Z. A. (2009). Preparing teachers for rural appointments. *The Rural Educator*, *30*(3), 10–15. https://files.eric.ed.gov/fulltext/EJ869310.pdf

Barley, Z. A., & Beesley, A. D. (2007). Rural school success: What can we learn? *Journal of Research in Rural Education*, *22*, 1. https://www.researchgate.net/profile/Zoe-Barley/publication/26449623_Rural_School_Success_What_Can_We_Learn/links/5a3ad4de0f7e9bbef9fd9fcb/Rural-School-Success-What-Can-We-Learn.pdf

Barrett, N., Cowen, J., Toma, E., & Troske, S. (2015). Working with what they have: Professional development as a reform strategy in rural schools. *Journal of Research in Rural Education*, *30*(10), 1. https://jrre.psu.edu/sites/default/files/2019-08/30-10.pdf

Beilock, S. L., Gunderson, E. A., Ramirez, G., & Levine, S. C. (2011). Female teachers' math anxiety impacts girls' math achievement. *Proceedings of the National Academy of Sciences*, *107*(5), 1860–1863. http://dx.doi.org/10.1073/pnas.0910967107

Bevan, B., Dillon, J., Hein, G. E., Macdonald, M., Michalchik, V., Miller, D., Rudder-Kilkenny, L., Xanthoudaki, M., & Yoon, S. (2010). Making science matter: Collaborations between informal science education organizations and schools. *Educational Policy*, *24*(4), 674–702.

Bowen, B., Shume, T., Kallmeyer, A., & Altimus, J. (2021). Impacts of a Research Experiences for Teachers program on rural STEM educators. *Journal of STEM Education: Innovations and Research*, *22*, 4. https://jstem.org/jstem/index.php/JSTEM/article/download/2541/2242

Bowman, F., Klemetsrud, B., Ozturk, E., Robinson, J., & Lacina, E. (2024). Impact of professional development in culturally relevant engineering design for elementary and middle school teachers [Conference session]. American Society for Engineering Education Annual Conference, Portland, OR, US.

Boz, T., Hammack, R., Lux, N., & Gannon, P. (2023). Empowering elementary students with community-based engineering: A teacher's experience in a rural school district. *Education Sciences*, *13*(5), 434. https://www.mdpi.com/2227-7102/13/5/434/pdf

Ciechanowski, K., Bottoms, S., Fonseca, A. L., & St Clair, T. (2015). Should Rey Mysterio drink Gatorade? Cultural competence in afterschool STEM programming. *Afterschool Matters*, *21*, 29–37. https://eric.ed.gov/?id=EJ1063856

Corbett, M., & Gereluk, D. (2020). *Rural teacher education: Connecting land and people*. Springer.

Cowen, J. M., Butler, J. S., Fowles, J., Streams, M. E., & Toma, E. F. (2012). Teacher retention in Appalachian schools: Evidence from Kentucky. *Economics of Education Review*, *31*(4), 431–441. https://doi.org/10.1016/j.econedurev.2011.12.005

D'Amico, L. K., West, H. S., Baker, M. A., Roy, G., Curcio, R., Harbour, K. E., Thompson, S. L., Guest, J., Compton-Lilly, C., & Adgerson, A. (2022). Using improvement science to implement and evaluate a teacher residency program in rural school districts. *Theory & Practice in Rural Education*, *12*(1), 83–104. https://doi.org/10.3776/tpre.2022.v12n1p83-104

Darling-Hammond, L. (2000). Teacher quality and student achievement. *Education Policy Analysis Archives*, *8*, 1. https://doi.org/10.14507/epaa.v8n1.2000

Darling-Hammond, L., Hyler, M. E., & Gardner, M. (2017). *Effective teacher professional development*. Learning Policy Institute.

DeFeo, D., Hirshberg, D., & Hill, A. (2018). It's more than just dollars: Problematizing salary as the sole mechanism for recruiting and retaining teachers in rural Alaska. *Alaska Native Studies Journal*, *4*(1). https://scholarworks.alaska.edu/bitstream/handle/11122/8323/Defeo%20et%20al.pdf?sequence=4&isAllowed=y

DeFeo, D. J., & Tran, T. C. (2019). Recruiting, hiring, and training Alaska's rural teachers: How superintendents practice place-conscious leadership. *Journal of Research in Rural Education*, *35*(2). https://jrre.psu.edu/sites/default/files/2019-06/35-2.pdf

Denton, M., & Borrego, M. (2021). Funds of knowledge in STEM education: A scoping review. *Studies in Engineering Education*, *1*(2), 71–92. https://pdfs.semanticscholar.org/8df8/d15afb00e2dba4aa6b2151821216eff9af56.pdf

Diaz, M. E., & Bussert-Webb, K. (2017). Latino youth's out-of-school math and science experiences: Impact on teacher candidates. *International Journal of Research in Education and Science*, *3*(2), 624–635. https://files.eric.ed.gov/fulltext/EJ1148427.pdf

Donaldson, M. L. (2012). The promise of older novices: Teach for America teachers' age of entry and subsequent retention in teaching and schools. *Teachers College Record*, *114*(10), 1–37. https://doi.org/10.1177/016146811211401008

Durr, T., Kampmann, J., Hales, P., & Browning, L. (2020). Lessons learned from online PLCs of rural STEM teachers. *The Rural Educator*, *41*(1), 20–26. https://scholarsjunction.msstate.edu/cgi/viewcontent.cgi?article=1049&context=ruraleducator

Education Commission of the States. (2023). *50-State comparison: Secondary career and technical education*. https://www.ecs.org/50-state-comparison-secondary-career-and-technical-education-2023/

Falk, J. H., & Dierking, L. D. (2010). The 95 percent solution. *American Scientist*, *98*(6), 486–493. https://www.jstor.org/stable/25766726

Filgona, J., John, S., & Gwany, D. M. (2020). Teachers' pedagogical content knowledge and students' academic achievement: A theoretical overview. *Journal of Global Research in Education and Social Science*, *14*(2), 14–44.

Fischer, L. W. (2024). Repairing the pipeline for rural career and technical educators in Wyoming. *The Daily Yonder*. https://dailyyonder.com/repairing-the-pipeline-for-rural-career-and-technical-educators-in-wyoming/2024/04/15/

Fowles, J., Butler, J. S., Cowen, J. M., Streams, M. E., & Toma, E. F. (2014). Public employee quality in a geographic context: A study of rural teachers. *American Review of Public Administration*, *44*(5), 503–521. https://doi.org/10.1177/0275074012474714

Gagnon, D. J., & Mattingly, M. J. (2016). Advanced Placement and rural schools: Access, success, and exploring alternatives. *Journal of Advanced Academics*, *27*(4), 266–284. https://doi.org/10.1177/1932202X16656390

Gallagher, S., & Woolard, C. (2022). *Professional development outcomes for rural teachers participating in a Research Experience for Teachers program in innovative transportation systems (evaluation)*. 2022 ASEE Annual Conference & Exposition. https://sftp.asee.org/40562.pdf

Gallivan, H. R. (2017). Supporting prospective middle school teachers' learning to revise a high-level mathematics task to be culturally relevant. *Mathematics Teacher Educator*, *5*(2), 94–121. https://doi.org/10.5951/mathteaceduc.5.2.0094

Garcia, A. (2020). *Grow your own teachers: A 50-state scan of policies and programs*. New America. https://files.eric.ed.gov/fulltext/ED609132.pdf

Glover, T. A., Nugent, G. C., Chumney, F. L., Ihlo, T. M., Guard, K., & Koziol, N. (2016). Investigating rural teachers' professional development, instructional knowledge, and classroom practice. *Journal of Research in Rural Education*, *31*(3). https://files.eric.ed.gov/fulltext/EJ1101917.pdf

Goe, L., & Stickler, L. M. (2008). *Teacher quality and student achievement: Making the most of recent research* (TQ Research & Policy Brief). National Comprehensive Center for Teacher Quality. https://files.eric.ed.gov/fulltext/ED520769.pdf

Goodpaster, K. P. S., Adedokun, O. A., & Weaver, G. C. (2012). Teachers' perceptions of rural STEM teaching: Implications for rural teacher retention. *The Rural Educator*, *33*(3), 9–12. https://doi.org/10.35608/ruraled.v33i3.408

Graue, E., Karabon, A., Delaney, K. K., Whyte, K., Kim, J., & Wager, A. (2015). Imagining a future in PreK: How professional identity shapes notions of early mathematics. *Anthropology & Education Quarterly*, *46*(1), 37–54. https://deepblue.lib.umich.edu/bitstream/handle/2027.42/110548/aeq12086.pdf?sequence=1

Grimes, L. E., Arrastía-Chisholm, M. A., & Bright, S. B. (2019). How can they know what they don't know? The beliefs and experiences of rural school counselors about STEM career advising. *Theory & Practice in Rural Education*, *9*(1), 74–90. https://doi.org/10.3776/tpre.2019.v9n1p74-90

Hammack, R., Gannon, P., Foreman, C., & Meyer, E. (2020). Impacts of professional development focused on teaching engineering applications of mathematics and science. *School Science and Mathematics*, *120*(7), 413–424. https://par.nsf.gov/servlets/purl/10285118

Hammack, R., Lux, N., Gannon, P., & LaMeres, B. (2021). Using ethnography to enhance elementary teachers' readiness to teach engineering. *Proceedings of the 2021 ASEE Annual Conference & Exposition*.

Hammack, R., Robinson, J., Boz-Togu, T., Lee, M. J., Summers, R., Iveland, A., Inouye, M., Macias, M., Zaman, M., Galisky, J., & Ringstaff, C. (2024). Board 298: Supporting elementary engineering instruction in rural contexts through online professional learning and modest supports [Conference session]. 2024 ASEE Annual Conference & Exposition, Portland, OR, US. https://peer.asee.org/46874

Hammack, R., Stanton, C. R., & Boyle, J. (2023). "Step Outside": A portrait of an exemplary rural K–8 science educator. *Journal of Research in Science Teaching*, *60*(3), 544–567. https://scholarworks.montana.edu/server/api/core/bitstreams/69125d4c-f310-471b-a133-e0b39438ea02/content

Hammer, P. C., Hughes, G., McClure, C. T., Reeves, C. A., & Salgado, D. (2005). *Rural teacher recruitment and retention practices: A review of the research literature, national survey of rural superintendents, and case studies of programs in Virginia*. Appalachia Educational Laboratory at Edvantia. https://files.eric.ed.gov/fulltext/ED489143.pdf

Hossain, M., & Robinson, M. G. (2012). How to motivate US students to pursue STEM (science, technology, engineering and mathematics) careers. *US-China Education Review, A*(4), 442–451. https://files.eric.ed.gov/fulltext/ED533548.pdf

Ingersoll, R. M., & Tran, H. (2023). Teacher shortages and turnover in rural schools in the US: An organizational analysis. *Educational Administration Quarterly, 59*(2), 396–431. https://doi.org/10.1177/0013161X231159922

Inouye, M., Macias, M., Boz, T., Lee, M. J., Hammack, R., Iveland, A., & Johansen, N. (2024). Defining rural: Rural teachers' perspectives and experiences. *Education Sciences, 14*, 645. https://doi.org/10.3390/educsci14060645

Johnson, J., & Howley, C. B. (2015). Contemporary federal education policy and rural schools: A critical policy analysis. *Peabody Journal of Education, 90*(2), 224–241. https://doi.org/10.1080/0161956X.2015.1022112

Kannapel, P. J., & DeYoung, A. J. (1999). The rural school problem in 1999: A review and critique of the literature. *Journal of Research in Rural Education, 15*(2), 67–79.

Kennedy, M. M. (2016). How does professional development improve teaching? *Review of Educational Research, 86*(4), 945–980. https://doi.org/10.3102/0034654315626800

Kier, M. W., & Khalil, D. (2018). Exploring how digital technologies can support co-construction of equitable curricular resources in STEM. *International Journal of Education in Mathematics, Science and Technology*, 6(2), 105–121. https://doi.org/10.18404/ijemst.408932

Krieg, J. M., Theobald, R., & Goldhaber, D. (2016). A foot in the door: Exploring the role of student teaching assignments in teachers' initial job placements. *Educational Evaluation and Policy Analysis, 38*(2), 364–388. https://doi.org/10.3102/0162373716630739

Leech, N. L., Haug, C. A., Rodriguez, E., & Gold, M. (2022). Why teachers remain teaching in rural districts: Listening to the voices from the field. *The Rural Educator, 43*(3), 1–9. https://scholarsjunction.msstate.edu/cgi/viewcontent.cgi?article=1340&context=ruraleducator

Lo, A. (2024, March). Lessons learned: Preparing rural teachers to design framework-aligned assessment tasks [Committee presentation]. Meeting 3, K–12 Rural STEM Education and Workforce Development (virtual). https://www.nationalacademies.org/event/42056_03-2024_k-12-stem-education-and-workforce-development-in-rural-areas-committee-meeting-3

Luebeck, J., & Downey, J. (2024). Cultivating rural mathematics teachers through place-attentive preparation. In B. Benken (Ed.), *AMTE handbook of mathematics teacher education: Reflection on past, present, future - paving the way for future of mathematics teacher education, Vol. 5.*

Lux, N., Hammack, R., Gannon, P., Windchief, S., Taylor, S., Richards, A., & Hacker, D. J. (2024). Culturally responsive energy engineering education: Campus-based research experience for reservation and rural elementary educators. *Journal of STEM Outreach*, 7(2), n2. https://files.eric.ed.gov/fulltext/EJ1415459.pdf

Lux, N., Hammack, R., Wiehe, B., & Gannon, P. (2022). Building primary preservice teachers' identity as engineering educators. *Education Sciences, 12*(10), 637. https://doi.org/10.3390/educsci12100637

Maina, F., Smit, J., & Serwadda, A. (2021). Professional development for rural STEM teachers on data science and cybersecurity: A university and school districts' partnership. *Australian and International Journal of Rural Education, 31*(1), 30–41. https://search.informit.org/doi/pdf/10.3316/informit.799074990568698

Malkus, N., Hoyer, K. M., & Sparks, D. (2015). *Teaching vacancies and difficult-to-staff teaching positions in public schools* (NCES No. 2015-065). U.S. Department of Education. https://nces.ed.gov/pubs2015/2015065.pdf

Marder, M., Brown, R. C., & Plisch, M. (2017). *Recruiting teachers in high-needs STEM fields: A survey of current majors and recent STEM graduates*. American Physical Society.

McLaughlin, D. S., & Calabrese Barton, A. (2013). Preservice teachers' uptake and understanding of funds of knowledge in elementary science. *Journal of Science Teacher Education, 24*(1), 13–36. https://doi.org/10.1007/s10972-012-9284-1

Mejia, J., Popov, V., Rodriguez, V., Ruiz, D., Myers, P., & Spencer, J. (2019). *Connecting to the physical space through funds of knowledge: Lessons learned from a STEM summer enrichment program.* 2019 ASEE Annual Conference & Exposition, Tampa, FL, US. https://doi.org/10.18260/1-2-32539

Miller, N. C., Elder, A. D., Seymour, D., Cheatham, D. A., & Brenner, D. (2019). Best practices article: Teacher recruitment for an alternate route program in a rural area—Methods and lessons. *Journal of the National Association for Alternative Certification, 14*(1), n1. https://files.eric.ed.gov/fulltext/EJ1218143.pdf

Mitchell, R., Wynhoff Olsen, A., Hampton, P., Hicks, J., Long, D., & Olsen, K. (2019). Rural exposures: An examination of three initiatives to introduce and immerse preservice teachers into rural communities and rural schools in the US and Australia. *The Rural Educator, 40*(2), 12–22. https://files.eric.ed.gov/fulltext/EJ1225138.pdf

Moeller, M. R., Moeller, L. L., & Schmidt, D. (2016). Examining the teacher pipeline: Will they stay or will they go? *The Rural Educator, 37*(1), 25–38. https://scholarsjunction.msstate.edu/cgi/viewcontent.cgi?article=1114&context=ruraleducator

Moffa, E., & McHenry-Sorber, E. (2018). Learning to be rural: Lessons about being rural in teacher education programs. *The Rural Educator, 39*(1), 26–40. https://scholarsjunction.msstate.edu/cgi/viewcontent.cgi?article=1087&context=ruraleducator

Monk, D. H. (2007). Recruiting and retaining high-quality teachers in rural areas. *The Future of Children, 17*(1), 155–174. https://files.eric.ed.gov/fulltext/EJ795884.pdf

National Center for Education Statistics (NCES). (2012). *The status of rural education.* Institute of Education Sciences, U.S. Department of Education.

Opper, I. M. (2019). *Teachers matter: Understanding teachers' impact on student achievement.* RAND Corporation. https://www.rand.org/pubs/research_reports/RR4312.html

Oyen, K., & Schweinle, A. (2021). Addressing teacher shortages in rural America: What factors encourage teachers to consider teaching in rural settings? *The Rural Educator, 41*(3), 12–25. https://files.eric.ed.gov/fulltext/EJ1303960.pdf

Player, D. (2015). *The supply and demand for rural teachers.* Rural Opportunities Consortium of Idaho.

Player, D., & Katz, V. (2016). Assessing school turnaround: Evidence from Ohio. *Elementary School Journal, 116*(4), 675–698.

Prusaczyk, J., & Baker, P. J. (2011). Improving teacher quality in southern Illinois: Rural Access to Mathematics Professional Development (RAMPD). *Planning and Changing, 42*, 101–119. https://files.eric.ed.gov/fulltext/EJ952395.pdf

Reagan, E. M., Hambacher, E., Schram, T., McCurdy, K., Lord, D., Higginbotham, T., & Fornauf, B. S. (2019). Place matters: Review of the literature on rural teacher education. *Teaching and Teacher Education, 80*(1), 83–93. https://doi.org/10.1016/j.tate.2018.12.005

Rhinesmith, E., Anglum, J. C., Parl, A., & Burrola, A. (2023). Recruiting and retaining teachers in rural schools: A systematic review of the literature. *Peabody Journal of Education, 98*(4), 347–363. https://doi.org/10.1080/0161956X.2023.2238491

Rooks, D. (2018). The unintended consequences of cohorts: How social relationships can influence the retention of rural teachers recruited by cohort-based alternative pathway programs. *Journal of Research in Rural Education, 33*(9). https://jrre.psu.edu/sites/default/files/2019-08/33-9.pdf

Rosenberg, L., Christianson, M. D., & Hague Angus, M. (2015). Improvement efforts in rural schools: Experiences of nine schools receiving school improvement grants. *Peabody Journal of Education, 90*(2), 194–210. https://doi.org/10.1080/0161956X.2015.1022109

Saw, G. K., & Agger, C. A. (2021). STEM pathways of rural and small-town students: Opportunities to learn, aspirations, preparation, and college enrollment. *Educational Researcher, 50*(9), 595–606. https://doi.org/10.3102/0013189X211027528

Schafft, K. A. (2016). Rural education as rural development: Understanding the rural school–community well-being linkage in a 21st-century policy context. *Peabody Journal of Education, 91*(2), 137–154. https://doi.org/10.1080/0161956X.2016.1151734

Schmitt, J., & deCourcy, K. (2022). *The pandemic has exacerbated a long-standing national shortage of teachers.* Economic Policy Institute. https://www.epi.org/publication/shortage-of-teachers/

Schulte, A. K. (2018). Connecting to students through place. *The Rural Educator, 39*(2), 13–20. https://doi.org/10.35608/ruraled.v39i2.201

Showalter, D., Hartman, S. L., Eppley, K., Johnson, J., & Klein, R. (2023). *Why rural matters 2023: Centering equity and opportunity.* National Rural Education Association. https://scholarsjunction.msstate.edu/cgi/viewcontent.cgi?article=1441&context=ruraleducator

Showalter, D., Hartman, S. L., Johnson, J., & Klein, B. (2019). *Why rural matters 2018-2019: The time is now.* Rural School and Community Trust. https://files.eric.ed.gov/fulltext/ED604580.pdf

Showalter, D., Klein, R., Johnson, J., & Hartman, S. (2017). *Why rural matters 2015-2016: Understanding the changing landscape.* Rural School and Community Trust. https://files.eric.ed.gov/fulltext/ED590169.pdf

Shume, T., Bowen, B. D., Altimus, J., & Kallmeyer, A. (2022). Rural secondary STEM teachers' understanding of the engineering design process: Impacts of participation in a Research Experiences for Teachers program. *Theory & Practice in Rural Education, 12*(2), 89–103. https://vtechworks.lib.vt.edu/bitstreams/4cc29f38-1627-4f51-ad9b-aa1b64b6af88/download

Skyhar, C. L. (2020). Thinking outside the box: Providing effective professional development for rural teachers. *Theory & Practice in Rural Education, 10*(1), 42–72. https://tpre.ecu.edu/index.php/tpre/article/download/42/49

Stoehr, K. J., & Civil, M. (2019). Conversations between preservice teachers and Latina mothers: An avenue to transformative mathematics teaching. *Journal of Latinos and Education*, 1–13. https://doi.org/10.1080/15348431.2019.1653300

Thiele, J., & Bogdon, O. (2022). Building a virtual STEM professional learning network for rural teachers. *Theory & Practice in Rural Education, 12*(2), Article 2. https://doi.org/10.3776/tpre.2022.v12n2p129-151

Thompson, S. L., Curcio, R., Adgerson, A., Harbour, K. E., D'Amico, L. K., West, H. S., Roy, G. J., Baker, M. A., Guest, J., & Compton-Lilly, C. (2022). Virtual summer institutes as a method of rural science teacher development. *Theory & Practice in Rural Education, 12*(2), 153–178. https://doi.org/10.3776/tpre.2022.v12n2p153-178

Tran, H., Hardie, S., Gause, S., Moyi, P., & Ylimaki, R. (2020). Leveraging the perspectives of rural educators to develop realistic job previews for rural teacher recruitment and retention. *Rural Educator, 41*(2), 31–46. https://files.eric.ed.gov/fulltext/EJ1277657.pdf

Tran, H., & Smith, D. (2019). Insufficient money and inadequate respect: What obstructs the recruitment of college students to teach in hard-to-staff schools. *Journal of Educational Administration, 57*(2), 152–166.

Ulferts, J. D. (2016). A brief summary of teacher recruitment and retention in the smallest Illinois rural schools. *The Rural Educator, 37*(1), 14–24. https://files.eric.ed.gov/fulltext/EJ1225312.pdf

Vernikoff, L., Schram, T., Reagan, E. M., Horn, C., Goodwin, A. L., & Couse, L. J. (2019). Beyond urban or rural: Field-based experiences for teaching residencies in diverse contexts. In T. E. Hodges, & A. C. Baum (Eds.), *Handbook of research on field-based teacher education* (pp. 256–279). IGI Global.

Versland, T., Will, K., Lux, N., & Hicks, J. (2020). Envisioning the rural practicum: A means to positively affect recruitment and retention in rural schools. *Theory & Practice in Rural Education*, *10*(1), 103–118. https://scholarworks.montana.edu/server/api/core/bitstreams/37609a4b-7380-466c-9fad-dcaf688c248f/content

Walker-Gibbs, B., Ludecke, M., & Kline, J. (2015). Pedagogy of the rural: Implications of size on conceptualisations of rural. *International Journal of Pedagogies and Learning*, *10*(1), 81–89. https://doi.org/10.1080/22040552.2015.1086292

Yoon, S. Y., Mihaley, K., & Moore, A. (2019). *A snapshot of educator mobility in Montana: Understanding issues of educator shortages and turnover*. Regional Laboratory Northwest. https://files.eric.ed.gov/fulltext/ED598943.pdf

7

STEM Education and Workforce Development Infrastructure and Materials

We turn now to a discussion of infrastructure and materials as important factors for driving change in rural science, technology, engineering, and mathematics (STEM) education and workforce development. Specifically, we examine material resources, facilities and spaces, and technology. Material resources include lab equipment and other dedicated space and materials for science investigations, purchased curricula for in-school and out-of-school learning, and learning resources (e.g., books, programs, supplies). Facilities and spaces include school STEM learning spaces (e.g., science labs, computer labs); museums; public libraries; parks and recreational spaces; local farms; and businesses and hospitals that may collaborate on experiential learning and workforce training opportunities with rural schools and districts. Technology includes broadband access, classroom and workplace technologies, virtual and remote learning technologies, and digital devices.

Infrastructure, material resources, and technology contribute to the academic and future success of students (Barrett et al., 2019; National Center for Education Statistics [NCES], 2018). But access to and quality of these resources vary significantly among rural schools, districts, and communities because of inequitable funding and opportunities (Showalter et al., 2023). We explore rural challenges related to policy, funding, and larger structural challenges (e.g., rural housing crisis, school and hospital consolidations and closures, economic and workforce changes). We then consider rural assets, resources, and opportunities—such as natural resources, tight-knit networks and communities, and community-employer-school partnerships—that can be leveraged and better supported to advance STEM education and workforce development. We end with promising and emerging strategies for improving infrastructure and access to resources.

INFRASTRUCTURAL AND MATERIALS-BASED CHALLENGES TO STEM EDUCATION IN RURAL SETTINGS

Material Resources

Material resources are often a barrier to offering high-quality STEM learning and workforce development programs in rural areas. High-quality STEM education requires a variety of instructional resources, such as lab equipment,[1] and acquiring and maintaining these materials can create challenges for rural schools. In fact, rural teachers have identified a lack of resources as a major barrier to implementing STEM teaching standards (Sandholtz & Ringstaff, 2020). Career and Technical Education (CTE) programs, for instance, often need specialized equipment that can be difficult to find or fund in rural areas and prevent schools from offering the programs (Advance CTE, 2017). Similarly, coding classes require computers and devices for students, and the lack of such equipment compromises rural schools' ability to offer the classes (Grimes et al., 2019). Rural public libraries also have fewer and older public access computers than urban libraries (Real & Rose, 2019); these computers may be a critical resource for patrons without a home computer or internet access to apply to college, for example, or research industry programs. Rural teachers and afterschool providers may have to use their own resources to equip their programs. Research indicates that, during the pandemic, school librarians who spent their own money on books and supplies worked at rural schools with high rates of students receiving free and reduced-price lunch (Kammer et al., 2022).

Time is another resource that rural students may lack (Grimes et al., 2019). Those who live far from school may spend hours in transit each day. Not only may STEM extracurriculars be difficult for them to travel to, but, with so much time spent on the bus, these students have little free time to devote to the activities.

Another major challenge is limited occupational diversity and relatively few industry partners in rural areas (Grimes et al., 2019; Lakin et al., 2021; Sutton et al., 2016). Rural communities can be economically dependent on a single industry, such as mining, agriculture, or prisons (Eason, 2010; Huling, 2001). Such dependence limits both students' exposure to the vast array of STEM industries and fields and the number of potential partners to hire interns, train apprentices, offer field trips, or cohost workforce development training.

---

[1] https://stemopportunityindex.com/

It also means that rural youth may have little exposure to STEM careers or opportunities for informal mentorship (Rogers & Sun, 2019).

Even spatial inequities that appear unrelated to STEM education and workforce training can impact them. For example, the rural housing crisis, especially a lack of high-quality, affordable rental properties (Housing Assistance Council, 2020), may make it difficult for schools to hire and retain teachers. (Chapter 2 discusses other spatial inequities related to rural communities.)

Education Deserts

Rural communities often lack the institutions—libraries, museums, and afterschool programs—that are important sites of informal STEM learning. Only 12 percent of children's museums are located in rural areas (Association of Children's Museums, 2015, quoted in Hartman et al., 2017). And although rural areas are well equipped with public libraries—about one third of all U.S. public libraries are in rural areas—they often provide fewer services than urban libraries, including fewer afterschool opportunities and STEM programming (Real & Rose, 2017). They also have fewer employees and older and smaller facilities than urban libraries, and their isolation can create unique challenges; for example, they are less likely than urban libraries to be part of a multiple-branch system, which can raise costs. A lack of local partners can also limit the STEM workshops and programming that libraries can provide (Davis et al., 2018), and transportation-related barriers can prevent rural residents from accessing library services (Real & Rose, 2017). Rural children also have fewer opportunities to participate in afterschool or summer programming, and when programming is available it can be cost prohibitive for low-income rural families (Afterschool Alliance, 2021).

Many rural communities are education deserts, which obviously shapes access to high-quality STEM education and workforce development. This limited educational access begins at a young age, with large swaths of rural America lacking early childhood education programs (National Advisory Committee on Rural Health and Human Services, 2023). About 60 percent of rural communities are childcare deserts—that is, areas without an adequate supply of licensed child care (Malik et al., 2018). Given the well-documented academic and employment benefits of early childhood education (Belfield, 2006; Campbell et al., 2002; Phillips et al., 2017), this lack can have profound short- and long-term effects on rural youth. It also matters for STEM education specifically. The incorporation of STEM activities in early childhood education settings can boost STEM skills, foster STEM career aspirations, and support children's and parents' positive attitudes toward STEM learning (Wan et al., 2020). Without childcare options, many rural youth and families may miss out on this formative STEM experience.

Researchers have also documented education deserts at the postsecondary level (Hillman, 2016; Hillman & Weichman, 2016; Rosenboom & Blagg, 2018). College deserts are places with no institutions of higher education or where a single community college is the only public option, and they are disproportionately located in rural places. In addition, rural areas have fewer four-year and more two-year colleges (Hillman, 2016). Proximity also matters: the likelihood that a student will apply to college increases with each additional school nearby (Turley, 2009), and more than half of students attend college within 50 miles of their hometown (Hillman et al., 2021). So the lack of nearby postsecondary options limits students' STEM and career opportunities and pathways. Furthermore, rural institutions of higher education may be underfunded, compromising their capacity for outreach and programming. Tribal colleges and universities, for example, enroll high proportions of students living in poverty, limiting their tuition revenue, and they receive little state support (Nelson & Frye, 2016).

Finally, many rural communities face the closure of their K–12 schools. These closures disproportionately affect poorer rural communities or rural areas with more students of color (Tieken & Auldridge-Reveles, 2019). District officials often make the decision to close schools because of low enrollment or budget shortfalls; policies that incentivize district consolidation are another major cause of school closures (Tieken & Auldridge-Reveles, 2019). Yet district consolidation and school closures may not create the efficiencies hoped for (Cooley & Floyd, 2013; Howley et al., 2011). For example, if teacher salaries differ, the higher pay scale often prevails, and increased capital expenditures can also reduce savings (Duncombe & Yinger, 2001). Consolidation and closure may also fail to improve student performance (Cooley & Floyd, 2013) and have long-term negative impacts on postsecondary attainment and employment (Kim, 2024).

School closure risks limiting educational access. Students whose schools are closed often face longer, more dangerous bus rides (Deeb-Sossa & Moreno, 2016; Spence, 1998), participate in fewer extracurricular activities (Graham et al., 2014; Lipman, 2014), and experience less parent involvement (Deeds & Pattillo, 2015; Lipman, 2014; Spence, 1998)—all of which may affect access to STEM learning. Finally, closure often eliminates an institution important to the community's economic, social, and political well-being (Tieken, 2014). "It is like having your arm chopped off one inch at a time," one rural superintendent said (Chance & Cummins, 1998, p. 4). It's not surprising, then, that policies promoting consolidation and closure erode trust in state government; local residents feel like the state is trying to "get rid of small rural districts" (Tieken, 2014, p. 108), limiting the potential for responsive and effective education and economic policymaking.

Broadband Access

One of the most critical inequities facing rural communities related to STEM education and workforce development is the lack of reliable high-speed internet access, which is essential for effective use of digital tools in education (Center for Public Education, 2023; Federal Communications Commission [FCC], 2024; Stenberg et al., 2009). Though more schools now have strong internet connectivity—in fact, nearly three quarters of all districts now meet or surpass the FCC's bandwidth recommendation of 1 Mpbs per student (NCES, 2023)—almost 25 percent of schools do not meet that limit, and many students do not have a robust connection at home.

According to the FCC (2024), approximately 19 million people in rural America still lack access to broadband internet. At the FCC's new benchmark speed of 100/20 Mbps, 72 percent of rural areas and 76 percent of tribal areas have access to fixed broadband (which includes technologies such as T1, cable, DSL, and FiOS and excludes cellular data), compared to 98 percent of urban areas (FCC, 2024, pp. 32–33).[2] Access is even more limited for rural students living in poverty (NCES, 2023). In addition, while about 63 percent of urban households have at least two provider options at this speed, fewer than 24 percent of rural households and 31 percent of households on tribal land do (FCC, 2024, pp. 37–38). Quoting the Wireless Infrastructure Association, the FCC (2024, p. 7) also notes the challenge of affordability: "For many Americans on the wrong side of the digital divide the biggest barrier is not the availability of service but the lack of resources to connect." In addition, rural households appear less likely to take advantage of subsidies than urban ones (Galperin, 2022). The spatial gap in access overlaps with a racial gap: rural Black and Latine households are significantly less likely to have access (Center for Public Education, 2023; Wright, 2023). For people without reliable internet access at home, rural public libraries are an important site for access to the internet, but they too are less likely than urban libraries to have high-speed internet connections (Real & Rose, 2017).

These limitations have serious implications for rural STEM learning and workforce development. One of several significant roles for internet technology in rural K–12 schools is the enhancement of educational resources and learning opportunities through digital learning materials, online courses, and virtual classrooms that can supplement traditional resources and practices. For instance, with reliable internet access students

[2]With increased attention to broadband access and new federal and state resources, the landscape of broadband access is changing quickly. However, although the gap in rural versus urban access has decreased over time, it persists (Vogels, 2021).

in remote areas can participate in Advanced Placement courses, advanced CTE courses, dual enrollment courses, or specialized programs not available locally, thereby expanding their academic horizons and improving their college readiness (Means et al., 2009). Related, the digital divide can also compromise training for STEM fields that rely on the internet, like coding (Grimes et al., 2019). In addition, teachers without adequate access to the internet are not able to access STEM professional development remotely—or colleagues, pedagogical resources, support services, or opportunities for collaboration with peers in other areas (Harris, 2016).

Even with adequate internet connectivity, rural schools encounter challenges in integrating internet technologies. One problem is inadequate schoolwide infrastructure. Limited budgets often mean that schools cannot afford the necessary hardware, software, and IT support required to implement and maintain modern technological systems. The cost of upgrading infrastructure, purchasing devices, and training staff can be prohibitive, leaving rural schools lagging behind their urban counterparts (Johnson, 2017). Furthermore, there are pedagogical challenges related to the integration of technology. Teachers in rural schools may not be adequately trained or resourced to incorporate digital tools effectively in their instruction. Professional development and support are often scarce, and without proper training, the potential of associated technologies to enhance learning may not be fully realized (Ertmer & Ottenbreit-Leftwich, 2010).

Addressing these challenges requires a multifaceted approach. Investments in rural broadband infrastructure are necessary but not sufficient to ensure that all students and educators have access to high-speed internet. Without ongoing support to routinely update and upgrade hardware and software, readiness for accessioning technology upgrades, professional development, and the like, rural schools will continue to struggle with resource gaps that interfere with competitive educational outcomes for their students. Policymakers have a role in prioritizing funding and support for rural schools to bridge financial and teacher resource gaps. Professional development programs that address rural contexts are also needed to equip teachers with the skills to integrate technology in their classrooms effectively and promote student success (Best & Cohen, 2014).

Funding

Rural STEM resources, facilities, and other infrastructure are often lacking because of insufficient funding. Rural superintendents cite low funds as one of their biggest challenges (Williams & Nierengarten, 2011; Yettick et al., 2014). Because much of school funding depends on property taxes, areas with low property wealth have trouble raising funds to adequately cover costs (Strange, 2011); many rural communities, especially those with high rates of poverty and larger Black, Indigenous, and Latine communities, have low property values (Tieken, 2017). In addition, federal Title I policy can disadvantage sparsely populated low-income rural districts. Many rural districts also have unique costs that can raise budgets, such as transportation, and small enrollments can limit economies of scale and inflate per-pupil costs (Sipple & Brent, 2012; Strange, 2003).

State and federal governments try to compensate for these funding inequities; states may offer additional funding for schools with small populations or in isolated areas (Kolbe et al., 2021; Sielke, 2004), and the federal government provides funds to support rural schools through the Rural Education Achievement Program[3] (Shavers, 2003). Yet concerns persist that these sources are inadequate for offsetting the higher costs and limited local resources of rural districts (Kim, 2021; Strange, 2011), and inadequate funding may be a major cause of educational inequities, including those related to STEM and workforce development.

INFRASTRUCTURAL AND MATERIALS-BASED ASSETS FOR STEM EDUCATION IN RURAL COMMUNITIES

Though rural communities face serious challenges and inequities in their efforts to provide STEM education, they also enjoy some important assets. Perhaps one of the most meaningful is access to the natural environment (Flora & Flora, 2008; Hellsten et al., 2011; Sandholtz & Ringstaff, 2020). Many rural communities have substantial natural resources with diverse plant and animal life in close proximity: forests, mountains, streams, fields, riverbeds, tundra, and lakes. These resources can provide rich opportunities for place-based education across STEM disciplines (Corbett, 2020; Grimes et al., 2019; Harris & Hodges, 2018; Lakin et al., 2021; NSF, 2024; Sobel, 2004), like studying frog life cycles in a local pond, coastal erosion at a local beach, or the impact of an invasive insect species on local crop production.

Natural resources shape the economies of many rural communities, and the associated economic activities can provide opportunities for STEM learning and workforce preparation (Smith & Sobel, 2010). Many rural youth learn STEM trades, like fishing or maple sugaring, by engaging in these practices at home. Because the natural resources that these industries rely on are accessible, and because local economies are so dependent on these trades, rural youth often have ample opportunities to develop these skills at a young age. These activities not only help develop the future workforce but also hone discrete STEM knowledge and skills: by observing

---

[3]https://www.ed.gov/grants-and-programs/formula-grants/rural-education-achievement-program

local fish counts, youth may learn about the impact of global warming, and by estimating how much syrup a bucket of sap will yield, youth may learn about ratios. This kind of continuous, informal STEM learning is often overlooked in assessments of rural youth achievement.

The rich cultural resources of rural communities can similarly support directed STEM learning (Moll et al., 1992; Topkok & Loon, 2021). Educators can leverage local rural knowledge (see Chapter 5 for a discussion of LRK) and Indigenous knowledge to create learning opportunities that are relevant and culturally sustaining.

Despite the relative lack of partnering institutions, those that are available in rural communities are often very committed to local education. For example, school staff and other educators work with local STEM-based industries to host events like career days or support afterschool programming (Grimes et al., 2019; Lakin et al., 2021). These events may help showcase the variety of paths—requiring college or not—to a STEM career, and they are "important in disputing the myth that STEM careers are far away and require a business suit" (Grimes et al., 2019, p. 81).

Local universities are also important partners (Crumb et al., 2022). They can help support postsecondary aspirations and connect local schools to governmental and private funding sources (Casto et al., 2016). Rural community colleges and tribal colleges are valuable sites for STEM learning and workforce development. They offer critical educational programs and training that build not only the workforce but also infrastructure and trust. In sparsely populated, underresourced rural places, they might be one of few institutions with the facilities and relationships necessary to spark economic development and drive economic activity. The Richmond Federal Reserve Bank, in fact, categorizes rural community colleges as "anchor institutions" (Norris et al., 2023). They may provide services, such as public computer labs and day care, and resources, such as an observatory or a library, that are critical to local STEM education and workforce development. In addition, the long-standing 4-H program[4] run through cooperative extension programs at over 100 public universities and available in every state, offers STEM and agricultural programming to students, including those in rural areas.

Rural community colleges and tribal colleges can also undertake infrastructure projects, like refurbishing a downtown, or house cultural projects, such as language preservation, that indirectly support a strong rural workforce (Bombardieri & Horwedel, 2022; Katsinas & Hardy, 2012; Norris et al., 2023). Some federal programs are expanding investments in education and workforce development at tribal colleges and universities (Head Start, 2023).

Although rural public libraries may lack the resources, capacity, and connectivity of more urban libraries, they play an outsized educational role

[4]https://4-h.org/programs/

in rural communities. They are more likely than urban or town libraries to offer patrons support in accessing online degree coursework, whether for high school, trade school, or certification programs (Real & Rose, 2017). And despite the relative lack of children's museums, there are other types of museums—in fact, as mentioned in Chapter 3, one in four U.S. museums is located in a rural area—and they serve as "community anchors" for cultural and STEM learning.[5]

In addition, many rural school districts partner to share services through education collaboratives (Brent et al., 2004; Broton et al., 2009). Through these collaboratives—known as *education cooperatives*, *educational service centers*, or *boards of cooperative educational services*—school districts pool resources and share opportunities. For example, students may take specialized STEM courses in other districts, districts may share a STEM coach, or STEM coordinators may share classroom materials or lab equipment between schools across district lines. These collaboratives can be critical in helping districts avoid consolidation and school closure (Howley et al., 2012).

Finally, more generally, rural K–12 schools are integral to the well-being of rural communities (DeYoung, 1995; Schafft, 2016; Tieken, 2014). They may be a community's largest employer, offering stable, well-paying, middle-class jobs to residents (Tieken, 2014). And they shape the social fabric of rural communities; they are a site for both youth and adults to gather, whether in classrooms or at Friday night basketball games or for community suppers, and, in these spaces, relationships are nurtured and grown. In some places, where schools pull together people across lines of race and class, they can have a significant influence on integration. Schools can help sustain cultural practices, such as maintaining home languages, or traditions, like homecoming events. They are also a source of political power, as schools are governed by a locally elected school board; this power may be especially important for historically marginalized populations. In all these ways, rural schools can have important social, cultural, political, and economic benefits to rural communities, and any reform to rural education must take into account this critical role.

PROMISING AND EMERGING STRATEGIES

This chapter ends with promising and emerging strategies for advancing infrastructure and material resources that could enchange rural STEM education and workforce development. The committee has identified strategies that leverage rural community assets and resources and that address inequitable infrastructure and technology access in rural communities.

[5]https://www.aam-us.org/wp-content/uploads/2024/02/Museum-Facts-2024.pdf

Research-Practice Partnerships for STEM Learning

Research-practice partnerships are "long-term, mutualistic collaborations between practitioners and researchers that are intentionally organized to investigate problems of practice and solutions for improving" learning, outcomes, and processes (Coburn et al., 2013, p. 2). They have been leveraged to specifically improve STEM learning, experiences, and outcomes (Bhaduri et al., 2022; Penuel, 2020) and can expand out-of-school spaces for STEM learning, relationships with local STEM-related businesses, and access to STEM technologies for rural youth (Bhaduri et al., 2022). In one such partnership, STEM Career Connections (STEMCC), researchers, educators (school district and postsecondary education), and STEM-related business leaders and professionals in a rural community collaborated to develop and implement STEM experiences for middle school youth through in- and out-of-school learning spaces, such as afterschool programs and summer camps (Bhaduri et al., 2022). In the out-of-school learning spaces, youth had the opportunity to engage in activities that advanced their knowledge of STEM technology (e.g., "designing, programming, and building sensor-integrated physical computing systems; designing, revising, and creating 3D printed animal prosthetics;" Bhaduri et al., 2022, p. 53). In addition, local STEM-related professionals served as mentors to the youth to support their STEM learning. STEMCC expanded students' STEM skills, increased their interest in STEM careers, and led to the development of STEM practices and resources that support STEM learning and pathways for rural youth (Bhaduri et al., 2022).

Work-Based Experiences for STEM Learning

Public-private-nonprofit partnerships can be essential for coordinating and collaborating on STEM learning opportunities such as internships and apprenticeships (Mathieson et al., 2023; Ross et al., 2020). One such example is a partnership codesigned by Rural Action and Building Bridges to Careers to offer a high school internship program in Appalachian Ohio (Ricket et al., 2023). Internship host sites include local businesses, nonprofits, community- and public-based organizations, and large employers, many of them in the agriculture, health science, and STEM sectors. Internship participants explore local career opportunities and can envision remaining in their communities. The internship experiences also help students expand their social networks and build soft skills.

STEM Learning in Rural Public Libraries

Rural libraries can be a critical learning space and facility for STEM learning and workforce development (Real & Rose, 2017). The national

STAR Net STEAM Equity Project—an U.S. National Science Foundation (NSF)-funded collaborative initiative of the American Library Association, National Center for Interactive Learning at the Space Science Institute, Twin Cities PBS, Institute for Learning Innovation, and Education Development Center—engages staff at 12 rural public libraries in largely Hispanic communities with community partners to collaborate on providing STEAM learning opportunities for rural youth.[6] The project hosts traveling STEAM exhibitions and the development of a STEAM learning space in each library.

STEM Learning in Outdoor Spaces

Many rural communities have access to natural resources and spaces that can be leveraged to enhance STEM learning (Corbett, 2020; Grimes et al., 2019; Harris & Hodges, 2018; Lakin et al., 2021; NSF, 2024). With NSF funding, the Center for Applied Special Technology (an education research organization), the University of New Hampshire, and outdoor recreational and STEM youth-based organizations in New Hampshire collaborated to investigate how outdoor recreation shapes STEM learning and identity development for rural youth in the state.[7] The findings indicate that outdoor recreation spaces can facilitate STEM interest and engagement (Bastoni et al., 2024). As described in Chapter 5, STEM learning ecosystems connect schools and community-based organizations to support outdoor STEM learning experiences.

Broadband and Technology Access Initiatives

Rural students, districts, businesses, and communities are often disadvantaged by lack of broadband access (FCC, 2024; Stenberg et al., 2009). Two FCC programs that demonstrated success with broadband and technology access were the Affordable Connectivity Program and Emergency Connectivity Fund; both ended in 2024 because of lack of renewed funding from Congress. The Affordable Connectivity Program (ACP) ran from December 2021 until June 2024 and provided eligible, low-income consumers "a discount of up to $30 per month toward internet service and up to $75 per month for households on qualifying Tribal Lands."[8] In addition, "eligible households could also receive a one-time discount of up to $100 to purchase a laptop, desktop computer, or tablet from participating internet companies if the household contributed more than $10 and less than $50 toward the purchase price." Over 23 million households participated in ACP, including approximately 3.45 million rural households (FCC, 2024).

[6]https://www.ala.org/news/2020/05/ala-announces-steam-funding-and-exhibitions-rural-libraries-serving-latino-populations

[7]https://www.cast.org/our-work/projects/outdoor-recreation-connecting-rural-youth-stem-careers

[8]FCC Affordable Connectivity Program has ended for now, https://www.fcc.gov/acp

The Emergency Connectivity Fund was authorized as part of the American Rescue Plan Act of 2021 and ended in June 2024. It provided "funding to schools and libraries for the reasonable costs of eligible equipment and services that can be provided to students, teachers, and library patrons who lack connected devices" such as laptop or tablet computers, Wi-Fi hotspots, modems, and routers. The initiative "funded nearly 13 million connected devices and more than 8 million broadband connections."[9]

Although these federal programs have ended, the Broadband Equity Access and Deployment Program (BEAD), funded by the Bipartisan Infrastructure Law of 2022, is a federal grant program aimed at getting all Americans connected to the internet with 100/20 Mbps by 2026. The 50 states, Washington, DC, Puerto Rico, and all U.S. territories were eligible to apply for BEAD funding to contract with local internet providers to build infrastructure for places not adequately or affordably connected to the internet. The National Telecommunications and Information Administration (NTIA) in the U.S. Department of Commerce provides guidance for states using BEAD dollars through a "cascade of options".[10] First, states are directed to pursue partnerships with providers offering Fiber to the Home infrastructure. In areas where fiber costs are prohibitive, NTIA suggests other reliable broadband technologies like coaxial cable or licensed fixed wireless. For very remote communities where none of these technologies may be feasible, NTIA advises that states fund providers of alternative technologies such as Unlicensed Fixed Wireless or Low Earth Orbit satellites (at this time Geostationary Orbit satellite is not eligible for BEAD funding).

Additionally, NTIA maintains a list of about 100 federal programs that support high-speed internet connectivity and adoption.[11] The programs are located across 13 federal agencies, and while some programs focus only on rural areas, many serve all communities. Because each has "its own application process and reporting requirements, definition of rural and other eligibility requirements, timeframe, and level of funding" (Pipa et al., 2023, p. 11), rural communities with few human resources may not be able to apply.

Separate from how states use federal grant money to support internet connectivity, state-level policies can affect access to and adoption of high-speed connectivity. A study of 2012–2018 data found that restrictions on cooperative and municipal connectivity efforts (i.e., privatization of broadband access) decreased availability but that offices and dedicated funding at the state level can improve it (Whitacre & Gallardo, 2020). More recently, states are administering federal funding to improve access and adoption. While states use a variety of efforts, such as offices or task forces (Read &

[9]https://www.fcc.gov/emergency-connectivity-fund-faqs

[10]NTIA.gov

[11]https://broadbandusa.ntia.doc.gov/resources/federal/federal-funding

Gong, 2022), the NTIA convenes a network of state broadband leaders to discuss best practices and improve coordination across federal agencies, states, and localities.[12]

Many state legislatures enacted policies and leveraged federal funding to expand broadband access and digital device access in response to the COVID-19 pandemic (Brixey, 2021). For instance, New Mexico appropriated funds from 2021 to 2026 "for the development of statewide broadband to support education" (Brixey, 2021, para. 8) and passed Connect New Mexico to expand broadband access across the state.[13] In Idaho the state legislature appropriated over $26 million to support "classroom technology, classroom technology infrastructure, wireless technology infrastructure, and learning management systems that assist teachers and students in effective and efficient instruction or learning" (Brixey, 2021, para. 10). In addition, states and school districts have begun investing in wireless routers and Wi-Fi hotspots on public school buses (Bartlett et al., 2023–2024; NCES, 2018), which supports students in doing and completing academic work (NCES, 2018).

SUMMARY AND CONCLUSIONS

This chapter provides an overview of infrastructure and access to material resources needed in rural areas to support effective learning experiences in STEM. Rural communities often lack easy and affordable access to material goods that affect their schools' ability to support STEM learning either directly (e.g., with lab equipment) or indirectly (e.g., through available and affordable housing for the STEM teacher workforce to buy or rent). Learning facilities themselves, both formal and informal, can be few and far between in rural America, especially as some rural schools, institutions of higher education, libraries, and museums close, reduce hours and/or services, or are understaffed because of policy and/or budget constraints.

Not only is physical infrastructure for STEM learning in rural areas often out of date or nonexistent, but digital infrastructure as basic as affordable access to broadband is slow to reach rural and remote areas. State and federal money can partially offset budgetary shortfalls contributing to this problem but is often not enough to make necessary improvements to physical or digital infrastructure and materials needed for effective, consistent STEM learning experiences in all rural places across the country.

Even with these infrastructural challenges (and in some cases because of them), rural areas have numerous, rich assets that educators can and do leverage to connect students to authentic STEM learning. Rural schools are often close to natural areas and students come to learning settings with a

---

[12]https://broadbandusa.ntia.doc.gov/resources/states

[13]https://connect.nm.gov/

deep understanding of the natural world as a result. Engineering and mathematical reasoning form a foundational part of how many rural students navigate through their daily lives. Educators and students alike draw on local rural knowledge in pursuing STEM learning goals.

Many of the promising strategies to connect rural communities to effective STEM learning opportunities for life, future education, and work leverage assets at the heart of rural communities. State and federally funded programs to address inequities in rural communities should empower local entities to design solutions for their problems by building on resources, assets, and strengths embedded in the diverse, vibrant places they seek to improve.

Conclusion 7-1: Many rural districts and schools lack adequate infrastructure and materials to support high-quality STEM education and workforce development. Specifically, they often have old buildings with outdated systems; lack dedicated space, equipment, and materials for science investigations; lack access to fast and affordable broadband; and have insufficient funding. Strategies for addressing these challenges include

- *research-practice partnerships;*
- *leveraging rural public libraries, government/business facilities, and outdoor spaces;*
- *online courses and resources; and*
- *initiatives to expand and enhance broadband access and speed.*

Conclusion 7-2: Inequitable access to broadband in rural communities leads to challenges with STEM education and workforce development and digital literacy in preparation for work and life. However, broadband access alone will not solve or fix access to STEM education and workforce development opportunities and resources.

Conclusion 7-3: Recent legislation has led to large investments in broadband connectivity across the United States, and many federal and state agencies are working to improve broadband access and adoption. But it is difficult to determine the extent to which these efforts will address broadband-related challenges for K–12 STEM education in rural areas because

- *the efforts are not well coordinated,*
- *some do not attend to affordability, and*
- *broadband access alone cannot address lack of or outdated computers, routers, or other hardware.*

REFERENCES

Advance CTE. (2017). *CTE on the frontier: Catalyzing local efforts to improve program quality*. https://careertech.org/wp-content/uploads/2023/01/CTE_Frontier_Program_Quality_2017_0.pdf

Afterschool Alliance. (2021). *Spiking demand, growing barriers: The trends shaping afterschool and summer learning in rural communities*. https://afterschoolalliance.org/documents/AA3PM/AA3PM-Rural-Report-2021.pdf

Barrett, P., Treves, A., Shmis, T., Ambasz, D., & Ustinova, M. (2019). *The impact of school infrastructure on learning: A synthesis of the evidence*. World Bank. http://dx.doi.org/10.1596/978-1-4648-1378-8

Bartlett, J. B., Beyenhof, N., & Wynn, A. (2023–2024). Digital divide: Iowa's K-12 broadband access. *Hawkeye Policy Report*, 48–64. https://politicalscience.uiowa.edu/sites/politicalscience.uiowa.edu/files/2024-03/Hawkeye%20Policy%20Report%202023_2024_Final.pdf#page=49

Bastoni, A., Johnston, S. C., Coppens, A. D., Seaman, J., & Hartman, C. (2024). *STEM pathways for rural youth: Experience sampling feedback and scoring manual*. University of New Hampshire Faculty Publications. https://dx.doi.org/10.34051/p/2024.04

Belfield, C. R. (2006). Financing early childhood care and education: An international review. Paper for the 2007 UNESCO *Global Monitoring Report on Education for All*. https://repository.upenn.edu/server/api/core/bitstreams/37d58d63-c7c7-4f8d-9f4d-adfd482a5cba/content

Best, J., & Cohen, C. (2014). *Rural education: Examining capacity challenges that influence educator effectiveness*. McREL International. https://files.eric.ed.gov/fulltext/ED557596.pdf

Bhaduri, S., Biddy, Q., Elliott, C. H., Jacobs, J., Rummel, M., Ristvey, J., Sumner, T., & Recker, M. (2022). Co-designing a rural research practice partnership to design and support STEM pathways for rural youth. *Theory & Practice in Rural Education*, *12*(2). https://doi.org/10.3776/tpre.2022.v12n2p45-70

Bombardieri, M. S., & Horwedel, D. M. (2022, November 18). For Native Americans, tribal colleges tackle the "present-day work of our ancestors." *Center for American Progress*. https://www.americanprogress.org/article/for-native-americans-tribal-colleges-tackle-the-present-day-work-of-our-ancestors/

Brent, B. O., Sipple, J. W., Killeen, K., & Wischnowski, M. W. (2004). Stalking cost-effective practices in rural schools. *Journal of Education Finance*, *29*, 237–256. https://www.researchgate.net/publication/312759363_Stalking_cost-effective_practices_in_rural_schools

Brixey, E. (2021). *Response to information request*. Education Commission of the States. https://www.ecs.org/wp-content/uploads/State-Information-Request_Broadband-Access-Legislation.pdf

Broton, K., Mueller, D., Schultz, J. L., & Gaona, M. (2009). *Strategies for rural Minnesota school districts: A literature review*. Wilder Research. https://files.eric.ed.gov/fulltext/ED511604.pdf

Campbell, F. A., Ramey, C. T., Pungello, E., Sparling, J., & Miller-Johnson, S. (2002). Early childhood education: Young adult outcomes from the Abecedarian Project. *Applied Developmental Science*, *6*(1), 42–57. https://doi.org/10.1207/S1532480XADS0601_05

Casto, H., McGrath, B., Sipple, J., & Todd, L. (2016). "Community aware" education policy: Enhancing individual and community vitality. *Education Policy Analysis Archives*, *24*, 50. https://doi.org/10.14507/epaa.24.2148

Center for Public Education. (2023). *Educational equity for rural students: Out of the pandemic, but still out of the loop*. https://www.nsba.org/-/media/CPE-Parent-and-Community-Supports-Are-Assets-of-Rural-Schools.pdf

Chance, E. W., & Cummins, C. (1998). School/community survival: Successful strategies used in rural school district consolidations. *The Rural Educator*, *20*, 1–7.

Coburn, C. E., Penuel, W. R., & Geil, K. (2013). *Research-practice partnerships: A strategy for leveraging research for educational improvement in school districts.* White paper prepared for the William T. Grant Foundation. https://files.eric.ed.gov/fulltext/ED568396.pdf

Cooley, D. A., & Floyd, K. A. (2013). Small rural school district consolidation in Texas: An analysis of its impact on cost and student achievement. *Administrative Issues Journal, 3*(1), 45–63. https://files.eric.ed.gov/fulltext/EJ1056898.pdf

Corbett, M. (2020). Place-based education: A critical appraisal from a rural perspective. In M. Corbett & D. Gereluk (Eds.), *Rural teacher education: Connecting land and people* (pp. 279–298). Springer. https://doi.org/10.1007/978-981-15-2560-5_14

Crumb, L., Chambers, C. R., Azano, A. P., Hands, A. S., Cuthrell, K., & Avent, M. (2022). Rural cultural wealth: Dismantling deficit ideologies of rurality. *Journal for Multicultural Education, 17*(2), 125–138. https://www.emerald.com/insight/content/doi/10.1108/jme-06-2022-0076/full/pdf?title=rural-cultural-wealth-dismantling-deficit-ideologies-of-rurality

Davis, K., Subramaniam, M., Hoffman, K. M., & Romeijn-Stout, E. L. (2018). Technology use in rural and urban public libraries: Implication for connected learning in youth programming. *Proceedings of the Connected Learning Summit, Pittsburgh, PA*, 47–56.

Deeb-Sossa, N., & Moreno, M. (2016). ¡No cierren nuestra escuela! Farm worker mothers as cultural citizens in an educational community mobilization effort. *Journal of Latinos and Education, 15*(1), 39–57.

Deeds, V. R., & Pattillo, M. (2015). Organizational "failure" and institutional pluralism. *Urban Education, 50*, 474–504. http://dx.doi.org/10.1177/0042085913519337

DeYoung, A. J. (1995). *The life and death of a rural American high school (1995): Farewell Little Kanawha.* Routledge.

Duncombe, W., & Yinger, J. M. (2001). Does school district consolidation cut costs? *Education Finance and Policy, 2*, 341–375. https://doi.org/10.1162/edfp.2007.2.4.341

Eason, J. (2010). Mapping prison proliferation: Region, rurality, race and disadvantage in prison placement. *Social Science Research, 39*(6), 1015–1028. https://doi.org/10.1016/j.ssresearch.2010.03.001

Ertmer, P., & Ottenbreit-Leftwich, A. (2010). Teacher technology change: How knowledge, beliefs, and culture intersect. *Journal of Research on Technology in Education, 42*, 255–284. http://dx.doi.org/10.1080/15391523.2010.10782551

Federal Communications Commission (FCC). (2024). Inquiry concerning the deployment of advanced telecommunications capability to all Americans in a reasonable and timely fashion (GN Docket No. 22-270). https://docs.fcc.gov/public/attachments/FCC-24-27A1.pdf

Flora, C. B., & Flora, J. (2008). *Rural communities: Legacy and change* (3rd ed.). Westview Press.

Galperin, H. (2022). *Estimating participation in the Affordable Connectivity Program* (Policy Brief No. 2). USC Annenberg. https://arnicusc.org/wp-content/uploads/2022/10/Policy-Brief-2-ACP-eligibility-final-1.pdf

Graham, B. C., Keys, C. B., McMahon, S. D., & Brubacher, M. R. (2014). Transportation challenges for urban students with disabilities: Parent perspectives. *Journal of Prevention & Intervention in the Community, 42*(1), 45–57. https://doi.org/10.1080/10852352.2014.855058

Grimes, L. E., Arrastía-Chisholm, M. A., & Bright, S. B. (2019). How can they know what they don't know? The beliefs and experiences of rural school counselors about STEM career advising. *Theory & Practice in Rural Education, 9*(1), 74–90. https://doi.org/10.3776/tpre.2019.v9n1p74-90

Harris, J. (2016). Inservice teachers' TPACK development: Trends, models, and trajectories. In M. Herring, M. Koehler, & P. Mishra (Eds.), *Handbook of technological pedagogical content knowledge for educators* (2nd ed., pp. 191–205). Routledge.

Harris, R. S., & Hodges, C. B. (2018). STEM education in rural schools: Implications of untapped potential. *National Youth-At-Risk Journal*, *3*(1). https://files.eric.ed.gov/fulltext/EJ1269639.pdf

Hartman, S. L., Hines-Bergmeier, J., & Klein, R. (2017). Informal STEM learning: The state of research, access and equity in rural early childhood settings. *Science Education and Civic Engagement*, 9(2), 32–39. https://seceij.net/wp-content/uploads/2017/07/SENCEIJSummer2017_FINAL.pdf#page=32

Head Start. (2023). *Biden-Harris administration announces increased investment in Tribal Colleges and Universities–Head Start Partnership Program*. Administration for Children & Families, U.S. Department of Health & Human Services. https://eclkc.ohs.acf.hhs.gov/about-us/press-release/biden-harris-administration-announces-increased-investment-tribal-colleges-universities-head-start

Hellsten, L. A. M., McIntyre, L. J., & Prytula, M. P. (2011). Teaching in rural Saskatchewan: First year teachers identify challenges and make recommendations. *The Rural Educator*, *32*(3), 11–21. https://scholarsjunction.msstate.edu/cgi/viewcontent.cgi?article=1189&context=ruraleducator

Hillman, N., Colston, J., Bach-Hanson, J., & Peek, A. (2021). *Mapping rural colleges and their communities*. University of Wisconsin–Madison.

Hillman, N., & Weichman, T. (2016). *Education deserts: The continued significance of place in the twenty-first century*. American Council on Education. https://www.acenet.edu/Documents/Education-Deserts-The-Continued-Significance-of-Place-in-the-Twenty-First-Century.pdf

Hillman, N. W. (2016). Geography of college opportunity: The case of education deserts. *American Educational Research Journal*, *53*(4), 987–1021. https://doi.org/10.3102/0002831216653204

Housing Assistance Council. (2020). *Taking stock: Rural housing, rural people, and their homes*. https://takingstockrural.org/taking-stock/rural-housing/

Howley, A., Howley, M., Hendrickson, K., Belcher, J., & Howley, C. (2012). Stretching to survive: District autonomy in an age of dwindling resources. *Journal of Research in Rural Education*, *27*(3). https://jrre.psu.edu/sites/default/files/2019-08/27-3.pdf

Howley, C. B., Johnson, J., & Petrie, J. (2011). *Consolidation of schools and districts: What the research says and what it means*. National Education Policy Center. https://nepc.colorado.edu/publication/consolidation-schools-districts

Huling, T. (2001). Building a prison economy in rural America. In M. Mauer, & M. Chesney-Lind (Eds.), *Invisible punishment: The collateral consequences of mass imprisonment* (pp. 197–213). Free Press. https://www.prisonpolicy.org/scans/huling_chapter.pdf

Johnson, K. (2017). Where is rural America and who lives there? In A. Tickamyer, J. Warlick, & J. Sherman (Ed.), *Rural poverty in the United States* (pp. 1–27). Columbia University Press. https://doi.org/10.7312/tick17222-003

Kammer, J., Atkins, C., & Burress, R. (2022). The personal cost of small budgets & underfunded libraries: Out-of-pocket spending by school librarians during COVID-19. *School Library Research*, *25*. https://files.eric.ed.gov/fulltext/EJ1362293.pdf

Katsinas, S. G., & Hardy, D. E. (2012). Rural community colleges. In J. C. Smart & M. B. Paulsen (Eds.), *Higher education: Handbook of theory and research* (pp. 453–520). Springer.

Kim, J. (2024). *The long shadow of school closures: Impacts on students' educational and labor market outcomes* (EdWorkingPaper No. 24-963). Annenberg Institute at Brown University. https://doi.org/10.26300/ax4m-3z14

Kim, R. (2021). Under the law: The rights of rural students. *Phi Delta Kappan*, *103*(4), 64–65. https://doi.org/10.1177/00317217211065836

Kolbe, T., Baker, B. D., Atchison, D., Levin, J., & Harris, P. (2021). The additional cost of operating rural schools: Evidence from Vermont. *AERA Open*, *7*. https://doi.org/10.1177/2332858420988868

Lakin, J. M., Stambaugh, T., Ihrig, L. M., Mahatmya, D., & Assouline, S. G. (2021). Nurturing STEM talent in rural setting. *Phi Delta Kappan, 103*(4), 24–30. https://doi.org/10.1177/00317217211065823

Lipman, P. (2014). Capitalizing on crisis: Venture philanthropy's colonial project to remake urban education. *Critical Studies in Education, 56*, 241–258. https://doi.org/10.1080/17508487.2015.959031

Malik, R., Hamm, K., Schochet, L., Novoa, C., Workman, S., & Jessen-Howard, S. (2018). *America's child care deserts in 2018*. Center for American Progress. https://cdn.americanprogress.org/content/uploads/2018/12/06100537/AmericasChildCareDeserts20182.pdf

Mathieson, D., Cotrupi, C., Schilling, M., & Grohs, J. (2023). Resiliency through partnerships: Prioritizing STEM workforce pathways amid macro challenges. *School Science and Mathematics, 123*(3), 137–149. https://doi.org/10.1111/ssm.12575

Means, B., Toyama, Y., Murphy, R., Bakia, M., & Jones, K. (2009). *Evaluation of evidence-based practices in online learning: A meta-analysis and review of online learning studies*. U.S. Department of Education. https://files.eric.ed.gov/fulltext/ED505824.pdf

Moll, L. C., Amanti, C., Neff, D., & Gonzalez, N. (1992). Funds of Knowledge for teaching: Using a qualitative approach to connect homes and classrooms. *Theory into Practice, 31*(2), 132–141. http://www.jstor.org/stable/1476399

National Advisory Committee on Rural Health and Human Services. (2023). *Childcare need and availability in rural areas: Policy brief and recommendations to the Secretary*. https://www.hrsa.gov/sites/default/files/hrsa/advisory-committees/rural/nac-rural-child-care-brief-23.pdf

National Center for Education Statistics (NCES). (2018). *Student access to digital learning resources outside of the classroom* (NCES No. 2017098). U.S. Department of Education. https://nces.ed.gov/pubs2017/2017098/index.asp

———. (2023). *Rural students' access to the internet: Condition of education*. Institute of Education Sciences, U.S. Department of Education. https://nces.ed.gov/programs/coe/indicator/lfc

National Science Foundation (NSF). (2024). *Making visible the invisible: STEM talent of rural America*. https://nsf-gov-resources.nsf.gov/files/CEOSE_STEM-Talent_of_Rural_America_Report.pdf?VersionId=Jr.NV_HxMT0eVnFm12wZA5EPZ0DgxAXJ

Nelson, C., & Frye, J. R. (2016). *Tribal college and university funding: Tribal sovereignty at the intersection of federal, state, and local funding*. American Council on Education. https://vtechworks.lib.vt.edu/server/api/core/bitstreams/7ca9c93e-3ef4-4150-b926-39797476cfcd/content

Norris, S., Ullrich, L. D., & Waddell, S. R. (2023). District digest: Community colleges as anchor institutions in rural areas. *Econ Focus, 23*(3Q), 26–30. Federal Reserve Bank of Richmond. https://www.richmondfed.org/-/media/RichmondFedOrg/publications/research/econ_focus/2023/q3/district_digest.pdf

Penuel, W. R. (2020). Promoting equitable and just learning across settings: Organizational forms for educational change. In N. S. Nasir, C. D. Lee, R. Pea, & M. M. de Royston (Eds.), *Handbook of the cultural foundations of learning* (pp. 348–364). Routledge.

Phillips, D. A., Johnson, A. D., Weiland, C., & Hutchison, J. E. (2017). *Public preschool in a more diverse America: Implications for next-generation evaluation research* (Working Paper No. 2-17). Poverty Solutions at the University of Michigan.

Pipa, A. F., Landes, L., & Swarzenski, Z. (2023). *Maximizing new federal investments in broadband for rural America*. Center for Sustainable Development, Brookings Institution. https://communitiesu.org/assets/uploads/2023/07/Rural_Broadband-Published-5.31.2023-Catherine-Krantz-contributer-1.pdf

Read, A., & Gong, L. (2022, June 28). Which states have dedicated broadband offices, task forces, agencies, or funds? *Pew Charitable Trusts*. https://www.pewtrusts.org/en/research-and-analysis/articles/2021/06/28/which-states-have-dedicated-broadband-offices-task-forces-agencies-or-funds

Real, B., & Rose, R. N. (2017). *Rural libraries in the United States: Recent strides, future possibilities, and meeting community needs*. American Library Association. https://www.ala.org/sites/default/files/advocacy/content/pdfs/Rural%20paper%2007-31-2017.pdf

Ricket, A. L., Yahn, J., & Bentley, E. (2023). Rural community and career connected learning: Impacts of high school internships prioritizing people and place. *Journal of Research in Rural Education, 39*(3). https://doi.org/10.26209/JRRE3903

Rogers, R. R., & Sun, Y. (Eds.). (2019). *Engaging STEM Students from rural areas: Emerging research and opportunities*. IGI Global.

Rosenboom, V., & Blagg, K. (2018). *Disconnected from higher education: How geography and internet speed limit access to higher education*. Urban Institute. https://www.urban.org/sites/default/files/publication/96191/disconnected_from_higher_education_1.pdf

Ross, D. A., Hinton, R., Melles-Brewer, M., Engel, D., Zeck, W., Fagan, L., Herat, J., Phaladi, G., Jacome, D. I., Anyona, P., Sanchez, A., Damji, N., Terki, F., Baltag, V., Patton, G., Silverman, A., Fogstad, H., Bangerjee, A., & Mohan, A. (2020). Adolescent well-being: A definition and conceptual framework. *Journal of Adolescent Health, 67*(4), 472–476. https://www.researchgate.net/publication/343629935_Adolescent_Well-Being_A_Definition_and_Conceptual_Framework

Sandholtz, J., & Ringstaff, C. (2020). Offering modest supports to extend professional development outcomes and enhance elementary science teaching. *Professional Development in Education, 48*(1), 1–16. https://doi.org/10.1080/19415257.2020.1725594

Schafft, K. A. (2016). Rural education as rural development: Understanding the rural school–community well-being linkage in a 21st-century policy context. *Peabody Journal of Education, 91*(2), 137–154. https://doi.org/10.1080/0161956X.2016.1151734

Shavers, A. W. (2003). Rethinking the equity vs. adequacy debate: Implications for rural school finance reform litigation. *Nebraska Law Review, 82*(1), 133–189. https://heinonline.org/HOL/LandingPage?handle=hein.journals/nebklr82&div=12&id=&page=

Showalter, D., Hartman, S. L., Eppley, K., Johnson, J., & Klein, B. (2023). *Why rural matters 2023: Centering equity and opportunity*. National Rural Education Association. https://wsos-cdn.s3.us-west-2.amazonaws.com/uploads/sites/18/WRMReport2023_DIGITAL.pdf

Sielke, C. (2004). Rural factors in state funding systems. *Journal of Education Finance, 29*(3), 223–236. https://www.jstor.org/stable/40704206

Sipple, J. W., & Brent, B. O. (2012). Challenges and strategies associated with rural school settings. In *Handbook of research in education finance and policy* (pp. 634–652). Routledge. https://www.researchgate.net/publication/262950112_Challenges_and_Strategies_Associated_with_Rural_School_Settings

Smith, G. A., & Sobel, D. (2010). *Place- and community-based education in schools* (1st ed.). Routledge. https://doi.org/10.4324/9780203858530

Sobel, D. (2004). Place-based education: Connecting classroom and community. *Nature and Listening, 4*(1), 1–7. https://kohalacenter.org/teachertraining/pdf/pbexcerpt.pdf

Spence, B. (1998). *Whatever happened to Pauley vs. Bailey? The story of the politics of education in West Virginia*. Covenant House. https://files.eric.ed.gov/fulltext/ED426839.pdf

Stenberg, P. L., Morehart, M. J., & Cromartie, J. (2009). Broadband internet service helping create a rural digital economy. *Amber Waves: The Economics of Food, Farming, Natural Resources, and Rural America*, 22–27. https://www.ers.usda.gov/amber-waves/2009/september/broadband-internet-service-helping-create-a-rural-digital-economy

Strange, M. (2003). Equitable and adequate funding for rural schools: Ensuring equal educational opportunity for all students. *Nebraska Law Review, 82*, 1. https://digitalcommons.unl.edu/cgi/viewcontent.cgi?article=1300&context=nlr

———. (2011). Finding fairness for rural students. *Phi Delta Kappan, 92*(6), 8–15. https://doi.org/10.1177/0031721711092006

Sutton, K., Patrick, K., Maybery, D., & Eaton, K. (2016). The immediate impact of a brief rural mental health workforce recruitment strategy. *Rural Society, 25*(2), 87–103. https://www.tandfonline.com/doi/full/10.1080/10371656.2016.1194327

Tieken, M. C. (2014). *Why rural schools matter*. University of North Carolina Press.

———. (2017). The spatialization of racial inequity and educational opportunity: Rethinking the rural/urban divide. *Peabody Journal of Education, 92*(3), 385–404. https://www.tandfonline.com/doi/epdf/10.1080/0161956X.2017.1324662?needAccess=true

Tieken, M. C., & Auldridge-Reveles, T. (2019). Rethinking the school closure research: School closure as spatial injustice. *Review of Educational Research, 89*(6), 917–953. https://doi.org/10.3102/0034654319877151

Topkok, S. A., & Loon, H. P. (2021). Uvvatuq Naluallangniaqtugut (I humbly hope we run into game): An Iñupiaq research process. *The Morning Watch: Educational and Social Analysis, 47*(1). https://journals.library.mun.ca/index.php/mwatch/article/view/2257/1792

Turley, R. N. L. (2009). College proximity: Mapping access to opportunity. *Sociology of Education, 82*(2), 126–146. https://doi.org/10.1177/003804070908200202

Vogels, E. A. (2021). Some digital divides persist between rural, urban and suburban America. *Pew Research Center*. https://www.pewresearch.org/short-reads/2021/08/19/some-digital-divides-persist-between-rural-urban-and-suburban-america/

Wan, Z. H., Jiang, Y., & Zhan, Y. (2020). STEM education in early childhood: A review of empirical studies. *Early Education and Development, 32*(7), 940–962. https://doi.org/10.1080/10409289.2020.1814986

Whitacre, B., & Gallardo, R. (2020). State broadband policy: Impacts on availability. *Telecommunications Policy, 44*, 102025. https://doi.org/10.1016/j.telpol.2020.102025

Williams, J. M., & Nierengarten, G. (2011). Recommendations from the North Star State: Rural administrators speak out. *The Rural Educator, 33*, 15–24.

Wright, R. G. (2023). The place of broadband within equal education opportunity. *Indiana Law Review, 56*(3), 519. https://heinonline.org/HOL/LandingPage?handle=hein.journals/indilr56&div=29&id=&page=

Yettick, H., Baker, R., Wickersham, M. E., & Hupfeld, K. E. (2014). Rural districts left behind? Rural districts and the challenges of administering the Elementary and Secondary Education Act. *Journal of Research in Rural Education, 29*(1). https://jrre.psu.edu/sites/default/files/2019-08/29-13.pdf

8

Conclusions, Recommendations, and Research Agenda

An effective K–12 science, technology, engineering, and mathematics (STEM) education prepares students for high-quality, well-paying careers in the STEM workforce and develops the STEM literacy that improves decision making and contributes to a well-functioning democracy. But as we have shown in this report, rural students face systemic barriers to that education, such as lack of technology or access to high-speed internet connections as well as challenges in recruiting and retaining qualified STEM educators. On the other hand, rural areas have abundant assets and provide a rich context for learning science and engineering; with access to the outdoors or work in agricultural industries many rural students naturally develop STEM-related skills in their daily lives. Connecting to STEM content in these forms provides opportunities for place-based education in rural areas, and use of learning through place increases access, engagement, and achievement in science content for rural students.

The committee examined the assets for and challenges to K–12 STEM education and workforce development that are unique to rural areas. In reviewing research on effective programs and approaches, the committee determined that few studies focus specifically on rural communities or explore variation across different rural areas. For this reason, the committee drew on the broad research literature related to effective STEM education and workforce development to make inferences about potential approaches in rural areas.

The committee's major conclusions and recommendations are summarized below, followed by recommendations for the U.S. National Science Foundation (NSF) in its programs, mentioned above, to support rural STEM education and workforce development and online STEM education. The committee also created a research agenda; it is presented at the end of this chapter.

THE DIVERSITY OF RURAL AMERICA AND DEFINING RURALITY

The information gathered by the committee shows that rural communities are diverse in every way—geographically, economically, and racially; the notion that rural America is largely White, agriculturally based, and uneducated is outdated. The rural diversity makes it understandably difficult to develop and implement programs that will improve K–12 STEM education and workforce development across all rural contexts: while some rural areas experience similar challenges to K–12 STEM education and workforce development, other challenges are specific to particular areas. It is therefore imperative for all actors in this space—federal and state agencies, nonprofit organizations, nongovernmental organizations, philanthropies and other groups with rural education portfolios, and rural education researchers—to consider the local context of each rural area.

The committee found that multiple definitions of *rural* are used by researchers and across and within federal agencies, and those definitions often focus on a false dichotomy of rural versus not rural. Improved, clear, and consistent definitions are critical to better understand rural communities and help ensure that they have access to the resources they need. Confusing or misaligned definitions can be a barrier for rural communities attempting to access state, federal, or philanthropic funding. Efforts to build a cohesive evidence base focused on rural STEM education also suffer from the multiple definitions of rural used by researchers.

> *Conclusion 2-1: Multiple definitions of* rural *are used across and within federal agencies, making it difficult to both accurately identify the number of districts and schools served by federal programs and ensure that resources are equitably distributed.*

> *Conclusion 2-2: Multiple definitions of* rural *are used by researchers, making it difficult to aggregate findings across studies in order to build a rigorous knowledge base about what works to improve rural STEM education and workforce development.*

> *Conclusion 2-3: Most federal agencies base their definitions of* rural *on one of two sources, one developed by the U.S. Census Bureau and the other by the Office of Management and Budget. Both define* rural *mainly as* nonurban. *This approach fails to adequately capture important characteristics that vary across rural areas, such as population density and remoteness.*

Recommendation 1: There is a need for a common measure of rurality that goes beyond a rural/nonrural dichotomy to capture dimensions such as population size, population density, extent of urban (built-up) area, and remoteness. This measure should be used both to monitor geographical disparities in STEM education and workforce development and to inform development and administration of programs for rural STEM education and workforce development.

- The federal government, through a statistical agency such as the National Center for Education Statistics or the Bureau of Labor Statistics, should develop this common measure.
- Federal agencies (including the U.S. National Science Foundation), state agencies, nonprofit organizations, nongovernmental organizations, philanthropies, and other groups with rural education portfolios should adopt and use this measure.

Recommendation 2: To monitor geographical disparities in STEM education and workforce development, federal statistical agencies (such as the National Center for Education Statistics, Bureau of Labor Statistics, and National Center for Science and Engineering Statistics) and state education agencies should regularly report indicators of STEM education and employment disaggregated by rurality (using a nondichotomous measure of rurality) in addition to other common demographics (e.g., race/ethnicity, gender, disability status, socioeconomic status).

Recommendation 3: When developing and administering programs for rural STEM education and workforce development, funders should use a nondichotomous measure of rurality to ensure that projects represent different dimensions of rurality and to enable them to target rural communities with specific characteristics when necessary.

Conclusion 2-4: Many rural areas are undergoing substantial demographic shifts and will continue to do so. While approximately 20 percent of those living in rural communities are people of color, almost a third of children under 18 in rural communities are people of color. K–12 STEM education and workforce development need to be responsive to these changes.

Recommendation 4: Education decision makers and leaders at all levels should monitor demographic and other changes in the rural communities they serve and take the changes into account when developing

programming and allocating funding. This might include adoption of culturally responsive and sustaining approaches to teaching, providing supports for multilingual learners, and diversifying the teacher workforce.

FEDERAL AND STATE PROGRAMS AND POLICIES

K–12 STEM education and workforce development programs in schools, districts, and communities are shaped by multiple layers of policy and funding streams based on federal, state, and district policies. Policies and funding streams at these different levels and across different policy domains (assessment, curriculum, graduation requirements, etc.) interact to facilitate or constrain how programs are implemented at the local level. Rural K–12 schools contribute to the broader well-being of their community and are often its largest employer, offering stable, well-paying, middle-class jobs to local residents. Because rural schools have important social, cultural, political, and economic benefits for rural communities, policies and programs that support their vitality also help sustain their communities.

The committee identified various challenges facing rural educational institutions and noted that, while there has been some progress in addressing barriers related to funding, federal and state entities need to provide support while recognizing the strengths of these communities. The policies in place have led some educational leaders to generate creative programs, offerings, or initiatives to provide high-quality STEM content to rural students.

Conclusion 3-1: All states have a significant population of rural students, but federal and state policies do not always attend to the unique needs and strengths of rural communities. Policy decisions and processes often do not take into account potential unintended consequences for rural districts and schools.

Recommendation 5: When developing state-level policy for STEM education and workforce development, education policy- and decision makers should ensure that representatives of rural districts are involved in the policymaking process or are given the opportunity to provide feedback on the policies and how they might impact rural districts and schools.

Conclusion 3-2: Rural districts and schools in remote areas with low population density and limited access to affordable and reliable broadband face unique challenges for supporting K–12 STEM education and workforce development initiatives, and these challenges are often not adequately addressed by federal and state programs. There is also limited research focused on these remote communities.

Conclusion 3-3: There are many federal programs in K–12 STEM education and workforce development that rural districts, schools, and out-of-school programs can apply to for funding, but few programs target rural districts and schools. In addition, rules for eligibility (including the definition of rurality), program requirements, and the demands of the application process can prevent rural schools, districts, and communities from applying for and receiving funding.

Conclusion 3-4: Some rural communities, districts, and schools lack the capacity (e.g., staffing, time, and expertise) to identify potential funding opportunities to advance STEM education and workforce development opportunities, complete the application process, and meet the reporting requirements if funding is awarded.

Recommendation 6: Because some rural communities (including youth-serving organizations), districts, and schools lack the capacity to identify potential funding opportunities, complete the application process, and meet the reporting requirements if funding is awarded, federal and state agencies, nonprofit organizations, nongovernmental organizations, philanthropies, and other groups with rural education portfolios should

- consider how timelines or burdens for preparing and submitting applications for funding might create barriers for applicants in rural areas,
- consider how requirements for receiving funding could create barriers for applicants in rural areas, and
- provide opportunities for rural communities, districts, schools, and teachers to build capacity to successfully respond to funding opportunities.

Recommendation 7: There is a need for coordinated attention to K–12 STEM education and workforce development in rural areas across existing federal agencies and initiatives. For example,

- the federal Rural Partners Network, led by the U.S. Department of Agriculture and the White House Domestic Policy Council, should prioritize issues related to K–12 STEM education and workforce development in their work; and

- **the White House Office of Science and Technology Policy's National Science and Technology Council's Committee on STEM Education should prioritize K–12 STEM education and workforce development in rural areas in their work.**

Conclusion 3-5: Out-of-school learning opportunities in STEM are an important complement to in-school learning. While many students in rural communities lack access to opportunities in museums or other out-of-school institutions, they often do have access to STEM learning opportunities at home or in nature.

ACCESS TO AND ENROLLMENT IN STEM COURSES IN RURAL SCHOOLS

Opportunities in rural STEM education are varied, cover a breadth of subjects, and may be rooted in the school's location. Just as there is no one-size-fits-all definition of *rural*, there is no one-size-fits-all approach to STEM education in rural schools. The committee examined trends in student achievement, aspirations, course taking, and persistence in STEM career pathways as well as access to STEM learning opportunities including coursework, out-of-school programs, and work-related experiences. Because of opportunity gaps in rural K–12 STEM education, students in rural areas generally have lower achievement in STEM courses and fewer aspirations to pursue a STEM college major or career, and they are less likely to enroll and persist in STEM courses throughout their educational pathways. Importantly, however, leveraging the assets of rural communities can provide K–12 students with engaging and effective STEM education and workforce development experiences.

Conclusion 4-1: Many rural students lack access to STEM coursework (e.g., computer science classes, Advanced Placement and International Baccalaureate courses in math) and programs (e.g., Talented and Gifted and Career and Technical Education [CTE] programs, dual enrollment, and third- and fourth-year CTE courses) that can better prepare them to pursue diverse STEM-related education and careers. These disparities in STEM learning opportunities translate into STEM achievement and aspiration gaps between rural and nonrural students, and these gaps grow as students move through K–12 schooling.

Conclusion 5-1: Rural students' competencies in STEM build over time beginning in the early grades (preK–2). Learning experiences in the core STEM subjects throughout the elementary grades are essential for building the knowledge, skills, and dispositions that develop STEM literacy and lead to later success including in STEM and related careers.

Conclusion 5-2: STEM learning experiences that connect to and leverage rural students' local experiences and knowledge are important components of effective K–12 STEM education in rural settings. Place-based learning experiences, often through local partnerships and the adaptation of instructional materials for local relevance, can be especially productive for building rural students' competence and motivation (e.g., interest, identity) in STEM.

Conclusion 5-3: High-quality instructional materials with connected professional development that can be adapted for local relevance are important for supporting effective K–12 STEM education in rural areas.

Conclusion 5-4: Pathways to and through STEM education in rural communities are enriched by STEM learning opportunities through schools, afterschool programs, summer camps and programs, public libraries, museums, local businesses, and virtual platforms. But these learning opportunities are sometimes constrained by limited funding and availability in rural communities.

Recommendation 8: Federal and state agencies should recognize that many students in rural areas lack opportunities in STEM education and therefore are not able to and/or do not pursue STEM careers at the same rate as their suburban and urban peers. These agencies should direct funding, resources, and policymaking designed specifically for rural districts and schools to address these disparities in STEM education and workforce development.

STRATEGIES FOR IMPROVING RURAL STEM EDUCATION AND WORKFORCE DEVELOPMENT

Drawing on the review of evidence related to implementing effective K–12 STEM education and workforce development, the committee developed recommendations targeted primarily to state and local actors to guide improvements in rural areas. These recommendations focus on the major components of education and workforce development—STEM learning experiences, pathways to STEM careers, the STEM educator workforce, and infrastructure and materials—where policymakers and education leaders can make impactful policy, programmatic, and funding decisions. In developing these recommendations, the committee took into account the unique assets and challenges of rural contexts and was attentive to the current and increasing diversity of rural communities.

Learning Experiences and Supportive Pathways

Given the geographic and economic diversity as well as the changing demographics of many rural areas, instructional approaches that connect to and leverage learners' cultural knowledge and experiences are especially important. To support teachers in providing effective STEM learning experiences, high-quality instructional materials with connected professional development that can be adapted for local relevance are essential.

Recommendation 9: STEM curriculum developers should take into account the assets, resources, and constraints of rural districts and schools when developing instructional materials and accompanying professional learning resources and opportunities. These materials should be designed to allow for the adaptability of instructional methods to leverage local rural funds of knowledge and take place-based approaches.

Pathways to and through STEM education in rural communities are enriched by STEM learning opportunities in or available through schools, afterschool programs, summer camps and programs, public libraries, museums, local businesses, and virtual platforms. The committee notes that strategic partnerships between educational institutions at all levels, community-based organizations, and industry can strengthen these K–12 STEM education and workforce development pathways. Examples of successful partnership models, presented in Chapters 3 and 5, should be beneficial to all parties as well as to rural students, and should maintain open communication lines between all partners. Rural school districts can also develop formal interdistrict agreements (e.g., consortia) to pool and maximize limited resources.

Conclusion 5-5: Promising models for designing STEM enrichment education and workforce development programs in rural areas (i) involve partnerships between K–12, local higher education institutions, Tribal Nations and other tribal leaders, and local government and business; (ii) provide students with job-relevant experiences (i.e., internships, apprenticeships); and (iii) target flexible and transferable knowledge and skills that are relevant to STEM education and local job opportunities.

Recommendation 10: Rural school districts should explore consortium models for STEM education and workforce development that pool resources to maximize opportunities across regions. Such consortia or other collaborative models could seek to provide

- opportunities for students to participate in advanced STEM coursework,
- job-embedded internships and apprenticeships for students,
- professional learning for preK–12 STEM educators, and
- improved access to out-of-school STEM learning experiences.

The 2015 Every Student Succeeds Act provided state education agencies more flexibility over measures of school accountability through their state accountability systems, and many state education agencies took advantage of the flexibility to develop innovative approaches to student learning pathways tailored to their state needs and goals. The innovative measures incentivize school districts to prioritize the state goals, including readiness for college and work and in STEM areas. Some states also provide funding to incentivize partnerships between districts and with higher education and industry to advance STEM readiness.

Recommendation 11: State education agencies should provide funding and other incentives, including in accountability systems, to encourage rural districts to partner with each other and with institutions of higher education, community organizations, out-of-school programs, and industry to advance K–12 STEM education and workforce development and better engage and support preK–12 students, parents, and educators in rural areas.

Recommendation 12: Rural districts should seek community and/or industry partners with whom they can develop a variety of STEM learning opportunities. These opportunities should include project- or placed-based learning experiences that build foundational knowledge in STEM disciplines for students across preK–12, exposure to STEM professions, access to rigorous courses in the core STEM disciplines, opportunities to develop job-related skills, and a requirement to complete a real-world internship, apprenticeship, or other work-based learning experience. Career-specific exploration and preparation could begin as early as middle school, should be based on an expanded definition of STEM that includes any job that requires proficiency

in STEM-related knowledge and skills, and should emphasize STEM fields that can contribute to the viability and sustainability of local areas.

Educators

Rural schools often receive few, if any, applicants for open teaching positions, despite devoting a great deal of time to recruiting. Many positions go unfilled or are covered by long-term substitute teachers. Recruiting, retaining, and developing STEM teachers in rural America requires a multifaceted approach that addresses the unique challenges of rural education. By offering competitive incentives, supportive professional environments, and continuous, context-specific professional development, rural districts can build a stable and effective teaching workforce. These efforts are essential for ensuring that all students, regardless of their geographic location, have access to high-quality education.

Conclusion 6-1: Teacher preparation programs often use a generalized approach for training and do not adequately prepare future educators for rural spaces. There are limited opportunities to do student teaching in rural areas, and some new educators may not be prepared to deal with issues such as how to identify and leverage local assets and knowledge related to STEM, isolation, lack of access to professional development opportunities, and how to enter and build relationships in tight-knit communities.

Conclusion 6-2: Rural schools, especially in remote locations and on reservations, greatly struggle to fill STEM teacher positions. As a result, a position may go unfilled and a specific course may not be taught or taught by a teacher who does not have the qualifications to teach it.

Conclusion 6-3: Many rural teachers lack local access to STEM-focused professional learning and mentorship opportunities. Promising strategies for addressing this lack include use of remote and online options (including repositories of resources and online opportunities to collaborate with other teachers), teacher-industry externships, consortia efforts among districts, and regional service centers.

Recommendation 13: Institutions that offer teacher preparation pathways should incorporate rural-focused coursework and opportunities for rural field placements in their licensure programs. These

rural-focused components should provide opportunities to learn about the diversity of rural communities and their assets, how to recognize those assets in different contexts, and ways to leverage the assets in STEM and STEM-based Career and Technical Education curriculum and instruction.

Recommendation 14: Institutions that offer school counselor preparation pathways should incorporate rural-focused coursework and rural internship opportunities for prospective counselors to learn about the diversity of rural communities and their assets, how to recognize those assets in different contexts, and ways to leverage the assets when advising students about STEM courses or career pathways.

Recommendation 15: Rural districts should work with regional teacher preparation programs to explore ways to address the shortage of STEM teachers in rural areas. Strategies to consider include

- housing assistance,
- transportation funds,
- "grow your own" programs in rural areas, and/or
- flexible and ongoing professional learning opportunities.

STEM Education Infrastructure and Materials

The committee's analysis of the research literature on rural schools shows that many have infrastructure and other material resources that are less robust than schools in nonrural areas. In particular, broadband access remains a challenge in rural communities, although the committee notes that access alone is not sufficient to improve STEM education using online tools and resources.

Conclusion 7-1: Many rural districts and schools lack adequate infrastructure and materials to support high-quality STEM education and workforce development. Specifically, they often have old buildings with outdated systems; lack dedicated space, equipment, and materials for science investigations; lack access to fast and affordable broadband; and have insufficient funding. Strategies for addressing these challenges include

- *research-practice partnerships;*
- *leveraging rural public libraries, government/business facilities, and outdoor spaces;*

- *online courses and resources; and*
- *initiatives to expand and enhance broadband access and speed.*

Conclusion 7-2: Inequitable access to broadband in rural communities leads to challenges with STEM education and workforce development and digital literacy in preparation for work and life. However, broadband access alone will not solve or fix access to STEM education and workforce development opportunities and resources.

Conclusion 7-3: Recent legislation has led to large investments in broadband connectivity across the United States, and many federal and state agencies are working to improve broadband access and adoption. But it is difficult to determine the extent to which these efforts will address broadband-related challenges for K–12 STEM education in rural areas because

- *the efforts are not well coordinated,*
- *some do not attend to affordability, and*
- *broadband access alone cannot address lack of or outdated computers, routers, or other hardware.*

Recommendation 16: When making decisions about adoption of new technology, online services, or equipment, states and districts should take into account the "total cost of ownership," including the initial investment, ongoing costs for access and maintenance, and professional development needed for teachers and administrators to use the technology, service, or equipment effectively. The total cost should explicitly account for challenges in rural areas that might affect costs (for example, costs of professional development for teachers who are spread out geographically, or of tech maintenance if schools are separated by long distances).

Leveraging Assets and Addressing Challenges in Rural K–12 STEM Education

Throughout the report, the committee describes the diversity of rural areas, assets embedded in those communities, and challenges they face. Two overarching conclusions arise from the evidence presented in the preceding chapters.

Overarching Conclusion 1: Rural communities vary tremendously across a variety of dimensions that shape their K–12 STEM education and workforce development landscape; these dimensions include remoteness; geography (i.e., mountainous, desert, island); racial, ethnic, and socioeconomic make-up of the population; and the types of STEM-related resources and industries that are present. This variation leads to differences in the types of challenges a community may face in implementing K–12 STEM education and workforce development initiatives, the kinds of assets that are available to leverage, and the strategies for improving STEM education and workforce development that will be successful.

Overarching Conclusion 2: While rural communities vary widely across the United States (including territories and Freely Associated States), some challenges to and assets for K–12 STEM education and workforce development are common across many of them. Common challenges include out-migration, difficulties with recruitment and retention of teachers in STEM, absence or low density of STEM-related institutions/organizations (e.g., museums, colleges and universities, industries), and closure and consolidation of schools. Common assets include proximity to the natural world, close social ties, community resources, and local rural knowledge.

The committee recommends continued funding of programs that support teaching preparation and training, new technologies in STEM education, and improved internet connectivity in schools and homes. When possible, funders should evaluate their portfolios to assess successful programs across rural areas.

Recommendation 17: The federal government should continue to support and expand programs that enhance preK–12 STEM education and workforce development initiatives in rural areas, with an emphasis on programs that

- **provide funding for training, placement, and continuing education (professional development) for STEM educators in rural schools;**
- **explore strategies for using technology, including improving internet access to online platforms and AI tools, expanding educators' abilities to teach robust, integrated STEM subjects, and expanding student opportunities to learn and gain experience in STEM fields, rather than as a technique to reduce staff, teachers, or costs, or to close schools; and**
- **complete connection of all schools and students' homes with internet access at minimal cost and using the technology (fiber optics, cable, satellite, mobile hotspots) available locally.**

Recommendation 18: Agencies that fund programs in STEM education and workforce development should conduct evaluations at the portfolio level that examine and document what makes a program or approach successful for rural populations and/or in rural settings. This could include assessing

- **how a program overcomes challenges that are unique to rural settings;**
- **how programs leverage assets of rural communities, including local rural knowledge;**
- **the capacity of rural organizations to apply for and manage grants (e.g., reporting requirements); and**
- **effective practices to increase the capacity of rural organizations.**

RECOMMENDATIONS TO NSF FOR IMPLEMENTING RURAL STEM EDUCATION AND WORKFORCE DEVELOPMENT PROGRAMS

In addition to the broad recommendations above for all federal agencies, as stipulated in the statement of task for this study the committee makes specific recommendations to NSF to inform the funding and implementation of programs under sections 10512 (National Science Foundation Rural STEM Activities) and 10513 (Opportunities for Online Education) of the CHIPS and Science Act, including rural STEM activities and online STEM education and mentoring in rural communities. We first provide general guidance for implementing the programs called out in the legislation, followed by more specific guidance related to each section of the legislation.

The committee recommends embedding a rural focus in existing programs in order to move forward more quickly and achieve results by 2027. Relevant programs are in the Directorate for STEM Education, such as the Robert Noyce Teacher Scholarship Programs, the Eddie Bernice Johnson Inclusion across the Nation of Communities of Learners of Underrepresented Discoverers in Engineering and Science Initiative (INCLUDES), Improving Undergraduate STEM Education, Discovery Research PreK-12, and Advancing Informal STEM Learning, Advanced Technological Education, or Innovative Technology Experiences for Students and Teachers. There are also opportunities to elevate rural STEM education and workforce development in other NSF directorates and programs, such as the Technology, Innovation, and Partnerships Directorate (TIP) program on Regional Innovation Engines (NSF Engines), and the Established Program to Stimulate Competitive Research (EPSCoR).

To qualify for this rural focus, an initiative needs to do more than just take place in a rural setting. It must clearly show how the questions asked, the programs implicated, and the knowledge generated are relevant to rural communities, schools, students, and families. If the results of the initial investments to existing programs indicate that a separate program dedicated to rural STEM education and workforce development is needed, NSF could explore developing and implementing such a program.

With longer-term investments, NSF could consider creating a center or centers for rural and rural Indigenous STEM education and workforce development to support relevant research through grants programs, curation of publications, professional development for researchers, and evaluation work to determine rural communities' needs. Such a center might be supported with funding across multiple existing programs.

Throughout its strategies and programs, NSF should attend to the different dimensions of rurality—population size and density, extent of urban (built-up) area, remoteness, and demographic diversity. This includes ensuring that the portfolio of funded rural projects reflects this diversity and reflects geographic diversity across the United States and its territories and Freely Associated States. Further, in describing their projects and in reporting, proposers and grantees should be required to describe the settings where the project takes place and the populations and communities involved in ways that will enable NSF to document different dimensions of rural diversity.

NSF should develop a strategy to encourage development and funding of projects that focus on rural Indigenous communities, including work on reservations and with Tribal Nations, Alaska Natives, Native Hawaiians, and Pacific Islanders. NSF should also develop a strategy to encourage development of projects focusing on rural migrant, Black, and Latine communities, and individuals with intersecting marginalized identities in rural communities.

In building programs focused on rural STEM education and workforce development, NSF will need to include individuals with expertise specific to rural STEM education throughout the process. Review panels for programs where rural STEM education has been highlighted should have at least two reviewers with specific expertise in rural STEM education and workforce development. It is NOT sufficient for these individuals to be from an institution in a rural setting. If possible, NSF should hire program officers who have specific expertise in rural STEM education and workforce development and make it possible for them to work across programs with a rural focus. To kick off development of the strategy for focusing on rural STEM education, it may be useful to convene experts in rural STEM education and workforce development to provide input on the needs and areas for research, building on this report.

As more grants are funded for rural preK–12 STEM education and workforce development, NSF should hold a meeting of the project principal investigators (PIs) to share insights and ideas (in addition to PI meetings for individual programs). This will allow for information exchange and deepening of a professional community around rural STEM education and workforce development.

To accomplish the goals outlined in the legislation, projects will need to include partnerships between institutions of higher education, nonprofits, preK–12 education, local industries, and communities. Building genuine, trusting, mutually beneficial relationships between different sectors and organizations requires time and resources. Applicants will need to demonstrate with documentation a functional partnership. Or the awards will need to build in time for partners to build these kinds of relationships. In addition, consideration should be given to how funding is shared with districts, schools, and communities to support their work. NSF may also need to consider the additional costs incurred for partnership with more remote rural communities, by, for example, providing funding for traveling longer distances or for enhancing technology to allow for virtual engagements.

As noted in this report, rural communities have many assets related to STEM education and workforce development that are often not leveraged sufficiently. In developing priorities focused on rural STEM education and evaluating proposals, NSF should explicitly call out the need to clearly describe how a program or project will identify and leverage community resources and be designed to connect to local community priorities and needs.

To jump-start work specific to STEM, NSF should consider using the Dear Colleague Letter mechanism, Early Concept Grants for Exploratory Research, and Ideas Labs; the latter could surface new ways to build connections across diverse rural environments. These opportunities would bring together research and development workers in K–12 STEM education to figure out the kind of connecting network rural education research communities need in order to advance.[1]

Recommendation 19: When implementing the suite of programs outlined in articles 10512 and 10513 of the CHIPS and Science Act, NSF should employ the following strategies:

- **Build on existing NSF programs when possible.**
- **Capture the diversity of rural settings and populations.**

[1]For an example: https://new.nsf.gov/events/life-leveraging-innovations-evolution-town-hall

- Elevate expertise related to rural STEM education and workforce development.
- Support mutually beneficial partnerships between institutions of higher education, nonprofits, preK–12 education, local industries, and communities.
- Emphasize an asset framing of rural communities.
- Create quick-turnaround, short-term funding opportunities to allow for pilot work and strategy development.
- Connect to existing rural STEM education and workforce development programs across other federal agencies.

Recommendation 20: As relates to Section 10512(a), Preparing Rural STEM Educators, NSF should expand the Robert Noyce Teacher Scholarship Program Tracks 1 and 2 to intentionally recruit STEM majors and professionals from rural areas; prepare them to leverage local, natural, and community assets in their STEM teaching; place them in rural areas for their teaching commitments; and support them after placement. In addition, NSF should expand the definition of eligible "STEM major" for the Noyce scholarships to include agricultural and health sciences, given their high relevance to rural areas.

Recommendation 21: As relates to Section 10512(a2B), Rural STEM Collaborative, NSF should leverage regional collaborative structures both within NSF (e.g., INCLUDES, TIP programs) and in higher education or nonprofit organizations (e.g., Regional Hubs in the Rural Schools Collaborative). The new regional structures should include preK–12 formal schooling institutions, organizations that provide informal or out-of-school STEM learning experiences, higher education institutions, and local industries.

Recommendation 22: As relates to Section 10512(b), Broadening Participation of Rural Students in STEM, the U.S. National Science Foundation should

- leverage existing programs like EPSCoR, Advanced Technological Education and other community college–focused programs, and the Division of Research on Learning in Formal and Informal Settings;
- be clear, nuanced, and inclusive when defining *rural*, by requiring use of either the Index of Relative Rurality or the definitional base for rural categorization in applications for funding;
- support longitudinal research in rural STEM education;

- fund participatory research that engages rural students in research methods or includes educators or educational leaders (e.g., research-practice partnerships); and
- consider a variety of partnership models, including fully virtual collaboration, to ensure that all rural areas, including remote areas with few colocated partners, can apply for funding.

Recommendation 23: As relates to Section 10513, Opportunities for Online Education, NSF should attend to the existing technological infrastructure in rural communities and fund research that examines

- the impact of differential connectivity on student and teacher STEM learning outcomes, and
- how online tools (including artificial intelligence) and communities can support students and educators in formal and informal settings.

DIRECTIONS FOR RESEARCH

The committee reviewed and analyzed current efforts to bring high-quality STEM education to rural schools. While reviewing the literature, it became clear that gaps need to be addressed to better understand who rural students are and how unique assets and challenges in their communities affect students' STEM participation and achievement. These assets and barriers present a complex narrative of rural STEM education and workforce participation. While it may be tempting to infer what rural STEM participation looks like based on certain characteristics of rural communities—such as higher poverty rates and lower adult educational attainment—these assumptions would be a disservice to rural students and may not accurately capture their lived experiences and outcomes.

There is an urgent need for more comprehensive, evidence-based, and broad-scale national research focused specifically on rural students in STEM. When developing research programs or priorities focused on rural STEM education, funders (federal agencies, foundations, and state agencies) should require applicants to describe how the research team will ensure that the needs and priorities of rural communities, districts, and schools are centered. Funders should also consider calling for research models that require equal partnership and collaboration between researchers and practitioners, such as research-practice partnerships.

Education researchers should engage in longitudinal research that examines the impacts of rural STEM and STEM-based CTE programs, including online learning programs, afterschool programs, teacher recruitment and retention, professional learning, industry internships and externships, and teacher mentorship or coaching efforts. Researchers should also examine how broadband infrastructure and affordability affects preK–12 STEM education and literacy in rural areas. Funders (federal agencies and philanthropic organizations) should develop programs that support longitudinal research in these areas.

The committee identifies the following three areas where more research is particularly needed. Only through rigorous, nuanced, and inclusive research can we hope to understand and ultimately improve STEM participation for rural students.

Intersecting Research on PreK–12 STEM Education and Workforce Development in Rural Areas

One of the major challenges in writing this report was the lack of studies examining preK–12 STEM education, especially in earlier grades, across the diversity of rural schools and communities. At times, rurality was a variable but not the study focus. There were no analyses of whether programs or partnerships were effective in ways that matter for the rural space. What may be effective in a school in rural Louisiana may not work in rural Appalachia or rural Washington state and it is imperative that researchers conduct studies that recognize these differences.

Research is needed to explore the challenges rural students face, how they impact students' outcomes, and what strategies might alleviate these challenges. This inquiry could uncover actionable insights and potential "low-hanging fruit" for improving outcomes for rural students. Such research must be conducted by scholars who have a deep understanding of rural contexts, who apply asset-based frameworks, and who recognize the diversity in rural communities as well as the important elements that distinguish rural from nonrural communities. It is crucial that any proposed solutions that emerge from this research incorporate and value local rural knowledge and the voices of rural people and avoid the pitfalls of standardization, which often reflect interventions designed for urban or suburban environments.

Robust research is needed to better understand the experiences and outcomes of rural students with intersectional identities, and the ways that the experiences and outcomes of Indigenous student populations differ from those of rural students or other populations. The barriers to this research are not insurmountable.

As research identifies best practices for teaching and learning in rural areas and leads to improvement in and development of STEM-specific programs, it is imperative to understand and anticipate the desired long-term outcomes for rural students and schools. Researchers should be encouraged to develop strategic plans that map to the outcomes they hope to see while studying online STEM learning programs, school-industry partnerships,

STEM teacher recruitment, retention, professional learning, and mentorship programs in rural areas.

Better Availability and Usability of Datasets

Work is needed to improve definitions of rurality to recognize that rural communities are not monolithic and that rurality exists on a continuum. Definitional improvements will help facilitate research on populations of interest, as well as make funding opportunities more accessible to rural communities. Some creative methods may also be needed to understand students with intersecting identities while protecting small cell size. Much of the data necessary to conduct further research are already available through federal data collections, and though the data are not without drawbacks, they offer a valuable starting point for further research.

New types of datasets are needed that are specific to rural students, teachers, and schools and that leverage the diversity of rural settings and STEM learning. For example, National Center for Education Statistics data are available for overall enrollment rates in rural spaces compared to suburban and urban spaces nationally, but not data on these differences at state and district levels or data disaggregated by other demographic characteristics.

Informal and Nonformal STEM Learning and Workforce Development in Rural Areas

Research is needed to enhance understanding of the impacts of informal and nonformal STEM learning and workforce development in rural areas. Informal and nonformal STEM learning is an underused pathway for rural students that may offset the lack of resources in their schools and provide access to other opportunities to sustain their interest in STEM or further their ability to enter a STEM career. Informal and nonformal STEM learning can also help show the variety of STEM jobs and help industry partners see the benefits of basing some STEM jobs in rural areas.

SUMMARY

As we have stated throughout the report, the diversity of rural areas and their assets and challenges can affect the development and implementation of programs that will improve rural preK–12 STEM education and workforce development. Agencies and other actors must therefore consider the localized context of each rural area when taking the actions recommended in this report.

In addition, multiple definitions of *rural* are used across agencies and other groups, and many focus on a false dichotomy of rural or not rural. This lack of consistency and clarity contributes to misunderstandings of rural students, teachers, schools, and districts; can result in lack of access to funding that creates opportunity gaps for rural students; and inhibits the development of a broad and consistent evidence base on rural K–12 STEM education and workforce development.

Finally, leveraging rural assets and knowledge, existing programs in this space, and partnerships and networks across education, industry, state and federal agencies, and community organizations will help support and strengthen K–12 STEM education and workforce development in rural areas.

Appendix A

Biosketches

COMMITTEE BIOS

KATHARINE G. FRASE (*Cochair*, she/her/hers) served in many roles over a 30-year career with the International Business Machines Corporation (IBM) since joining as a postdoctoral fellow in the IBM Research Division, retiring as vice president of business development in which she spearheaded the development of new education solutions to support teachers and student outcomes with individualized, data-driven recommendations. She has previously served as chief technology officer in the IBM Public Sector and as vice president in IBM Industry Solutions Research. Frase holds three patents and 15 refereed publications in the fields of solid electrolytes, ceramic powder synthesis, neutron diffraction and small angle scattering, high Tc superconductors, and ceramic packaging. She received an AB degree in chemistry from Bryn Mawr College and a PhD in materials science and engineering from the University of Pennsylvania. Frase was elected to the National Academy of Engineering (NAE) for engineering contributions, including the use of lead-free materials, to the development of electronic packaging materials and processes. She has served as an NAE councillor and on the National Academies' Committee on Science, Engineering, Medicine, and Public Policy; Committee on the Status, Role, and Needs of Engineering Technology Education in the United States (Cochair); Committee on the Study of Education, Training, and Certification Pathways to a Skilled Technical U.S. Workforce (Cochair); and many other National Research Council panels and studies.

TIFFANY NEILL (*Cochair*, she/her/hers) has been a longtime leader in STEM education and education policy and currently serves in a variety of roles continuing to advance and advocate for quality learning experiences for students. She currently serves as a Curriculum Manager at OpenSciEd focused on integrating computer science and science through free and open curriculum at the middle school level. She also serves as a research scientist at the University of Washington on an U.S. National Science Foundation (NSF) funded grant, *Advancing Coherent and Equitable Systems of Science Education* and as the Director of Accelerated Cohorts for Teaching Success at the University of Central Oklahoma offering pathways of support for those seeking to change careers and enter the education profession. Neill began her career in education as a middle and high school teacher serving in both traditional and nontraditional school settings. She later assumed a position as an instructional specialist at the K20 Center for Community and Educational Renewal at the University of Oklahoma where she developed a statewide program known as K20alt designed to support alternative education teachers around the state with innovative and effective approaches to instruction for at-promise students. In 2002 she joined the Oklahoma State Department of Education as the Director of Science and Engineering Education and served in the role for five years before becoming the Executive Director of Curriculum and Instruction and later the Deputy Superintendent of Curriculum and Instruction, serving on Cabinet for the State Superintendent of Public Instruction. For over a decade, Neill led agency strategies on academic matters including state and federal policies and state and federal funds to drive student achievement for Oklahoma's 700,000 public school students. She served as the President of the Council of State Science Supervisors from 2017 to 2019, on the President's STEM Advisory Board for NSF from 2020 to 2022, and on the National Assessment Governing Board's Development Panel to update the 2028 NAEP Science Assessment Framework. Neill earned a bachelor's degree in biology from Northeastern State University in Oklahoma and a master's in instructional leadership and academic curriculum from the University of Oklahoma, and a doctorate of philosophy in education from the University of Oklahoma where her research emphasis was on STEM integration.

JUAN-CARLOS AGUILAR (he/him/his) is the director for innovative programs and research at the Georgia Department of Education. He provides internal evaluation support for innovative projects awarded to the state Department of Education as well manages a portfolio of projects funded by the National Science Foundation, the U.S. Department of Education, and private foundations. Aguilar previously served as the state science program manager where he oversaw the development and adoption of the current Georgia Standards of Excellence for Science and was the state liaison for science, engineering, and STEM with several national and state professional organizations. He has served as a member of the National Academies of Sciences, Engineering, and Medicine's America's Lab Report committee and the Steering Committee on Exploring the Overlap Between "Literacy in Science" and the Practice of Obtaining, Evaluating, and Communicating Information. Aguilar is the past president of the Council of State Science Supervisors (CSSS) where he coordinated projects designed to support states as they made their own plans to adopt and implement the Next Generation Science Standards and oversaw the development of a set of Professional Development Standards in collaboration with CSSS Higher Education partners. He has worked as an advisor for the Experiential Citizen Science Training for the Next Generation an Emory project funded under the National Institutes of Health SEPA 2015. Aguilar was the principal investigator (PI) for the Georgians Experience Astronomy Research in School a project funded by NASA under their K–12 Competitive Grants Opportunity program and was the co-PI of the Science Learning Integrating Design, Engineering, and Robotics, a project funded by the National Science Foundation's Discovery Research K–12 program. He has served as a member of the Board of Directors for the Georgia Youth Science and Technology Centers, the Valdosta STEAM Board of Advisors, the Board of Directors of the Triangle Coalition for STEM Education, and as the chair of the Alliance of Affiliates, a group of nine national organizations focused on science education that support the work of the National Science Teachers Association. Aguilar taught in Guatemala, working in two 6–12 schools teaching mathematics and science, then, upon moving to the United States, he pursued a postgraduate degree in physics and began teaching middle school science and mathematics in the Fayette County School system in Lexington, Kentucky, in the Spanish Immersion Program housed at Bryan Station Middle School. He later became the team leader of the Spanish Immersion Team and assumed the responsibilities of science department chair for the school. Later, Aguilar moved to Atlanta, Georgia, where he began working at the Georgia Department of Education as the region 3 science implementation specialists regional coordinator, later being promoted to science program manager for the State of Georgia. He received his undergraduate degree in physics from the Universidad del Valle of Guatemala and PhD in physics from the University of Kentucky.

BRADLEY S. BARKER (he/him/his) is a professor and youth development specialist for Nebraska 4-H Extension in the Institute of Agriculture and Natural Resources at the University of Nebraska–Lincoln. Previously, he served as a program director (Intergovernmental Personnel Act) at the National Science Foundation (NSF), in the Division of Research and Learning in Formal and Informal Environments. Barker's primary research interests are the use of technology and digital manipulatives (i.e., robotics, e-textiles) for teaching and learning. He has also researched the use of technology to connect rural learners to academic experiences through virtual reality and telepresence robotics. Barker was principal investigator (PI) on two NSF grants that encouraged middle school youth to explore STEM through hands-on activities centered on precision agriculture and robotics. He has published two books on the formation of learning communities in the Maker Movement and was coeditor for the 2012 book *Robots in K–12 Education: A New Technology for Learning*. While at NSF, Barker managed a portfolio of projects focused on formal and informal rural learning in STEM. He was awarded the NSF Director's Team award for his work with the Navigating the New Arctic program and earned a secondary social sciences teaching endorsement. Throughout his career, Barker has provided professional development for educators in formal and informal learning environments around educational technology. Currently, Barker is the PI on the NSF Advanced Informal STEM Learning award grant Informal Biodiversity Education Models for Rural and Tribal Youth designed to enhance science identity and environmental stewardship participants and develop a framework that can be leveraged by rural and Tribal communities across the country to engage youth, families, and practitioners in local scientific research practices. Barker received his PhD from the University of Nebraska–Lincoln in curriculum and instruction with an emphasis in instructional technology.

GLORIA BURNETT (she/her/hers) currently serves as an associate professor in the University of Alaska Anchorage's College of Health Department of Human Services. She is the director of the Alaska Center for Rural Health and Health Workforce as well as the director of the Alaska Area Health Education Centers (AHEC) Program. Burnett previously served as dean of students, allied health program coordinator, and NW Alaska AHEC director at Ilisagvik College, Alaska's only tribal college, located in Utqiagvik, Alaska. She also has prior experience in K–12 education serving as a prekindergarten, fourth grade, and K–6 substitute teacher in Pennsylvania prior to relocating to Alaska. Throughout her career, Burnett has spearheaded a variety of projects focused on health career pathways and exploration for youth and adults. She also has experience with health professions training student exposure to rural and frontier communities and continuing education for rural healthcare providers. This work has included K–12 curriculum and program development, strategic partnership, and administration of federal, state, and local grants and contracts. Further, Burnett has experience with continuing education and professional development for teachers, administrators, and healthcare professionals. All of these training opportunities have a special focus on those practicing in rural or underserved communities. She is recipient of the Alaska Association of Career & Technical

Educators Community Contribution Award, Barbara Berger Excellence in Public Health Education and Promotion Award, and Alaska Primary Care Association Sockeye Award for Workforce Development. Burnett is also a HERS Institute graduate. She holds a BA in psychology with a minor in human development and family studies from Pennsylvania State University, and both an MS in the science of instruction and an instructional technology specialist certification from Drexel University. Burnett is also a certified adult and teen mental health first aid instructor.

LINDA FURUTO (she/her/hers) is currently a professor of mathematics education at the University of Hawai'i at Mānoa (UHM) where she directs the MEd Curriculum Studies, Mathematics Education, and the world's first degree program in ethnomathematics, which received an official add-a-field licensure in ethnomathematics from the Hawai'i Teacher Standards Board. Before joining UHM, she was an associate professor of mathematics and head of mathematics and science at the University of Hawai'i - West O'ahu, as well as a middle and high school mathematics teacher. Furuto's publications and work have appeared in Oxford University Press, Mathematical Association of America, and the International Congress on Mathematical Education Invited Lectures, among others. Her activities include being a visiting scholar of mathematics at the University of Tokyo, research-practitioner in the Boston Public Schools as part of Harvard University's Inventing the Future project, secondary mathematics teacher at the Fiji Technical College, secondary mathematics teacher in the Hawai'i State Department of Education, Obama Foundation Asia-Pacific Leader, and National Assessment of Educational Progress Visioning Panel Member. Furuto is an education specialist and apprentice navigator with the Polynesian Voyaging Society in the 2023–2027 Moananuiākea Voyage for Island Earth by celestial navigation on the traditional canoe Hōkūle'a. Furuto was born and raised in the rural town of Hau'ula, Ko'olauloa, O'ahu (population ~3,300) and grew up farming and fishing from the ocean. Her family and community instilled in her values such as kindness, compassion, strength, aloha, and the importance of visioning beyond the horizon. She strives to live by the 'ōlelo no'eau (Hawaiian proverb) 'A'ohe hana nui ke alu 'ia (No task is too big when done together by all). Furuto completed her bachelor's degree at Brigham Young University in mathematics education, master's degree at Harvard University, and PhD at the University of California, Los Angeles, with her main research interests including quantitative methodology, mathematics achievement, ethnomathematics, and access and equity.

REBEKAH HAMMACK (she/her/hers) is an assistant professor of science education in the College of Education at Purdue University where she also serves as an advisor to the Purdue Center for Rural Research, Education, and Outreach. She serves as principal investigator (PI) or co-PI on four federal projects focused on enhancing STEM education in rural schools and communities. Prior to joining the faculty at Purdue University, Hammack was an assistant professor in the College of Education, Health and Human Development, at Montana State University, an affiliate faculty of the Montana Engineering Education Research Center, and a faculty fellow of the Montana Center for Research on Rural Education. She also spent 11 months as an Albert Einstein Distinguished Educator Fellow at the National Science Foundation (NSF). Prior to her fellowship at NSF, Hammack spent 12 years as a middle school science and engineering teacher in Oklahoma. Her research focuses on the connection of local knowledge and context to STEM interest and identity development in youth, particularly rural and Indigenous youth in elementary and middle grades, as well as how elementary and middle grades teachers develop teaching efficacy and identity as STEM educators. Hammack holds a BS degree in agriculture from the Ohio State University, an MS in animal science from Oklahoma State University, and a PhD in professional education studies with a concentration in science education from Oklahoma State University.

ERIC J. JOLLY (he/him/his) is president and CEO of the Saint Paul & Minnesota Foundation—an organization working to create an equitable, just and vibrant Minnesota where all communities and people thrive. He is a cognitive psychologist with a background that includes engineering and mathematics. Previously, as vice president and senior scientist at Education Development Center, Jolly led technical assistance for the National Science Foundation's office of system reform for STEM education. As president of the Science Museum of Minnesota he led both a significant science education center and the nation's largest exhibit construction group, bringing groundbreaking science programming to major museums around the nation. He has previously served as a member of the Mathematical Sciences Education Board, Committee for Equal Opportunities in Science and Engineering, chaired the American Association for the Advancement of Science's (AAAS's) Education and Human Resources division, as well as chair or service to numerous panels for the National Science Foundation and the National Academies. He is a member of several academic honor societies, a senior member of the Institute of Electrical and Electronics Engineers, life fellow of AAAS, life appointee to the Hendrickson Institute for Ethical Leadership, life member of Society for the Advancement of Chicanos/Hispanics and Native Americans in Science, and recipient of two honorary doctorates and numerous scholarly awards.

JOHN P. McNAMARA (he/him/his) taught general education biology as Pet Nutrition, Advanced Nutrition and Biochemistry, and wrote a text in Pet Nutrition for introductory college and high school biology/animal sciences/advanced placement biology. He has provided leadership, professional development, and content background for K–12 life, chemical, physical, and earth sciences as well as all aspects of food systems education. McNamara is presently a member of the Food Animal Science Societies Science Policy Committee, and actively plans and presents professional development on all aspects of food systems to K–12 teachers especially in small and rural schools. He works across the spectrum of educational content and pedagogy, all grades; plant and animal sciences, consumer nutrition and education, rural and agricultural businesses; farms and farm support companies; and including Future Farmers of America, 4-H, Career and Technical Education, Washington Science Teachers Association, and National Science Teaching Association. McNamara was elected to the Washington State Academy of Sciences for research in nutritional physiology of farm animals and his work to help prepare teachers in integrated STEM teaching. He worked on the Next Generation Science Standards adoption in Washington State, including item writing and reviewing, performance expectation reviews, STEM teacher professional growth plans, and the National Science Foundation-funded NextGen STEM teacher preparation program in Washington State. McNamara is recognized as a fellow of the American Dairy Science Association as well as the American Society of Animal Sciences and received the American Dairy Science Young Scientist, Zoetis Physiology, and American Society of Animal Science Corbin Companion Animal Biology awards. He earned his BS in agricultural sciences and MS in dairy science from the University of Illinois at Urbana-Champaign and a PhD in human foods and nutrition from the University of Georgia, Athens. McNamara is on the Board on Agriculture and Natural Resources (BANR) at the National Academies of Sciences, Engineering, and Medicine, and served on the National Animal Nutrition Program/National Research Support Project committee in partnership with BANR.

AUDREY MEADOR (she/her/hers) is an assistant professor of mathematics in the College of Engineering at West Texas A&M University. She was previously a K–12 mathematics educator for grades 9–12 in Texas before moving into higher education, where she currently teaches mathematics content and STEM methods courses for pre- and in-service teachers. Meador's research interests include preservice teacher pedagogical content knowledge development, Number Talks, and the recruitment and retention of underserved and underrepresented populations in rural STEM education. Currently, she is actively pursuing funding for her research initiative to support formal and informal robotics instruction in Hispanic-serving, rural high schools. Through Meador's research projects, she has participated in partnerships with administrators, teachers, and other higher education institutions to provide professional development in the delivery of instructional routines and STEM education through robotics. Her scholarly contributions include several journal articles and four book chapters, and she is currently a co-primary investigator on two funded National Science Foundation grants in the Division of Undergraduate Education. Meador's work has been recognized with the Outstanding Dissertation Award from the School Science and Mathematics Association and the Intellectual Contributions Award from West Texas A&M University's College of Engineering. She has received fellowships through the Service, Teaching, and Research program from the Association of Mathematics Teacher Educators and the Institute for Measurement Methodology in rural STEM education at the University of South Carolina. Meador received her BS and MS degrees in mathematics from West Texas A&M University and her PhD in curriculum and instruction from Texas Tech University.

DARRIS R. MEANS (he/him/his) is a professor of education leadership in the College of Education at Clemson University. Across his faculty career, he has supported and led rural education initiatives at Clemson University, University of Pittsburgh, and University of Georgia. Prior to becoming a faculty member, Means was an administrator for a college access program, Elon University's Elon Academy, working with high school and college students from low-income families and/or students with no family history of college to support their postsecondary education enrollment, persistence, and graduation. He has been engaged in qualitative and mixed-methods research on rural education and STEM education for a decade. Means' current research focuses on two areas: (a) science learning, opportunities, and resources that support rural students and Black students in their science degree career trajectories and (b) postsecondary education access and completion for rural students. He currently serves on the Executive Committee for the National Rural Education Association, a leading voice for rural schools and communities nationwide. Means previously served in several advisory and leadership capacities related to rural education, including serving on the advisory board for the Ascendium Education Group to help develop a National Rural Research Agenda and serving as the chair of the Committee on Justice, Equity, Diversity, and Inclusion for the American Educational Research Association's Rural Education Special Interest Group. He earned a BA in political science and sociology from Elon University, MEd in counselor education from Clemson University, and his PhD in educational research and policy analysis from North Carolina State University.

STEPHEN L. PRUITT (he/him/his) is the sixth president of the Southern Regional Education Board (SREB). He started his education career as a high school chemistry teacher in Fayette County, Georgia. During his career, Pruitt has amassed education policy, assessment, and instructional background at the local, state, and national levels. Before coming to SREB, Pruitt was Kentucky's state commissioner of education. At the national level, he had worked closely with state agencies and educators around the country to improve policy and practice in science education. In Georgia, Pruitt served as science and mathematics program manager, director of academic standards, associate state superintendent for assessment and accountability, and chief of staff for the Georgia Department of Education. He also served as a board member to the Council of Chief State School Officers, as president of the Council of State Science Supervisors, and as a member of the writing team for the College Board Standards for College Success for science. Pruitt holds a bachelor's degree in chemistry from North Georgia College and State University, a master's degree in science education from the University of West Georgia, and a doctorate of philosophy in chemistry education from Auburn University. He was named to the National Research Council's Board on Science Education and served on the National Academies Committee on Conceptual Framework for New Science Education Standards that developed the Framework for K–12 Science Education.

JESSICA SAMPLEY (she/her/hers) is a 20-year veteran educator who currently serves as the Academies and Career and Technical Education (CTE) director at Gulf Shores City Schools (GSCS). She is a National Board Certified Teacher who previously taught English Language Arts at the secondary (grades 8–12) and postsecondary levels, coached athletics, and served as technology coordinator and assistant athletic director. Sampley has committed her entire career to serving rural schools and districts in Alabama. She grew up in rural Alabama and is a first-generation college graduate; in her current role, she leverages that experience and focuses on bridging the gap between CTE and core academics. Sampley has successfully developed and implemented innovative projects through the GSCS "Sustainability: Full STEAM Ahead" initiative by leveraging partnerships, resources, and grant funds. Highlights include scuba certification; dune restoration; STEAM Thinking Across the Curriculum; plane building and flight training; Summer WAVE; CTE vertical alignment professional development; an outdoor rock-climbing wall; biking for STEAM learning; and the "Small Town, Big Garden" Project. Her research interests include integrating design/STEAM thinking with a focus on sustainability across the curriculum to increase student engagement and achievement, as well as overcoming disparities in achievement and discipline referrals of historically marginalized groups in Alabama's education system. Recent honors and awards include the U.S. Green Ribbon School District, over $1,000,000 in grants for related projects, Governor's Award in WBL Regional Best Practices, and Council for Leaders in Alabama Schools' Banner School Award. Sampley holds an MFA in creative writing from North Carolina State University and an EdS in instructional leadership from the University of West Alabama.

GUAN KUNG SAW (he/him/his) is an associate professor in the School of Educational Studies at Claremont Graduate University. His work focuses on diversity, equity, and inclusion in STEM education and workforce development, STEM mentorship and social capital, as well as college access and success. Saw teaches courses on inequalities in education, sociology of education, and quantitative research methods. A former science teacher in a rural high school and a fellow at the Institute for Measurement Methodology in Rural STEM Education, he investigates the disparities in opportunities to learn, motivation, and career pathways in STEM among rural and small-town students. Saw co-leads the STEM Pathways Research-Practice Partnership to study and improve STEM programs/practices that support underrepresented students from diverse geographical areas. His work has been supported by the National Science Foundation, Institute of Education Sciences, National Institute of Justice, and American Educational Research Association. Saw has published in journals such as *Educational Researcher*, *Journal of Research in Science Teaching*, *International Journal of Science and Mathematics Education*, *Journal for STEM Education Research*, and *Policy Insights from the Behavioral and Brain Sciences*. His paper titled "STEM Education and Pathways of Rural and Small-Town Students: Disparities by Geographical Remoteness" was selected for the Best Research Award by the National Rural Education Association in 2024. He received his PhD from Michigan State University.

MARA CASEY TIEKEN (she/her/hers) is an associate professor of education at Bates College. Her research focuses on educational equity for rural students and communities, including the rural school/community relationship, rural college access, rural school closure, and rural racial justice. Tieken has written two books, *Why Rural Schools Matter* (2014, University of North Carolina Press) and *Educated Out: How Rural Students Navigate Elite Colleges—And What It Costs Them* (to be published spring 2025, University of Chicago Press). She is working on a project designed in partnership with Arkansas's Rural Community Alliance, that documents, examines, and communicates the impacts of school closures on rural Black communities in the Arkansas Delta. Tieken won the Lynton Award for the Scholarship of Engagement for Early Career Faculty and she routinely provides professional development to teachers and administrators on supporting rural college access and success, adopting inclusive practices for rural schools, and understanding rural demographics and poverty. She serves as an associate editor of the *Journal of Research in Rural Education* and is an active member of the Rural Sociological Society, the Rural Education Special Interest Group of the American Educational Research Association, and the Rural Youth Catalyst Project's Rural Youth Working Group. Tieken received her EdD from the Harvard Graduate School of Education. Before beginning her graduate work, she taught third grade and adult education in rural Tennessee.

STAFF BIOS

BETH CADY (she/her/hers) is a senior program officer with the Board on Science Education in the Division of Behavioral and Social Sciences and Education at the National Academies of Sciences, Engineering, and Medicine. She conducts studies, workshops, and other projects focused on equitable, inclusive, and effective STEM education at all levels. From 2006 to 2023 she worked in the National Academy of Engineering Program Office on projects focused on equitable and inclusive engineering education and related research at the precollege and higher education levels. She earned MS and PhD degrees in cognitive and human factors psychology from Kansas State University and a BA in psychobiology and political science from Wheaton College in Massachusetts.

LETICIA GARCILAZO GREEN (she/her/hers) is an associate program officer for the Board on Science Education at the National Academies of Sciences, Engineering, and Medicine. As a member of the board staff, she has supported studies focusing on criminal justice, science education, science communication, and climate change. Garcilazo Green has a BS in psychology and a BA in sociology with a concentration in criminology from Louisiana State University and an MA in forensic psychology from The George Washington University.

HEIDI SCHWEINGRUBER (Board Director, she/her/hers) is the director for the Board on Science Education at the National Academies of Sciences, Engineering, and Medicine. In this role, she oversees a portfolio of work that includes K–12 science education, informal science education, and higher education. Schweingruber joined the National Academies starting as a senior program officer for the Board of Science Education. In this role, she directed or co-directed numerous projects including the study that resulted in the report *A Framework for K–12 Science Education* (2011) which served as the blueprint for the Next Generation Science Standards. Most recently, she co-directed the study that produced the report *Call to*

Action for Science Education: Building Opportunity for the Future (2021). Schweingruber is a nationally recognized leader in leveraging research findings to support improving science and science, technology, engineering, and medicine education policy and practice. She holds a PhD in psychology and anthropology, and a certificate in culture and cognition from the University of Michigan.

LACHELLE THOMPSON (she/her/hers) is a senior program assistant with the Board on Science Education at the National Academies of Sciences, Engineering, and Medicine. In this role, Thompson provides comprehensive operational and logistical support for high-impact initiatives focused on advancing education and workforce development. She is currently supporting two critical consensus studies: K–12 STEM Education and Workforce Development in Rural Areas and Developing Competencies for the Future of Data and Computing: The Role of K–12. Thompson brings expertise in coordinating complex projects, including managing logistics for meetings, webinars, and conferences; creating and maintaining databases and records; and preparing polished materials for both internal and external audiences. She is skilled in process documentation, program monitoring and evaluation, and ensuring compliance with organizational policies, such as processing invoices and travel expense reports. Prior to joining the National Academies, Thompson spent eight years in the telecommunications and banking industries, honing her skills in operations management, client relations, and business administration.

AUDREY WEBB (she/her/hers) is a program officer with the Board on Science Education (BOSE). Since she joined the BOSE staff in April 2023, she has supported two congressionally mandated consensus studies and the Collaborative on Advancing Science Teaching and Learning in K–12. Before joining the BOSE team, she served as the K–12 Science supervisor for the Nebraska Department of Education. In this position, she supported district selection and implementation of instructional materials for science, provided professional learning opportunities across the state, and supported the development of the statewide phenomenon-based performance assessment system, including large-scale, interim, and classroom formative assessments and implementation toolkits. Previously, Webb designed and implemented project-based curricula for secondary biology, physiology, and physical science in the San Francisco Unified School District. She holds a MA in education from Stanford University and a BA in both biology and sociology/anthropology from St. Olaf College.

Appendix B

Analysis of Current Federal Funding for Rural STEM Programs and Research

The committee was tasked with evaluating the quality and quantity of current federal programming and research in preK–12 science, technology, engineering, and mathematics (STEM) and workforce development in rural areas. Dan Aladjem from Policy Studies Associates was contracted to conduct this analysis and communicated throughout the process to establish methodology, variable creation, and cross tabulations. The committee developed criteria for determining the quality of identified programs guided by previous work in the Board on Science Education on effective STEM education and guidelines for rigorous education research like those laid out in *Scientific Research in Education* (National Research Council, 2002) and in the Common Guidelines for Education Research and Development (2013) developed by the U.S. National Science Foundation (NSF) and the Institute for Education Sciences in the U.S. Department of Education. This appendix presents portions of the commissioned paper; the committee's analysis, interpretation, and use of the information from the following material is in Chapter 3.

APPROACH AND METHODS

The reach of the federal government is broad, so constructing an inventory of federal programs requires certain assumptions and simplifications to identify, inventory, and assess the quality of current federal support for rural preK–12 STEM education and workforce development. The following describes the process used.

Federal programming is defined here as federal assistance as catalogued in the System for Award Management (SAM.gov; General Services

Administration, 2023). The Federal Assistance Listings (AL) are considered "the single, authoritative, governmentwide comprehensive source of Federal financial assistance program information produced by the executive branch."[1] The AL cover 56 federal agencies, including all cabinet-level agencies. The Office of Management and Budget has aggregated AL data from SAM.gov into the Federal Program Inventory (FPI) to provide a "coherent picture of all Federal programs, and the performance of the Federal Government as well as individual agencies."[2] The Office of Management and Budget launched the FPI earlier this year, so there remain inconsistencies in the data and as yet incomplete capabilities. Nonetheless, for the purposes of this analysis, the FPI provides the most valid and comprehensive source of data on federal programs.

This analysis draws on the publicly available data on the FPI website, collected from SAM.gov as of February 2, 2024. Although the FPI includes many types of assistance, this review focuses on formula grant programs and project grant programs. The FPI data for each program include

- AL number
- program title
- agency/subagency
- objective
- URLs to SAM.gov, usaspending.gov, and grants.gov
- assistance type
- beneficiary types
- applicant types
- a categories designation.

NSF programs do not have individual AL numbers. Rather, each directorate has a unique AL number. To better capture the full inventory of federal programs, the committee analyzed datasets provided by NSF. Awards made in fiscal year (FY) 2024 (October 1, 2023, through September 30, 2024) with the word "rural" in either the title or the abstract were examined.[3] Importantly, awards were not considered to be related to rural issues merely by being awarded to an institution in a rural area. In addition, the award amount references "Awarded Amount to Date" so solely reflects the award amount for FY 2024. In other words, some grants may have had only part of their funding awarded for FY 2024.

Binary variables for preK–12 education, STEM fields, rural communities, and workforce development were created for the FPI data (described

[1]Requirement to Provide Public Notice of Federal Financial Assistance Programs, 2 CFR §200.203(a)(1), amended October 2, 2024. https://www.ecfr.gov/current/title-2/section-200.203

[2]Office of Management and Budget, Federal program inventory, https://fpi.omb.gov/about/about-the-data

[3]NSF Awards Advanced Search, https://www.nsf.gov/awardsearch/advancedSearch.jsp

below), which was then analyzed in Excel to create counts of programs in each analytic category (preK–12, STEM, rural, and workforce) and of programs across combinations of categories.

Data on program quality were drawn primarily from program websites, the Federal Register, SAM.gov, and the federal budget. A full analysis of all programs in the FPI was beyond the scope of this paper. A small number of programs at the intersection of preK–12, STEM, and rural were selected for the quality analysis.

Variable Construction

For both datasets, binary variables to code each program as related to preK–12 education, STEM fields, rural communities, and workforce development were created by coding a cell as 1 if the search found one of the terms listed for the variable and 0 if none of the terms were found.

FPI Data

Tables B-1, B-2, and B-3 show the search terms used for each of the variables in the FPI data. The variables chosen below are those that occur in the FPI data. Each was searched in the program title, popular name, agency, subagency, objective, beneficiaries, and categories.

The formula for the rural variable searched for the word *rural* in the program title, popular name, agency, subagency, objective, beneficiaries, and categories.

Limitations

While this analysis draws on the most valid set of data to inventory federal programs supporting preK–12 STEM education and workforce efforts in rural communities, certain limitations must be considered when assessing its overall contribution.

First, the FPI is a newly launched resource. The Office of Management and Budget (2024) acknowledges its current limitations and has outlined

TABLE B-1 Search Terms Used for PreK–12 Education Variable

Beneficiary Type	Categories: Education
Child (6–15), Education (0–8), Education (9–12), Juvenile Delinquent, Preschool, School, Youth (16–21)	Elementary and Secondary; Indian Education; Resource Development and Support - Elementary, Secondary Education; Special Education; Teacher Training; Vocational Development

SOURCE: Committee generated from commissioned paper.

TABLE B-2 Search Terms Used for STEM Variables

Objective	STEM; Science; Technology; Engineering; Math; Mathematics
Agricultural	Forestry; Production and Operation; Research and Development; Resource Conservation and Development; Stabilization and Conservation Service
Business and Commerce	Commercial Fisheries; Maritime; Statistics
Community Development	Construction, Renewal and Operations; Fire Protection
Disaster Prevention and Relief	Disaster Relief; Emergency Health Services; Emergency Preparedness, Civil Defense; Flood Prevention and Control
Education	Dental Education and Training; Health Education and Training; Nuclear Education and Training; Nursing Education; Resource Development and Support - Sciences
Employment, Labor, and Training	Bonding and Certification; Job Training; Employment
Energy	Conservation; Research and Development
Environmental Quality	Air Pollution Control; Pesticides Control; Radiation Control; Research, Education, Training; Solid Waste Management; Water Pollution Control
Food and Nutrition	Food Inspection
Health - Alcoholism, Drug Abuse and Mental Health	General; Law Enforcement; Planning; Research
Health	Communicable Diseases; Facility Planning and Construction; General Health and Medical; Health Research - General; Health Services Planning and Technical Assistance; Indian Health; Maternity, Infants, Children; Mental Health; Occupational Safety and Health; Physical Fitness; Prevention and Control; Veterans Health
Housing	Construction Rehabilitation; Site Preparation for Housing
Natural Resources	Community Sewage Treatment Assistance; Community Water Supply Services; Land Conservation; Mineral Research; Recreation; Water Conservation and Research; Wildlife Research and Preservation
Regional Development	Energy; Health and Nutrition; Transportation
Science and Technology	Information and Technical; Research - General; Research - Specialized
Transportation	Air Transportation; Highways, Public Roads, and Bridges; Rail Transportation; Urban Mass Transit; Water Navigation

SOURCE: Committee generated from commissioned paper.

TABLE B-3 Search Terms Used for Workforce Variable

	Workforce Variable
Objective	Workforce; Work force; Career
Education	Dental Education and Training; Health Education and Training; Nursing Education; Resource Development and Support - Vocational Education and Handicapped Education; Vocational Development
Employment, Labor, and Training	Job Training; Bonding and Certification; Equal Employment Opportunity; Job Training, Employment

SOURCE: Committee generated from commissioned paper.

plans for future iterations; no doubt a similar analysis in the future will yield more refined results. The Office of Management and Budget further acknowledges—and the data suggest—that agencies completed the data input to SAM.gov in ways that were not wholly consistent and not necessarily ideal for the analyses undertaken in this chapter.

The coding of the binary variables indicating preK–12 education and STEM may have overidentified programs, including some only tenuously connected to common conceptions of preK–12 education and STEM as envisioned for this study. The structure of the FPI data and variability in agency categorization suggest that it would be better to err on the side of casting a wider net for preK–12 education and STEM than looking only very narrowly at those constructs.

Conversely, the coding for rural programs may undercount programs serving rural communities. As opposed to preK–12 education and STEM, looking narrowly for programs that explicitly target rural communities seemed not just reasonable but appropriate.

More fundamentally, the choice to define federal assistance as the object of the inventory means that direct federal operations are excluded, most notably, perhaps, STEM education and workforce development efforts of the U.S. Department of Defense Education Authority. Another consequence of the design choices is that important programs authorized by major legislation (such as the Elementary and Secondary Education Act and the Individuals with Disabilities Education Act) may not be adequately reflected because of the limitations in the FPI data, despite their clear relevance to understanding federal investments.

The quality assessment relies in part on examination of programs' performance indicators. Use of such indicators presents multiple challenges, ranging from access to program performance data to the debatable validity of many indicators (Gerrish, 2016; Government Accountability Office, 2018; Heinrich, 2002; Moynihan & Pandey, 2010).

INVENTORY OF FEDERAL STEM INVESTMENTS

The tables below present the numbers of federal programs in different groupings, from an overall count of programs to counts for each analytic group: preK–12 education, STEM (defined broadly as discussed), rural, and workforce development. The paper reviews the federal government as a whole first, then explores NSF, and finds the following:

- Federal assistance is broad in scope, concentrated in cabinet-level agencies, and weighted toward project grants.
- There is an abundance of STEM-related programs across the federal government, but just three agencies administer over half of all STEM-related programs.
- Relatively few programs prioritize rural communities.
- Even fewer programs prioritize preK–12 STEM education in rural communities.
- Unsurprisingly, the vast majority of NSF grants (in the directorates included here) serve preK–12 STEM but, again, relatively few also serve rural communities.
- There is untapped potential scholarly capacity among NSF grantees outside the STEM Education directorate.

Federal Formula Grant and Project Grant Programs by Agency

Federal agencies provide assistance, as shown in Table B-5, predominantly through project grants rather than formula grants. The use of project grants necessarily implies that agencies likely have greater flexibility to target resources effectively by leveraging expertise within the agencies. The FPI dataset catalogues 1,946 formula and project grant programs across all federal agencies. Of these, 1,689 (87%) are project grant programs and 257 (13%) are formula grant programs. Seven (of 44) agencies—the Departments of Agriculture, Education, Health and Human Services (HHS), Justice, Interior, Transportation, and the Environmental Protection Agency (EPA)—account for almost 70 percent of the grant programs across all agencies. HHS accounts for over 21 percent of all programs, administering 334 project grant programs and 75 formula grant programs. Interior and Agriculture account for about 12 percent each (238 project grants and 10 formula grants, and 215 and 27, respectively).

Numbers of Federal Programs Related to PreK–12, STEM Education, and Workforce Development in Rural Communities

Cabinet-level agencies operate all but a few of the federal programs related to preK–12, STEM, rural communities, and workforce development.

This is unsurprising as noncabinet-level agencies tend to be smaller and focused on highly specific policy issues. NASA and NSF stand out among other agencies: both are organized into directorates and AL numbers are assigned at the directorate level rather than to individual programs in the directorates. As such, it appears that NASA and NSF fund very few programs and the data do not fully reflect the breadth and depth of their work.

Table B-4 displays the number and percentages of preK–12, STEM, rural, and workforce grants by agency. It is important to note that these are duplicated counts; that is, a single program can be counted in none, one, multiple, or all of the analytic categories.

PreK–12: Over half (58%) of all federal preK–12 education programs are administered by just three agencies: Education (90 programs, 29.6%), Health and Human Services (62 programs, 20.4%), and Agriculture (25 programs, 8.2%). These 339 programs constitute 15.6 percent of all federal programs.

STEM: In contrast, almost 70 percent of all federal programs relate directly or indirectly to science, technology, engineering, or mathematics. Three agencies account for about half (52%) of all 1,355 STEM-related programs: Health and Human Services (351 programs, 25.9%), Interior (198 programs, 14.6%), and Agriculture (154 programs, 11.4%).

Rural: While STEM abounds across federal programs, a mere 13.6 percent (265) of federal programs explicitly mention rural communities as a focus, target, context, or beneficiary. These programs are highly concentrated in a few agencies. Agriculture alone accounts for 34 percent (90 programs) of federal rural programs. Agriculture, HHS, and Interior combined account for 54.3 percent of federal programs. Transportation and EPA bring the total to 68.3 percent of rural programs in five departments.

Workforce: Workforce development follows a similar pattern of concentration in a similar set of agencies. Four agencies—Health and Human Services (107 programs, 36.8%), Education (39 programs, 13.4%), Labor (26 programs, 8.9%), and Agriculture (19 programs, 6.5%)—administer two thirds (66%) of federal workforce development programs.

PreK–12 and STEM Programs

Of the 170 programs (8.7% of all programs) that can be characterized as concerning both preK–12 and STEM, almost two thirds (63.5%) are administered by Health and Human Services, Education, Commerce, Agriculture, and the Environmental Protection Agency (Table B-5).

TABLE B-4 Number and Percentage of PreK–12, STEM, Rural, and Workforce Programs by Federal Agency

Agency	PreK–12		STEM		Rural		Workforce	
	Number	Percent	Number	Percent	Number	Percent	Number	Percent
Agency for International Development	0	0.00	5	0.37	0	0.00	1	0.34
Appalachian Regional Commission	0	0.00	4	0.30	2	0.75	0	0.00
Consumer Product Safety Commission	0	0.00	0	0.00	0	0.00	0	0.00
Corporation for National and Community Service	3	0.99	3	0.22	0	0.00	1	0.34
Denali Commission	1	0.33	1	0.07	2	0.75	1	0.34
Department of Agriculture	25	8.22	154	11.37	90	33.96	19	6.53
Department of Commerce	12	3.95	60	4.43	16	6.04	5	1.72
Department of Defense	10	3.29	41	3.03	3	1.13	10	3.44
Department of Education	90	29.61	26	1.92	5	1.89	39	13.40
Department of Energy	2	0.66	38	2.80	1	0.38	6	2.06
Department of Health and Human Services	62	20.39	351	25.90	33	12.45	107	36.77
Department of Homeland Security	1	0.33	51	3.76	1	0.38	6	2.06
Department of Housing and Urban Development	2	0.66	31	2.29	9	3.40	4	1.37
Department of Justice	16	5.26	65	4.80	12	4.53	4	1.37
Department of Labor	9	2.96	29	2.14	4	1.51	26	8.93

Department of State	14	4.61	32	2.36	12	4.53	8	2.75
Department of the Interior	20	6.58	198	14.61	21	7.92	12	4.12
Department of the Treasury	1	0.33	7	0.52	7	2.64	2	0.69
Department of Transportation	3	0.99	88	6.49	14	5.28	9	3.09
Department of Veterans Affairs	0	0.00	13	0.96	1	0.38	2	0.69
Election Assistance Commission	0	0.00	2	0.15	0	0.00	0	0.00
Environmental Protection Agency	13	4.28	109	8.04	23	8.68	9	3.09
Executive Office of the President	0	0.00	2	0.15	0	0.00	0	0.00
Federal Communications Commission	0	0.00	0	0.00	0	0.00	0	0.00
Federal Financial Institutions Examination Council Appraisal Subcommittee	0	0.00	0	0.00	0	0.00	0	0.00
Federal Permitting Improvement Steering Council	0	0.00	0	0.00	0	0.00	0	0.00
Gulf Coast Ecosystem Restoration Council	0	0.00	2	0.15	0	0.00	0	0.00
Institute of Museum and Library Services	5	1.64	5	0.37	0	0.00	8	2.75
Inter-American Foundation	2	0.66	1	0.07	2	0.75	1	0.34
Japan-US Friendship Commission	0	0.00	0	0.00	0	0.00	0	0.00
Library of Congress	1	0.33	2	0.15	0	0.00	0	0.00
Millennium Challenge Corporation	0	0.00	0	0.00	1	0.38	0	0.00

(continued)

TABLE B-4 Continued

Agency	PreK–12		STEM		Rural		Workforce	
	Number	Percent	Number	Percent	Number	Percent	Number	Percent
National Aeronautics and Space Administration	7	2.30	7	0.52	5	1.89	2	0.69
National Archives and Records Administration	0	0.00	0	0.00	0	0.00	0	0.00
National Credit Union Administration	0	0.00	1	0.07	0	0.00	0	0.00
National Endowment for the Arts	0	0.00	0	0.00	0	0.00	0	0.00
National Endowment for the Humanities	2	0.66	4	0.30	0	0.00	0	0.00
National Science Foundation	1	0.33	11	0.81	0	0.00	5	1.72
Northern Border Regional Commission	0	0.00	1	0.07	0	0.00	0	0.00
Nuclear Regulatory Commission	0	0.00	3	0.22	0	0.00	1	0.34
Small Business Administration	0	0.00	1	0.07	1	0.38	0	0.00
Social Security Administration	1	0.33	2	0.15	0	0.00	1	0.34
Southeast Crescent Regional Commission	0	0.00	0	0.00	0	0.00	1	0.34
United States Institute of Peace	0	0.00	0	0.00	0	0.00	0	0.00
Unspecified	1	0.33	5	0.37	0	0.00	1	0.34
Total	**304**	**100.00**	**1,355**	**100.00**	**265**	**100.00**	**291**	**100.00**

SOURCE: Tabulation of data from Office of Management and Budget (2024).

TABLE B-5 Number and Percentage of PreK–12 and STEM Programs, by Federal Agency

Agency	Number	Percent
Corporation for National and Community Service	2	1.18
Denali Commission	1	0.59
Department of Agriculture	12	7.06
Department of Commerce	12	7.06
Department of Defense	8	4.71
Department of Education	25	14.71
Department of Energy	2	1.18
Department of Health and Human Services	47	27.65
Department of Homeland Security	1	0.59
Department of Housing and Urban Development	1	0.59
Department of Justice	10	5.88
Department of Labor	7	4.12
Department of State	8	4.71
Department of the Interior	6	3.53
Department of the Treasury	1	0.59
Environmental Protection Agency	12	7.06
Institute of Museum and Library Services	3	1.76
Inter-American Foundation	1	0.59
Library of Congress	1	0.59
National Aeronautics and Space Administration	6	3.53
National Endowment for the Humanities	1	0.59
National Science Foundation	1	0.59
Social Security Administration	1	0.59
Unspecified	1	0.59
Total	**170**	**100.00**

SOURCE: Tabulation of data from Office of Management and Budget (2024).

PreK–12 and Rural Programs

Sixty-five programs (3.3% of all programs) at the intersection of preK–12 education programs in rural communities can be characterized as both preK–12 and rural (Table B-6). They are relatively evenly distributed across 15 agencies, although 46 percent are in Agriculture, Health and Human Services, State, Commerce, and the Environmental Protection Agency.

TABLE B-6 Number and Percentage of PreK–12 and Rural Programs, by Federal Agency

Agency	Number	Percent
Denali Commission	1	1.54
Department of Agriculture	9	13.85
Department of Commerce	6	9.23
Department of Defense	3	4.62
Department of Education	4	6.15
Department of Health and Human Services	8	12.31
Department of Housing and Urban Development	1	1.54
Department of Justice	6	9.23
Department of Labor	3	4.62
Department of State	7	10.77
Department of the Interior	3	4.62
Environmental Protection Agency	7	10.77
Inter-American Foundation	2	3.08
National Aeronautics and Space Administration	5	7.69
Total	**65**	**100.00**

SOURCE: Tabulation of data from Office of Management and Budget (2024).

PreK–12 and Workforce Development Programs

Twenty agencies administer 95 programs at the intersection of preK–12 education and workforce development (Table B-7). Education and Health and Human Services administer about half (50.5%). Together with Labor and Defense, four agencies administer 64 percent of the federal preK–12 education and workforce programs.

PreK–12, STEM Programs in Rural Communities

Eleven agencies offer 39 programs—37 project grant programs and 2 formula grant programs at the intersection of preK–12 education and STEM programs in rural communities (Table B-8).

PreK–12, STEM, Workforce Programs

Fourteen agencies offer 62 programs—51 project grant programs and 11 formula grant programs—at the intersection of preK–12 education, STEM, and workforce (Table B-9). The Departments of Health and Human Services and Education together offer half of these programs.

TABLE B-7 Number and Percentage of PreK–12 and Workforce Development Programs, by Federal Agency

Agency	Number	Percentage
Corporation for National and Community Service	1	1.05
Denali Commission	1	1.05
Department of Agriculture	3	3.16
Department of Commerce	2	2.11
Department of Defense	5	5.26
Department of Education	33	34.74
Department of Energy	2	2.11
Department of Health and Human Services	15	15.79
Department of Homeland Security	1	1.05
Department of Justice	1	1.05
Department of Labor	8	8.42
Department of State	2	2.11
Department of the Interior	4	4.21
Department of the Treasury	1	1.05
Department of Transportation	3	3.16
Environmental Protection Agency	4	4.21
Institute of Museum and Library Services	4	4.21
Inter-American Foundation	1	1.05
National Aeronautics and Space Administration	2	2.11
National Science Foundation	1	1.05
Unspecified	1	1.05
Total	**95**	**100.00**

SOURCE: Tabulation of data from Office of Management and Budget (2024).

PreK–12, STEM, Workforce Programs in Rural Communities

A search for federal efforts supporting preK–12 STEM education and workforce development in rural areas reveals 11 programs (Table B-10). These 11 illustrate the main conclusion of this analysis: that while the federal government invests broadly (in terms of the sheer number of programs), very many of these programs are at best tangentially related to preK–12 education, STEM, rural communities, or workforce development. And many of those that are more directly relevant rely on grantees' choice to focus on preK–12 education, STEM, rural communities, or workforce development (see, for example, the Community Services Block Grant; U.S. Department of Health and Human Services, 2022). NASA's Office of STEM

TABLE B-8 Number of PreK–12 STEM Programs in Rural Communities, by Federal Agency

Agency	Formula Grants	Project Grants	Total
Denali Commission		1	1
Department of Agriculture		5	5
Department of Commerce		6	6
Department of Defense		3	3
Department of Education		1	1
Department of Health and Human Services	1	6	7
Department of Housing and Urban Development		1	1
Department of Labor		2	2
Department of the Interior		2	2
Environmental Protection Agency	1	5	6
National Aeronautics and Space Administration		5	5
Total	**2**	**37**	**39**

SOURCE: Tabulation of data from Office of Management and Budget (2024).

TABLE B-9 Number of PreK–12, STEM, Workforce Formula Grant and Project Grant Programs by Federal Agency

Agency	Formula Grant	Project Grant	Total
Corporation for National and Community Service		1	1
Denali Commission		1	1
Department of Agriculture		3	3
Department of Commerce		2	2
Department of Defense		4	4
Department of Education	5	10	15
Department of Energy	1	1	2
Department of Health and Human Services	4	11	15
Department of Labor	1	6	7
Department of the Interior		2	2
Environmental Protection Agency		4	4
Institute of Museum and Library Services		3	3
National Aeronautics and Space Administration		2	2
National Science Foundation		1	1
Total	**11**	**51**	**62**

SOURCE: Tabulation of data from Office of Management and Budget (2024).

TABLE B-10 Number of PreK–12, STEM, Workforce Formula Grant, and Project Grant Programs by Federal Agency

Agency	Formula Grant	Project Grant	Total
Denali Commission		1	1
Department of Health and Human Services	1	3	4
Department of Labor		2	2
Department of the Interior		1	1
Environmental Protection Agency		1	1
National Aeronautics and Space Administration		2	2
Total	**1**	**10**	**11**

SOURCE: Tabulation of data from Office of Management and Budget (2024).

Engagement (which is actually a collection of programs) offers a different, strategic, and intentional approach to supporting preK–12 STEM education and workforce development. Even this program, however, could be more strategically targeted toward rural communities.

REFERENCES

General Services Administration. (2023). *About SAM.gov.* https://www.gsa.gov/about-us/organization/Federal-acquisition-service/technology-transformation-services/integrated-award-environment-iae/about-samgov

Gerrish, E. (2016). The impact of performance management on performance in public organizations: A meta-analysis. *Public Administration Review*, *76*(1), 48–66. http://www.jstor.org/stable/24757491

Government Accountability Office. (2018). *Managing for results: Further progress made in implementing the GPRA Modernization Act, but additional actions needed to address pressing governance challenges* (GAO-18-609). https://www.gao.gov/products/gao-18-609

Heinrich, C. J. (2002). Outcomes-based performance management in the public sector: Implications for government accountability and effectiveness. *Public Administration Review*, *62*(6), 712–725. http://www.jstor.org/stable/3110329

Institute of Education Sciences (IES), U.S. Department of Education, & National Science Foundation (NSF). (2013). *Common guidelines for education research and development.* https://ies.ed.gov/pdf/CommonGuidelines.pdf

Moynihan, D. P., & Pandey, S. K. (2010). The big question for performance management: Why do managers use performance information? *Journal of Public Administration Research and Theory: J-PART*, *20*(4), 849–866. http://www.jstor.org/stable/40925882

National Research Council. (2002). *Scientific research in education.* National Academies Press. https://doi.org/10.17226/10236

Office of Management and Budget. (2024). *Appendix budget of the US government, fiscal year 2025.* The White House. https://www.whitehouse.gov/wp-content/uploads/2024/03/budget_fy2025.pdf

U.S. Department of Health and Human Services. (2022). *Community Services Block Grant (CSBG) fact sheet.* Administration for Children and Families, Office of Community Services. https://www.acf.hhs.gov/sites/default/files/documents/ocs/COMM_OCS_CSBG%20FactSheet_FY2022.pdf